A Practical [barcode] are for the
Primary School: 50 Lesson Plans using Drama

Shakespeare is one of our key historical figures, but so often he remains locked behind glass and hard to reach. The purpose of this book is to unlock Shakespeare, to remove the tag of 'high art' that has surrounded his work and return him to the heart of popular culture, where his plays began in the first place. In his foreword, playwright **Edward Bond** says of *Shakespeare for the Primary School*, 'It is written with knowledge and experience of its subject – but also with knowledge of the young people with whom that experience was shared'.

John Doona will inspire and motivate pupils and teachers alike to engage with Shakespeare in a fresh and accessible manner. He provides clear, tried and tested schemes of work that demonstrate how engagement with the plays and their language can have a dramatic impact on children's literacy and writing. As well as providing practical guidance to classroom delivery and performance, techniques, approaches and attitudes, this handbook also promotes learning outcomes linked to literacy targets and cross-curricular units of learning.

The central chapters of the book form a comprehensive cross-curricular unit of work on four plays – *The Tempest*, *Macbeth*, *A Midsummer Night's Dream* and *Romeo and Juliet* – providing background notes and historical facts linked to the plays, along with comprehensive schemes of work for immediate implementation and ideas for generating performance.

Features unique to this resource include:

● free electronic 'info-blasts' for all book buyers, containing electronic versions of key elements of the book as well as additional resources and lesson plans
● 'drama for the petrified' – a crash course for teachers in the techniques, approaches and attitudes required to bring Shakespeare to life
● a chapter on Shakespeare, including 'Fifteen-minute Will', a short, comic, scripted account of his life
● comprehensive schemes of work, each including a 'teacher's crib sheet', 'Story Whoosh!', 'story jigsaw', 'scheme structure map', plus edited scenes and additional classroom resources.

Shakespeare for the Primary School is an essential resource for all primary teachers, trainee teachers and drama practitioners, offering guidance, insight and compelling schemes of work for the study of Shakespeare through drama in the primary classroom.

John Doona is the creator and director of the **Children's Shakespeare Festivals**, a series of projects now in its fourth year. He is a qualified advanced skills teacher with a wide experience of secondary and primary drama practice; a visiting lecturer in drama at the University of Chester; and a professional writer, with dramatic work broadcast on Radio 4 and performed by the Royal Court Young People's Theatre and elsewhere.

A Practical Guide to Shakespeare for the Primary School: 50 Lesson Plans using Drama

John Doona

Routledge
Taylor & Francis Group

LONDON AND NEW YORK

Dedication

To Chris, Tom, Mia and Heather
'...such stuff...'

First published 2012
by Routledge
2 Park Square, Milton Park, Abingdon, Oxon OX14 4RN

Simultaneously published in the USA and Canada
by Routledge
711 Third Avenue, New York, NY 10017

Routledge is an imprint of the Taylor & Francis Group, an informa business

British Library Cataloguing in Publication Data
A catalogue record for this book is available from the British Library

Library of Congress Cataloging in Publication Data

Doona, John.
Shakespeare for the primary school : 50 lesson plans using drama / by John Doona. -- 1st ed.
p. cm.
Includes bibliographical references.
1. Shakespeare, William, 1564-1616--Study and teaching (Elementary) 2. English drama--Study and teaching (Elementary) 3. Drama in education. I. Title.
PR2987.D66 2011
372.66'044--dc22
2011009660

ISBN: 978-0-415-61042-1 (pbk)
ISBN: 978-0-203-81792-6 (ebk)

Typeset in Helvetica, Caslon Antique & ILLShakeFest by FiSH Books, Enfield, Middx.

MIX
Paper from
responsible sources
FSC
www.fsc.org   FSC® C004839

Printed and bound in Great Britain by the MPG Books Group

Contents

Foreword: A playwright's introduction

Edward Bond

Edward Bond is perhaps the closest the contemporary world has to the great mind of Shakespeare. That's quite a claim, but no other playwright we know of offers a canon of work with such depth and breadth, which enquires into the human condition with such a razor wit, and which offers theatrical experiences that compel, entertain and challenge in equal measure.

To be

A teacher was staging *Romeo and Juliet* with her class. They had rehearsed for weeks. It was the dress rehearsal. Romeo was speaking on a ladder at Juliet's window. The rest of the cast and crew sat round the edge of the stage space. Romeo came to the moment when Juliet has called his name and he says 'It is my soul that calls upon my name!' He stopped short – and said 'That is the most **** beautiful thing I've ever heard.' The unexpected intricacy hidden in the simple words had suddenly revealed iwebtself to him. He jumped off the ladder and walked round the stage saying 'That is beautiful! Beautiful! The most beautiful thing I've ever heard!' In one moment all our dreary TV chat show–Hollywood/Bollywood–two-for-the-price-of-one culture was swept away. He might just have landed on another planet, standing at dawn on the shore of a brave new world. He had not suddenly discovered Shakespeare – he had been saying this line for weeks. He had discovered himself.

At last we are learning that feeding children junk food bloats their bodies and weakens their brains. We still almost poison them by force-feeding them junk culture. How often, to take one small example, is the end-of-term school play an identi-copy of a West End musical money-spinner? The young cast enjoy it, it's an escape from maths, it releases their energy and they do it well – but they will never stand, like the young man playing Romeo, in the dawn of a new world and in the presence of one of the greatest of all human minds and know that they are at home in it. Only the young can have such revelations. It's the gift of youth. If it doesn't happen then, it can never happen. If it happens it will remain. It will always be there when it's needed. And without it, when youth has gone, everything will always be slightly stale and unprofitable and tainted by junk.

A class society such as ours creates barriers between people. '*They* do Shakespeare in public schools, *we* aren't interested in it. We sneer at anyone of *our* class who is.' Junk knows how to defend itself! – indeed it's a way of surviving with some self-respect. Be honest: we even teach Shakespeare with almost a sense of shame and hopelessness. He has no place in our increasingly junk society, no hope of surviving beyond the school-gate. And most corrupting of all: often we feel our own concern with him alienates us from those we teach.

The truth is, Shakespeare cannot be 'taught'. How can you overcome the barrier of four centuries? Of a pre-industrial world? Of chanting witches and talking ghosts? Even the language is a trap. 'To be or not to be' – yes, in a sense that's a label on half the acts children do every day.

But a few lines later – what is a fardel? And how do you make your quietous with a bare bodkin? You cannot be pushed back into his world. Yet he is universally acknowledged, even by junk culture, 'to be' one of the greatest of all human minds – I use the present tense because he has recorded his abiding presence with us in his plays. Perhaps what he gives us might have been given in other ways. But then the problem is still that he exists – and even if there are 'other ways', if we ignore him we create a huge gap in our understanding of ourselves and our world. We may ignore him, but others possess him – and that leads to the inverted snobbery I have described above. We become rancorously proud of our ignorance.

Shakespeare is a problem. And as this book says, 'It is always better to do no drama than to do drama badly.' How do we get out of the trap? Shakespeare has a super-ordinate power to enter into other people's minds. He creates his characters from *inside* their minds. He knows what it is '*to be*' the king, the servant, the nurse, the child, the adolescent, the lover, the sage, the judge, the condemned man, the dying soldier, the monster – and to find what is human in all of them, even the wicked and damned. And as that is so, he must be in us, in all of us – in every child in front of you in the room. That is where we begin.

We create *his* world. It cannot be – certainly not at first (that may come later when our interest has been aroused) – his world of 400 years ago. It must be the world we are in, and all human beings have been in since our beginning. The world of change, movement, isolation, belonging, survival, apprehension, risk, excitement, pride, anxiety, intrigue – all the natural responses and initiatives that allow and require us to live in the situations in which we find ourselves. This is what this book does – it is the 'invisible globe', which the young people enter and which is created by the exercises and games that are at its centre. It is written with knowledge and experience of its subject – but also with knowledge of the young people with whom that experience was shared. The author approaches these young people with a friendship and respect that I would call a sort of 'practical awe' – because that is the way he approaches Shakespeare himself. What he respects in Shakespeare and in his pupils is their shared human creativity. It is the book's simple but majestic secret. You do not have to drag, cajole, persuade or even encourage children to enter Shakespeare's world. You have to create *their* world so that Shakespeare may enter *it*. He will do that readily and easily because that is the power of drama.

No sort of drama can be taught. You can teach students the name of a river or the population of a continent. But who can teach anyone anything about themselves? Even Shakespeare cannot do that. The 'self' has to be *created*. That is the point of drama. It confronts the self with the self – it does it by placing the self in the extreme situations of drama because that is where the self must define itself and know itself. In drama the 'I' looks itself in the 'eye'. When the self stands in the dawn of the new world, it knows that at dawn the shadows are longest but that the sun will rise. Personally and socially this is a world more profound than the visceral, effervescent stimulation of West End musicals or the sports field – because it means this: that when the self confronts itself it has to define not just what it itself is, but what a human being is, what all human beings are, what it is 'to be' human. When Hamlet puts his question he is asking whether he should die. When Shakespeare says 'to be' he is asking us how we should live. Drama cannot teach anything, but if you deny children this confrontation you deny them all education. You may pack them with knowledge but they will be as dead as a book that is never read. Shakespeare created the situations of our lives, of being, with an almost unique precision and thoroughness. In his plays Shakespeare met himself. This book is a key. With it he can enter our lives. He cannot be shut out.

Edward Bond

Preface: Author's introduction

The purpose and shape of the book

This is a book about working with Shakespeare. It is also a book about working with the approaches of educational drama. The purpose throughout is to use the power and possibilities of drama to explore the power and possibilities of Shakespeare's work.

Following an introduction to Shakespeare's life and work and a 'crash course' in educational drama, we will go on to look at four plays: *The Tempest*, *Macbeth*, *A Midsummer Night's Dream* and *Romeo and Juliet*. The plays are explored through comprehensive schemes of work, which you are invited to use as the heart of your own compelling classroom experiences. The schemes use drama as their exploratory form, but embedded within them are a host of opportunities for creative learning tasks in a wide range of other curriculum areas. As you begin to translate the schemes into your own classrooms, we hope that you will develop opportunities to meet the needs and interests of each unique group of children. You might offer a scheme as an intense week-long project or as the heart of a term's thematic exploration; make of them as you will.

The schemes have been used extensively with primary schools in the north-west of England as part of the continuing 'Children's Shakespeare Festivals'. As such, they are tried and tested and, we hope, have proven the possibilities they contain. In a final short section we offer 'Notes for a festival' and invite you to make a public show of the extraordinary work we hope will ensue.

In creating the schemes, the process has been to absorb ourselves in the rich world of each play and to look for the doorways that offer compelling points of access for children, opportunities for learning activity, and possibilities for drama. The texts summon a profound world of human living and our drama offers access to both its fun and its profundity – a heady mix!

At the heart of our work are three simple aims – by the end of each scheme your children will:

- have a good understanding of the key narrative of the play
- know the nature of the main characters and their role within the story
- have experienced hearing and speaking Shakespeare's language.

On top of these clear and practical aims sit a second set of perhaps less tangible outcomes – your children will:

- be simply excited by the study of Shakespeare
- no longer fear such study
- have a new sense of ownership of the text and the writer
- have been asked *his* important questions and formulated their *own*.

Shakespeare

Shakespeare is our key historical and literary icon. He is the centre of western culture in art and literature; initially within English language culture, but now crossing linguistic barriers to be global in his reach. In England, he is a key *national* icon, helping to define what it is to be English. So often, however, Shakespeare remains locked behind glass and difficult to reach. Actors and their theatre chums often seem to have entered his world in a much more concrete and compelling way than most of their audiences. They have picked the lock. In truth, most audiences take his greatness on trust; it takes an effort to access his art and his wisdom, an effort that often eludes the contemporary mind. To educationalists, however, it is exactly this effort that makes his work such an exciting prospect for learning.

The distance is a terrible shame because, as they say, all human life is there, and because when the work emerged in sixteenth-century London it was a *popular* form, speaking to kings and illiterate peasants alike. The separation between high and popular culture was an innovation still only just emerging. In the words of modern playwright Edward Bond, it was art capable of speaking 'to the kitchen table and the edge of the universe'. Now, however, Shakespeare has been appropriated by a cultural elite and is generally regarded as 'high art'. Of course, in tackling big questions and exploring the difficult edges of life (in 'speaking to the universe') his work *is* 'high art' – but he is also a popular communicator; it is also 'entertainment'. He asks questions and offers insight not of exclusive interest to an intellectual elite, but of proper interest to us all; questions and insight central to what it is to be human. Shakespeare is ours and we want him back.

The purpose of this book is to unlock Shakespeare, to take him from his glass case and let him live amongst us again. To find a new form that will allow him to ask his questions of us, to challenge, to provoke, to rekindle a love of words, to show us the edges of things, and to share some rollicking good fun. In a sense, our schemes are like protracted actors' rehearsals in which the work of picking the lock is begun.

A living curriculum

In addition, this book is perhaps as much about enlivening the school curriculum through drama as it is about rediscovering Shakespeare. Shakespeare is the flag we gather around; as an icon he lends our work status, credence and value. We use the romance of him and his theatre, but the twin purpose of our work is the development of quality classroom learning through drama under the pretext of Shakespearean study. It is a task given real richness and depth by its drawing upon the weighty seams of human experience that his work offers. We want to achieve challenging and significant learning through drama, and Shakespeare's worlds license exploration of extreme situations, profound questions, fascinating lives and critical choices. After 400 years, he remains a wonder and a wonderful educational resource.

Through our explorations, we hope to develop understanding and experience of the drama form. The coming together of the potential of the drama form and the richness of the Shakespearean canon will hopefully prove a powerful and magical source of deep learning in our classrooms.

Making the most of the book

To achieve maximum benefit from this book you will need to enter into a creative relationship with it, to accept the imaginative challenge of working within these dramatic structures and to begin a dynamic conversation with Shakespeare, his people, his ideas and his language, but also – and most importantly – with your children. It is a creative, learning journey you will make together.

We propose that you give yourself a clear, realisable aim and explore the book through the prism of a piece of imminent new work. For example, decide to use *Romeo and Juliet* in a forthcoming term as an overarching theme and look to the book as your key resource. It might be enough to make this an imaginary task ('*if* I were to do *Romeo and Juliet* next term *then*...'), but why not test yourself for real? There is nothing like a practical deadline for focusing the mind! However you choose to proceed, it is important to regard the book as a practical resource.

A note on layout

We have tried to find the most user-friendly layout for these highly practical pieces and have arrived at an approach that involves two distinctive voices:

● the **descriptive and reflective voice**, which describes the activity in detail and gives an account of some background thinking for the particular element
● the **teacher's voice**, which is an account of the language in which the delivery might be expressed – not a 'script' that should be learnt and followed slavishly, but an indication of an approach, and a modelling of language... your most important tool.

The effect is something reminiscent of a script: stage direction and actors' lines. This dramatic presentation also gives the *reading* of it some theatrical impact. As you might with a script, we suggest that, as you read each account, you should try to picture the activities happening in your most familiar large teaching space; let the voice already be your own and give the participants the faces of your most familiar children. We hope you will find the approach useful.

Online resources

We have made the reasonable assumption that readers will have access to the internet. The vast repository of resources, ideas, images and texts available online is a staggering opportunity that has, in a blink, become accessible to just about all of us. We have been confident, to the point of the cavalier, in assuming that if we cite (as in the first workshop) the Elizabethan song 'Rose', a few moments 'clicking' will deliver to you the lyrics, the history, and even a recording of the song in many various forms. The internet has become part of the human landscape in which teaching and learning now operate. Finding such resources is the easy part of our project; putting them to work within a compelling structure and making them useful and meaningful is where the artistry and the craftsmanship come to matter.

Session timings

Rather than trying to anticipate the length of your drama sessions or the pace at which individual groups will progress through the units, we have not given indications of the start and end of sessions; they will start and end dependent upon the constraints you work within and the responses of your children. We would simply commend to you the fact that, if children are engaged and motivated in their work, it is possible to stop sessions at a variety of places and pick up exactly the same moment at a later date; the thinking and settling time offered by such interruption can be made a real bonus.

Curricular mapping

During the preparation of the book we have considered trying to map each scheme onto the requirements and demands of the primary curriculum; an early vision would have seen each activity given a gloss which demonstrated the curriculum links and relevance of each element. We have stepped back from this cumbersome task for two reasons.

● Such a mapping could only be relevant for the specific schooling system in which it was created, in this instance the English system. Being so specific would have been unhelpful to readers operating outside this system, and might have distracted from the clarity of the drama being explored.
● The same point can be made about our specific location in time, as the language of educational parlance and the conceptual framework that underlines it is constantly in flux. To pin our work

to *this* moment's particular educational language-game would ultimately make the book age very quickly.

In lieu of such a mapping, what we do offer for each scheme is a table that captures the structure of the scheme and, in general terms, makes suggestions about the curriculum areas towards which the activities might point. The table also lists the resources you might need in your delivery. Each of these 'scheme structure maps' (at the end of each chapter in Part Two) offers space for you to make your own notes on the uses to which *you* will put them.

Infoblast

As an adjunct to the text, we have also prepared a number of additional materials and electronic versions of elements of text. Our intention is to offer as much support as we can to facilitate you in implementing the schemes. These will available online at www.routledge.com/cw/doona.

Finally

In our creativity, in engaging our imaginations, we are most human. We learn best when we are engaged as physical, emotional, social, as well as rational and intellectual beings. In the firm coupling of the work of our richest writer with the dynamic approaches of educational drama, we give ourselves a learning engine of formidable forward momentum.

To make a favourite paraphrase from Dorothy Heathcote, the original great spirit of educational drama, in accepting the challenge of drama we place ourselves in 'the zone of possible adventures'.

My friends, let us adventure well!

Acknowledgements

Drama

To the leaders in the field of drama who have provided a lifetime of support in text and in person and aided the development of this powerful and important approach. Special thanks to the illustrious professors, Dorothy Heathcote, Jonothan Neelands and Alan Owens.

Vying for significance alongside these names are the pupils, students and staff of the various classrooms where our work together has challenged, provoked, inspired and offered understanding to the author; it is the daily contact with the drama form and the exploration of its possibilities that have allowed for the development of the approach represented here. Thanks to the students and staff of Oakwood High School and Egerton Park Arts College, in particular Jude Ellson, Graham Mercer, Phil Robinson, John Hart, Darren Randle, Stacey Morley, Jan Linnik and Alison Rudd.

Edward Bond; for his wisdom, inspiration, support and friendship.

Festival

Egerton Park and associated primaries.

Festival primary schools, their children, teachers and heads:

Cheshire – Huxley CE, Oakefield, Hurdsfield, Prestbury, Dorin Park, Havannah, Shavington, Dee Point, Winsford High Street, Pear Tree, Hungerford, Haslington, Warminham, Kingsley St John, Great Budworth, Leighton

Manchester – Chapel Street, St Chads, Irk Valley

Tameside – Micklehurst All Saints, Flowery Field

Oldham and Rochdale – Burnley Brow, St James, Holy Family, Belfield, Sandbrook, Mayfield, Broadfield, Alexandra Park, Greenhill

At the Royal Exchange Theatre: Amanda Dalton, Philip Lord, Jackie and all the technical staff for their professional support.

At the Conway Centre: Debbie, Andy and all the staff for making inspiration possible.

Cheshire East Council, Fintan Bradley and John Weeks.

Colleagues, friends and excellent practitioners of drama and so many other things: Jan Linnik, Sarah McAdam and Richard Hall.

Bruce Roberts and Hamish Baxter at Routledge, for their patience and support.

Richard Folse and Yvette Huddlestone of the Illinois Shakespeare Festival, for permission to use their 'IllShake Fest' type font.

Keen-eyed members of the proofing committee, Julie, Heather, Cath, Mark, Jan and Jenny.

Finally, to my wife and family for their patience, love and support.

Part One: Drama for the petrified* – a crash course

(*or the keen but unsure)

1 Why drama?

This chapter prepares the ground for your extensive use of drama during the delivery of the schemes. After exploring the uses and powers of the drama approach, we look in detail at some of the practicalities of working with a wide range of drama techniques, followed by some 'practical wisdom' and some handy hints. This chapter gives its attention to some big ideas and some simple groundwork. While reading it, you are invited to think through the ideas offered as you might deliver them yourself.

Drama is a powerful form of engagement and learning. It offers an alternative 'way of knowing' and ensues simply when teachers invite children to enter *into* a story/event/character rather than think *about* the story/event/character.

Consider the following.

Drama and the 'I'

As Dorothy Heathcote has pointed out, drama is such an ordinary thing. We cross over into drama when, instead of saying 'There once was a captain of a ship', we say, '*I* am the captain of this ship and you are my crew. . .', or when we ask 'Will you be the captain of this ship. . .', to which *you* then say, '*I* am the captain of this ship'. Alongside 'this', 'I' is perhaps the identifying mark of drama: 'I' indicates I am 'living though as another person'; 'this' identifies that we agree the *place* of the fictional situation we are to share. Drama reclaims the ability to speak as first-person subject in the service of learning; to identify with the people of the fiction; to think, feel, act as these 'others' within the constraints of their world, to learn by living through an alternative world. Drama is simply 'I-ness'.

Drama is an extension of play

We all recognise the experience of childhood imaginative play: playing schools, playing soldiers, playing mums and dads, giving out footballers' names before a match in the park. This innate, uniquely human ability to take on a role and act 'as if' is, evolutionarily speaking, a profound way of preparing for life within the safety of fiction. It is a compelling, natural mode of behaviour, and in classroom drama we harness its power and allow it to thrive in the service of learning.

Drama and knowing

What is it to 'know' a thing? Is it simply to be able to recall it? Repeat it? Is it to pass a paper test in it? Or to demonstrate a skill in it? The Caribbean saying 'Who feels it, knows it' beats the theory of multiple intelligences (by some distance) to an awareness that, in reality, there are many ways of knowing; we can *know* with our bodies, our senses, our emotions, our imaginations. And although the *demonstration* of this 'knowing' might, in our current situation, usually only show itself in concrete, 'institutional' tasks (in written outcomes, for example), even these written tasks are enhanced and deepened through the opportunity to 'know' in the widest range of possibilities. Drama offers us the chance to *know* in many diverse ways.

Preparing your arguments for drama

Rather than attempting a comprehensive statement for the case for drama... let's pretend. Let's rehearse four real-world arguments for our special kind our work; four 'clinchers'. Choose from the following a scenario to imagine ourselves in.

- *The staffroom.* Staff are scoffing at your need for the hall on Wednesday morning... again! A serious educational discussion ensues. What are you messing about at?
- *The school office.* A parent has come in to see you. They are concerned that their child's learning is being interrupted by 'fashionable' teaching approaches – your drama sessions.
- *The head's office.* Your head teacher would like you to account for yourself; noise coming from the hall, lights dimmed, candles lit (heaven forefend!), classroom desks empty – again. They are willing to support you, but only if you can give a clear account of why it is necessary and how it promotes effective learning.
- *The parents' room* – this week allocated to OFSTED*. You bravely invited OFSTED into yesterday's drama session on the mechanicals' village life. It was a lively session... but they would like to discuss the impact on learning before deciding on a grade for your teaching.

The clinchers – which we propose you consider elaborating yourself in order to develop your own account of why drama is important to your classroom – have the headings: Engagement and motivation, Admitting the whole child, Social health, and Improving outcomes. The voice is yours!

Why drama is necessary

Engagement and motivation

I need the children to care about their learning. Drama offers the possibility of making our learning tasks urgent. Pupils might ordinarily 'care' because it is simply good to do well, or to gain the approval of adults or the respect of their peers, but there is another possibility: they care because they have entered and accepted the urgency of a fictional situation; a drama has made our learning uniquely urgent. During the drama we will enter an imagined world. The compelling nature of simply being *in* a well constructed imagined world will seize my children's attention. They will identify with fictional people and begin to feel as they feel, to do as they do, to deal with the situations they need urgently to deal with. They will experience the tensions and problems of this 'new' world, facing jeopardy and dangers which are 'beyond-real but safe' – jeopardy that is more than we can generate here in the classroom in our real life, but safely contained within the fiction. Of course, making learning urgent and active means making learning fun and promoting

---

*   OFSTED is currently Britain's national agency for school inspections.

enjoyment. Do we need to argue that children learn best the things that they enjoy... and that offer the gentle pressure of fictional urgency?

The sheer liberation of 'pretend you are...' is a powerful invitation (again) in the service of learning.

The following are some examples from the Shakespeare work.

Example 1

I want the children to write a poem about an environment – a forest. The lights in the hall are low. Lamps cast shadows on the wall. The children are seated in a circle, and they are told in portentous tones:

Before there were people in this land, there was forest. Before the human creature cut space for homes, fires, farmland... and later, roads, cities... before this there was forest. And if, one day... every human adult and child were to vanish from this place... what would return? (It is waiting at the gates...)... The Forest.

Imagine sitting in this ancient forest right now, it is night... what would you hear?

We create the sounds with our bodies and voices; a soundscape.

Now, it is twenty-thousand years in the past... we are the first people to ever step into this forest. What will we see, hear, feel, smell, taste?

The children step into the forest one at a time. The group provides the soundscape. Turns are taken. The teacher freezes the action and asks each child to describe their experience; the things that each hears, sees, feels, tastes, smells. *Now* we are ready to write our poem about this compelling environment.

The experience of the fiction in drama engages the children physically, aurally, emotionally, intellectually, socially, spiritually. It builds commitment, motivates response, and provides vocabulary in context and material for the writing task.

Example 2

I want the children to consider a story from contrasting perspectives.

We have built Macbeth's castle. We have walked its dank corridors. We have heard of the king's murder and felt the presence of walking, bloody ghosts. We have trained as soldiers in the courtyard, and woven magic around fires as heathen witches. Now we will write as one of the soldiers seeing the trees of Burnham Wood approach; we will write as witches flying invisibly over the turrets, scoffing at the chaos they have brought; we will write as Macbeth's forgotten child Lullach, seeing the world crumble around him as the English army approach. The drama has offered us the possibility of experiencing the single literary event from a multitude of perspectives. We are ready to write. Each child's experience has been shared within the group, but is also unique.

Admitting the whole child

All too often, our classrooms are simply 'rational' places; we honour the ability to recall, process, compute, spell, follow patterns, etc. These are valuable things – and good drama is also urgently rational – but they represent only a small part of the totality of what it is to be human. I want to allow children to bring into the classroom the neglected aspects of themselves as human creatures. When we exclude the possibility of our children as physical, emotional, imaginative, social beings, we not only impoverish the possibilities of their responses and unnecessarily exclude children whose strengths are elsewhere, we also limit their capacity to learn. Drama offers the possibility of being able to address the multiplicity of aspects that are all part of our human make-up. Drama makes our schools more human.

To go a little further into current thinking…

Even a glance in the direction of 'brain-friendly' learning suggests new insights into our understanding of the drama approach. Our lay-person reading of popular accounts of recent neuroscience research into the human brain and the micro-mechanics of learning, points us to a few pertinent ideas.

- The brain is evolved for activity and learning in the 'real' world. We learn best in our natural habitat – a rich, human landscape. A good learning environment offers real-world challenges and real-world contexts for challenge. In addition, the brain's experience of the 'real' seems to be identical to its experience of the 'fictional'. Enter good drama!
- The brain cannot escape being multi-sensory. It thrives in a multi-sensory environment. Enter good drama!
- The whole person learns – the greater the involvement of the whole, the greater the learning. Enter good drama!
- The brain accepts 'knowledge' as fact only when verified by emotional experience; on 'verification', information is admitted to a deeper level of 'knowing'. Enter good drama!

Example

Immortal spirits are drawn to the mortal human child. Titania, Queen of the fairies, has stolen a beautiful Indian child. King Oberon is desperate to have the child for his own, and an argument erupts that is so fierce it changes the weather.

Where is the stolen child? S/he is kept in a high hollow of a tree, guarded by a kindly fairy. The fairy promises to deliver a single letter to the child's home. What note will the child write?

In this tender moment of drama, we acknowledge the schoolchild's emotional life and invite an emotionally specific response: the schoolchild is offered the chance to explore, through analogous experience, their own fears of loss, abandonment, separation, perhaps drawing on experience of real estrangements, real 'child-stealing' incidents they may know of. The situation is at arm's length; the response is real. The writing task is charged, meaningful and motivated by the fiction.

Social health

I want my class to be drawn together as a group. They are a diverse range of children, from a diverse range of backgrounds. There have been tensions between the sub-groups, with some hostility and unhappiness. Through this specific drama, I wish to look at the mechanisms of group formation and conflict – to explore the management of conflict and, importantly, to build a fictional analogous situation in which the *whole* group is forced to face an extreme jeopardy under the threat of a common enemy. I want the *group* to be the basic unit, and its members to demonstrate capability, resilience and perseverance through their shared experience of prevailing through community action. Drama is a deeply social activity; the rich *shared* experiences it offers are capable of transforming groups and building mutually supportive communities.

Example

Verona. Two houses, alike in dignity, are at war. Can we remember where the conflict began? Is it just something that *has always been*? Is there a way through it?

The families are drawn together through the shared grief of losing their youngest children – Romeo and Juliet.

Social learning: if conflicts go unchecked, they tend to escalate towards consequences that are far beyond the 'wrong' that began the conflict.

Improving outcomes

I want my children to be challenged; to be driven upwards in a spiral of improvement in their basic skills, and particularly in the quality of their expression in literacy: speaking, listening and writing. I believe that, through using a drama approach at key moments in the development of learning programmes, I can motivate, enrich and inspire more detailed, precise, insightful responses. Good drama is enjoyable and beneficial in itself; it is also a pretext for the enhancement of other educational outcomes.

The medium of drama is language – sometimes it is the language of space or movement... but primarily it is the spoken word. The drama I share with my children gently forces them to use language in new ways, and gives them opportunities to expand their vocabulary; to deepen their responses; and to explore variant uses of language and the language of variant times, characters and places. When the situation has given them experience of the rich use of language, they are much more likely to transfer this new experience onto the page in more elaborate, accomplished and mature forms of expression. We shall be amassing evidence to support this assertion as we progress through the schemes.

Example

We 'live through' Caliban's capture by Prospero, the banishment of his mother and his enslavement to his new master. We speak with his spitting, visceral voice, mixed with the Shakespearean idiom. We stand in his shoes, seeing the mighty Prospero lord it over the kingdom that he knows should be *his*.

We speak failed spells, express our anger, plot our revenges, devise our tortures, and dream of life when we regain our crown.

How do we achieve all this without expanded, elaborate, glorious, character-specific and moment-specific language? We can't – we create it. The children will write 'in-role' and 'for-role'.

A final flourish

Good drama is an urgent, living, human enterprise. It looks us squarely in the face and heart and centre and, with a hearty, insistent laugh, demands of us who we are. Good drama finds a place in schools for real, complete joy. Good drama makes us agents in our lives in a world that would only have us be objects. Good drama pushes us forward; it does what all education should do, it drives us towards full maturity, it makes us more human. Good drama is an important force for good as well as a force for learning.

We hope this brief tour of some ideas in support of the drama approach will ignite your interest and commitment. As your experience develops through these schemes, be alert to the impact of your work together. Gather your own ideas, your own examples and your own narratives. Be reflective and take your own thoughts seriously. Become an advocate; an expert. Keep a journal. Blog! Drama is a movement that has developed quietly through an accumulation of rich experience in the privacy of classrooms. It needs to be experienced, and that experience then needs to be shared in whatever forms we can muster. We hope you will join the movement.

The field of drama

When we set about developing drama as a resource to enhance our teaching, we are entering into a tradition of 'drama-in-education' that originates in Britain and has, over the past fifty years, developed into a powerful toolkit of available approaches that together are capable of opening up the curriculum and learning in an exciting, profoundly human way. In entering into drama as an approach, there is a body of work waiting to be mined. The leading lights of drama have been Dorothy Heathcote, Gavin Bolton, Jonothan Neelands, Allan Owens and many more practitioners. Begin there. We offer a select bibliography for further reading at the end of this book.

So – why drama for exploring Shakespeare?

It seems obvious.

Drama is Shakespeare's proper form. Drama is Shakespeare in his element.

Shakespeare's mastery involves the creation of compelling new worlds, inhabited by complex human characters, who are driven to moments of glorious or terrible illumination where their worlds disintegrate or are reborn, and who speak in precise, wonderful words that capture the essence of the moment and speak to us of ourselves.

The worlds of Shakespeare's plays are rich, diverse and extreme. His characters are often at the edge of things, forced to confront life in extraordinary ways. Through the dramas we create here, we give children (and ourselves) the chance to enter into these worlds: to walk the land, speak *with* the characters and *as* the characters, to hear and deliver the language, to live through the developing stories and their often tragic ends.

As well as wonderful opportunities for language and learning, the plays offer such rich pictures of life that they invite us and our children to ask the *big questions* and explore the outer reaches of what it is to be human. If you work with children, and if you listen, you will recognise the truth of Bond's statement that 'children ask the questions of Plato'. Here is a space for the questions to be revealed and wrestled with.

The nature of Shakespeare's language offers particular opportunities for learning and development. The thoughts expressed are sometimes experienced by readers and listeners as 'ideas in knots'. This isn't to disparage the texts, it is part of their power: they are beautiful, lyrical, intriguing knots, which require precise listening and provoke a tender struggle of mental untangling. The reward of *solving* the language seems similar to the reward of mathematical problem-solving. In the schemes that follow, we aim to create the circumstances for children to gain access to some key elements of the text, and to offer experiences that contain the *need* to accomplish the untangling.

Drama and Shakespeare: a long, happy, happy marriage.

2 Conventions and techniques

Throughout the development of the drama-in-education approach, some activities that teachers have found effective and used repeatedly have become established as 'drama conventions'. You'll know their names: hot-seating, thought-tracking, freeze-frame, etc. Indeed, there is a form of classroom drama which seems to involve the simple enacting of these conventions – 'I hot-seat, therefore I am (doing drama)' – but we hope the schemes outlined here demonstrate something beyond the basic application of techniques. Simply *implementing* or even *stringing together* conventions might enliven your classroom, but will not in itself allow us to generate compelling, inspiring, human learning opportunities. The schemes in this book (chapters 4–7) represent the artful construction of rich *sequences* of experiences. The schemes do use recognisable drama conventions – they are the bones of drama – but they are smart about their use, adding ligament, sinew, flesh, heart and blood.

The following practical accounts of drama conventions will be of use when you come across them in the schemes. Here we give each approach individual attention in isolation from its application in the schemes. We hope to paint a clear picture of the techniques and offer some practical insight into their use.

Tableaux/still images/freeze frames

How? Ask pupils to create a 'statue' or 'frozen picture' of a particular moment, or character, or emotion. Can be accomplished individually, in pairs, in a small group, in a large group, or as a whole group. Sometimes usefully introduced with: 'If I had been there with a camera at that moment and taken a picture… what exactly would I have seen?'

Why? Allows pupils to distil an idea, or character, or moment. Forces them to concentrate on the essentials of a scene or moment. Who are these people? What are their relationships? What precisely is the situation in which they are trapped at this moment? How do they feel? How do they feel about the other people around them? How is this shown 'in space'?

Other things

- We have a preference for the more specialised word 'tableau' over 'freeze frame', 'frozen picture', etc., just for its 'otherness'. Of course, as we are developing the use of this more unusual term, we will support understanding with the simpler terms as well. (Note: the plural of 'tableau' is 'tableaux'.)
- Tableaux can be useful in slowing down the development of a drama to allow pupils to focus on the key elements. For example, use 'create a tableau of…' as a preliminary stage to making a full piece of drama that might include action and words.
- A preliminary series of tableaux of the beginning, middle and end of a narrative can be very useful and underlie the necessary structure of a piece.
- Tableaux have a mechanism of control built into them, which helps to maintain focus and a sense of seriousness when it is needed.

- Demonstrate yourself how *still* a 'still image' needs to be, and *insist* on this level of stillness.
- Make stillness (as well as silence) an important, readily achieved feature of your drama classroom. Teach the word 'freeze' as your central control mechanism and insist on a speedy response.
- Anticipate an approaching 'freeze' call with an audible countdown. This gives pupils the chance to complete their conversations and activities under the gentle pressure of time: '5, 4, 3, 2, 1 . . . *freeze*'.
- Holding tableaux across a whole room also helps bring a sense of seriousness to the drama classroom.
- Couple creating tableaux with 'reading' of the tableaux. Look at them closely: the details are critical. Invite pupils to join you in careful 'reading'. What can you see? What is happening here? How do the people feel? What are they thinking?
- Tableaux lead effortlessly into 'thought-tracking' – see below.

A specialised form of tableau, which is made great use of in the schemes that follow, is the whole group tableau.

Whole group tableaux

How? Define a space clearly. This might be the centre of a circle, or a specific space ('on the carpet'; 'between these two chairs'; 'within this boundary marked with paper tape on the floor'). The space is our empty stage and it is waiting to be filled – calling us! Speak about the place to be created in preparation; allow images to build in the group's mind; suggest characters, situations, shapes, to add 'scaffolding' for children who might find the process more challenging. Explain, and demonstrate yourself, that one at a time, in silence, each person is going to enter the empty space, take up a position, and make a simple action (with a word, if they choose and if it is appropriate) that makes clear just *what* they are doing, or *who* they are, and then freeze. Other pupils entering the space can build upon earlier images, or start their own image in a new, empty space.

Why? To create a comprehensive image of a specific place. A good tool for setting the scene and building belief. Also a very controlled activity, which might build your own and your pupils' confidence in the drama approach. It allows the group to work as a unit in a careful way and builds group reliance. Because each person must enter alone, it is a powerful technique for safely distributing high focus and supporting pupils through it.

Other things

- Once created, you could turn the sound of this place on and off – use a gesture of your hand to signal the switch.
- Or you could bring it to life (action) for a few seconds and then freeze it again, or return it to the beginning.
- Explore separate sections of the scene by *spotlighting* areas one at a time and allowing them to come alive, or the sound to be heard. As this section 'enacts', the rest of the group remains fixed in the tableau.
- You might visit individuals in the scene and give them back the power of speech ('thought-track' them). Explain that tapping them very gently on the shoulder will trigger speech.
- It can also be a controlled way of building a sense of seriousness before giving a signal for the scene to come alive and allowing the group the chance to 'live through' this moment in some

absorbing occupational mime, which you might yourself enter in-role to add greater depth or a new direction.

Thought-tracking/inner thoughts

How? A gentle touch on the shoulder is established as the trigger for speech... often while in a tableau. Allows a pupil to speak their character's thoughts.

Why? A good way of allowing characters to emerge slowly or, often, spontaneously, in a spirit of seriousness.

Other things

- You may find it useful, or necessary, to give pupils the chance to rehearse their statement silently in their head before speaking.
- You might helpfully give pupils a 'sentence root' (see below) to complete in their speech: for example, 'I feel...', 'I can see...'. The use of 'I' is important – it indicates that the 'actor' is now *being* the character, not reporting *about* a character.
- Leave space between each piece of speech. This adds value to what has been spoken and develops the dramatic tension of the moment.
- You may wish to repeat each statement yourself, both to add value and drama to the statement, and to make sure everyone has heard every contribution.

Interviews/hot-seating

How? Place a character in a specially chosen space (such as a chair separated from a circle or group). Members of the group question the character. You might play the character yourself (see 'Teacher in-role' below), or hand the role to a pupil.

Why? Good for building belief and developing understanding of, and empathy for, a character. Good for creating the information a group might feel they need for further work. A way of dramatically moving a story on, or presenting new information in a spontaneous, compelling manner.

Other things

- You might play the character yourself, if you have definite information you wish to present.
- If you are at a point where the next critical 'turn' in the narrative could be the free choice of the pupil being hot-seated, be prepared to think on your feet... always with an eye on the *dramatic* possibilities of the decision as well as on *learning* opportunities.
- Think carefully about the choice of character to interview; choosing not a central character but an auxiliary one (for example, not the king but a servant in the court) offers an entirely new perspective.
- If a pupil is being hot-seated and you need a certain direction to be taken, don't be afraid to take the pupil into your confidence and brief him/her on the key points to get across, or even to make it a thoroughly 'assisted interview' during which, as *critical* questions are asked, you hand notes or whisper to the interviewee, who uses your intervention to guide their answer. You operate as a kind of 'solicitor to the accused'.

Distributed hot-seat/whole group monologues

How? At a character's key moment, the whole group becomes the main character and speaks his/her thoughts. *You* pose the questions, and anyone can answer. When a person has spoken, others are invited to add to this strand of thought, or to begin a new one. This can be developed into creating a 'whole group monologue', in which the character speaks, with individual pupils offering successive lines.

Why? Can add real depth by allowing individual contributions to accumulate to become a fuller statement of the character's thoughts and situation. Can be a powerful way of sharing the attention and responsibility of a hot-seat and making use of the wisdom of the group.

Other things

- To add focus, try sitting the group in a circle, in tableau, with an actor in the centre as the character; '*this* is the character, *we* are his/her mind'.
- Alternatively, have the group spread around the room, isolated in their own space. Make sure, as they look forward, that they are not looking into the face of another person. This gives each person the chance to focus on the character.
- Often members of the group are given time to prepare a statement and then, by raising a hand, to speak their thoughts one at a time.
- Sometimes you might think it useful to allow the group to speak *alternative* rather than *accumulating* thoughts. For example, accumulating thoughts: 'She said ... *and then* she thought and continued...'; or alternative thoughts: 'He thought this ... *but could have* thought this ...'.
- At the end of such a sequence, you might summarise by repeating all the offerings yourself in a continuous stream: the character's single speech that you 'perform'.
- Or, once developed, ask the group to repeat their statements as a continuous speech.
- Or you might have a note-taker to write it all down for future use. You could give the 'speech' to one actor to deliver.
- Again, encourage silence between statements to add value and 'ritual tension'.

Teacher in-role

How? Many moments can be enriched by your adopting a character and entering the drama 'in-role'. It is your most powerful tool. Hot-seating (above) is perhaps a good starting point. You might also enter into an ensuing drama (whole group or small group) as a new character, whose attitude might be passive, inquisitive or hostile, or who might introduce new, urgent information – a new twist.

Why? A way to deepen the response and commitment of a group; to move a drama on while perhaps provoking a turning point or decisive moment in the narrative. It can be a dramatic way of internally engineering a critical plot development.

Other things

- The group will need to be prepared for your entering the drama. You should explain that you are going to behave and speak differently. The group has to 'allow' you to do this and be able to maintain the fiction.

- Normalise the idea that you can drop in and out of character at will... and that you will *need* to if the class doesn't allow you to continue.
- You might find it useful to give yourself a simple prop (such as a hat) to indicate whether you are *in* or *out* of role.
- Taking on a role is not an 'acting job' in the same sense as a professional actor's role might be understood. Generally speaking, all that is required of you as a teacher in-role is a demonstration of the character's basic attitude. You might find a simple change of posture or vocal pitch, or a discreet suggestion of accent, is enough. You needn't become absorbed in the role. The character serves the drama, and you need to be able to step in and out of characters and reflect upon them in an instant.
- When choosing characters to adopt, experiment with playing low status as well as high status. You might be the emperor, or chairperson of an important meeting; but you might also be a nervous peasant farmer, or a lowly, anxious maid. A low-status role is recommended for engendering a 'caring' response from the group. It is also a great demonstration of the teacher's confidence and commitment.

Meetings

How? Every member of the group either creates, or is given, a role to play in a critical meeting that is to take place (usually) at a decisive moment in a developing drama. The characters may already have been involved in the drama, or they may be new to it; they may be 'hotly' involved in the drama, or more detached and 'cool'. Discuss the composition of the meeting group with the class before entering into the drama. Encourage the development of a diverse group with a variety of statuses and perspectives. After preparing the ground, explain that the meeting group will look and behave differently from this group (the class)... invite pupils to sit differently on their chairs and prepare a new voice. Give a very clear signal that the meeting and your role are about to begin (see 'Teacher in-role' above). Around the circle, ask everyone to introduce themselves. You are either in a chairing role yourself, or you have handed this over, with clear guidance, to a pupil. The chair needs to think through a number of critical issues to begin the meeting: set the scene, recap the background and situation, then launch and manage the meeting.

Why? Deepens commitment and understanding. New characters discover and offer new understandings. Good opportunities for problem setting and problem solving. Good for revealing the crux of the situation or conflict. Can lead to a real flow of language when pupils become absorbed as a group in the situation. In some circumstances, a meeting is a great exercise in consensus-building, in finding settlement: 'We must agree to...'.

Other things

- Community meetings (such as a village assembly) are good for making what begins as an individual problem into a community problem, placing it in a wider social context.
- Pupils might be encouraged to take 'expert' roles as part of the group meeting (such as a professor of history in a meeting about evacuees; or a child psychologist, head teacher or GP at a meeting about a troubled child). Be prepared for some surprisingly expanded vocabulary and language from pupils! This has been called the 'mantle of the expert', a term coined by Dorothy Heathcote.

- Often, after the ground-establishing phase of a meeting, it becomes necessary to 'turn up the heat' and offer a provocative statement or position that will bring forward more strident responses. You might do this yourself, or you might think about 'priming' a pupil to take on the role of provocateur.
- It will probably be necessary to give the meeting a clear task to complete: 'We must decide tonight...'; 'The danger is approaching...'; 'The king has given this meeting the power to decide... and expects an answer by dawn...'. A sense of urgency can be a wonderful thing.
- After the meeting, you and the class might analyse how the group at the meeting operated together. This can be a good way of thinking about how groups work.

Small group play-making

How? Break up into small groups and set pupils a clear task of making their own response to the dramatic situation. Ask groups to make a play or a drama to explore/complete/ elaborate/explain the precise question/moment/situation at hand. Give the groups a specific amount of time to complete their task. At the end of this period (see 'Time in drama' in Chapter 3), ask the groups to perform their dramas (for one example see 'Into performance' below).

Why? Pupils' own play-making is an opportunity for them to process the flow of information that the drama has fostered. They have the chance to make their own creative responses, assimilate information, experiment with ideas and solutions, and solve problems in negotiation. It is a moment in which they become solely responsible for their own creativity; they become their own playwrights, directors and actors. It is *their* space. Within the flow of the drama, it is sometimes necessary to break the whole group down into smaller units, with the simple aim of relieving a 'focus overload' – both on you and on the whole group.

Other things

- In making sure the task is as focused as possible, you might engineer the 'lead-in' task to end at a critical moment, and then pose a clear but challenging question. 'What could have happened next?' is the obvious, but probably least interesting, one. Others might be:
  - 'A new person is about to enter... who is it, and how does the scene change?'
  - 'Someone has just overheard this scene. What happens?'
  - 'Why is this happening? Show me an event two days/one week/three years before that helps explain why this happened.'
  - 'At this decisive moment, what are the consequences of the possible decision? Show me a moment one day/one month/fifteen years later.'
- It may be useful at times to stage the development of small group play-making by asking groups first to create just a *tableau* of a moment... and once this has been achieved to allow the layering-in of movement and speech as groups move towards a full, living piece.
- Offering limitations to the play-making is often very productive. You might, for example, exclude the *obvious* solution to a problem; allow only five, or ten, or thirty seconds of action; allow only four words or three sentences, or one line per character; or make the scene happen over a telephone. Imposing such limits forces the play-makers to *choose* more carefully and promotes artistic selection.
- When constituting groups, you will need to consider the most appropriate form of grouping for the task. You might want to make systematically created, random, non-friendship groups (for example by numbering off around a circle), or allow free choice (which is likely to lead to

friendship groups). Our preference is for 'rationally engineered' groups which are negotiated openly with the class in order to fulfil the needs of the task. For example, if it is a family scene, it might be important for the groups to be mixed gender; or you might negotiate that today is a day when the group needs to look at the issue from a new perspective and therefore non-friendship groups are best. Of course, when necessary, retain the right to outlaw any groups that you feel will not be productive ('it's for your own benefit!'). Finally, you might use spatial criteria for creating groups: for example, wherever the previous activity has left the group in the space, gather together teams of pupils who are closest to each other, or within certain boundaries that you might draw (with an eye to the composition of the groups) as you go.

Forum theatre

How? During the performance of a drama, the teacher and the class have the power to freeze the action and to question characters, or to suggest alternative actions or words. Suggestions are implemented immediately.

Why? A way of really exploring and dissecting a situation, character or set of characters. Dynamic and powerful.

Other things

- The changes suggested are usually enacted by the person suggesting the change, but perhaps alternatively by the actor on stage, or by a volunteer. The scene changes in response.
- The suggestions made by the audience may come about in response to the questions you pose: Why did this happen? Why did this character decide to do that? How might it have been different? Choose such questions carefully.
- Depending on the nature of the consideration you are exploring, we might take the drama back to the start and replay it with the suggested changes made to the action. Sometimes a suggestion or question might take us to a completely different time or place.
- You might choose to hot-seat a particular character (see above). It is a free-wheeling, animated dialogue and exploration; we don't have to discuss ideas . . . we explore them by enacting them. It is a process of experimentation, enquiry and clarification.
- 'Forum theatre' is a term coined by Augusto Boal, a Brazilian drama and theatre-maker who pioneered the idea of a whole theatre performance being improvised and created by the audience in this way. He calls the audience 'spectactors' – a term we like!

Soundscaping

How? To evoke a particular environment, we imagine all the sounds we might hear in this place. In a *landscape*, an artist captures and recreates everything they can *see* before them; in a *soundscape*, we capture and recreate everything we can *hear* in this place.

Why? A very engaging method that can really cement a feeling of purpose for a group and set a powerful backdrop for an emerging setting or event. It is also a demonstration of the power of the community working together – the effect is a fragile thing that needs everyone's support.

Other things

- You might think about beginning with a relaxation activity that gets pupils lying down and attentive to sound.
- Prepare the group by asking them to 'hear' the sounds of the fictional place, and prepare to begin creating the sounds when you invite them.
- It is an activity that might be accomplished in a circle or with the group spread around the room. It might be evoked with the pupils' eyes closed or open.
- The noises made must be possible with their voices or hands, though you might consider offering percussion instruments.
- Sometimes noises are contributed which dominate the soundscape. Explain that some noises are distant (and quieter) and some are close (and louder) – just as, in a landscape, more distant things are smaller. Similarly, you might ask for several pupils to contribute together to a more dominant sound (for example, a gathering storm).
- You may need to ask pupils to repeat their sounds, either continuously (the sea) or intermittently (an owl hooting).
- Establish your hand as a volume control.
- You might usefully 'narrate' the soundscape in order to encourage its development, or 'conduct' it with gestures as a conductor might an orchestra.
- Give the soundscape some dramatic structure: a sense of development over time, from silence to silence, building, climaxing and then fading.
- Once you have created the landscape by improvising it, you might repeat it from the beginning as a 'score', perhaps making a simple digital recording of it for later use in the drama.
- A soundscape can become a repeatable item that you can summon from the group with a minimum effort, to great effect.

Decision corridor/conscience alley

How? Ask pupils to line up in two parallel, facing lines. A character will begin at one end of the line and pass down the 'corridor' to the other. As they move through, the pupils in the lines speak to the character, giving a diverse range of advice and opinions with the intention of influencing the character. When the character reaches the end of the corridor, they will announce their decision and the drama may continue from the decision taken, or it may end.

Why? It is a vehicle for decision-making and for getting to the crux of the problem. It also demonstrates the complexities of real decisions. It allows every member of a group to contribute perspectives.

Other things

- A conscience alley will normally happen when the drama has arrived at a point of critical decision for a character.
- Make sure the decision to be made is clear. Don't be afraid to run the process through more than once until it feels as though the group has exhausted the possibilities and arrived at a conclusive end point.
- There are a number of options for how it might be run, including the following.
  - Allow the main character to *not* speak back to those in the 'walls', but just to listen and consider until the second run or the end.

- Allow all of the 'walls' to speak their thoughts at once and 'loop' their thoughts in endless repetition – this gives them the chance to rehearse their lines in a kind of noisy privacy.
- Try encouraging pupils to express their thoughts with heightened emotion; to develop a real emotional commitment to the idea they are promoting. This might be thought of as the hot version of the technique, rather than something cooler and more thoughtful. Both have their place, depending upon the moment of drama.
- You might line up pupils with opposing views on one side of the corridor or the other, so that one side is, for example, *yes* and the other is *no*. This is likely to encourage a more passionate episode of decision-making.
- Invite pupils to offer a 'shape' or gesture to show how they feel physically about the main character before (or even instead of) speaking. It can be useful to show their basic attitude.
- Try not letting the main character speak their final decision until after all of your trial runs, during which the ideas will have developed in complexity.

Mind trap

How? This is similar to a conscience alley, but is not necessarily determined by a moment of decision. Ask the group to sit in a circle with a character in the middle. The circle is the mind in which the character is trapped. The character wants to escape. The pupils in the circle express the rush of thoughts that might be swirling about the character's mind. Sometimes the thoughts are the character's own thoughts; sometimes they are things they have heard other people say around or to them.

Why? It can be a powerful way of capturing the complex mental state of a person at a particularly difficult moment in their story. It gives every individual the chance to contribute to a whole group sense of the central character.

Other things

- The 'mind trap' is a term we have coined ourselves to capture an activity that has presented itself as useful during the flow of many dramas; it springs from the needs of our practice, as must all these techniques which have become formalised as 'conventions'.
- As with conscience alley, the activity might be played out with various degrees of passion and emotional attachment – hot or cool.
- The sense of the character being trapped and trying to break free might be dramatically interesting. As the character moves towards a particular arc of the circle-wall, that arc can repel them with the ferocity or significance of their offering.
- The walls might achieve some greater solidity by linking arms.

Story Whoosh!/animated story-telling

How? During a Story Whoosh! the group stands in a wide circle and the centre is indicated as the 'stage' onto which the story will be summoned. As you read or tell the story, pupils step into the circle and create tableaux of every character or object that you mention. This builds a picture of the place, characters and situation. When you reach the end of a particular 'unit' of story and the stage is full, you wave your hand over the stage, give a call of 'Whoosh!' and clear the stage. At this the pupils return to their places in the circle and the building of the stage-picture begins again.

> **Why?** A really great, energetic and stimulating way of having a narrative told in its entirety. It is active, involving and 'democratic' in as much as a large number of pupils can play the key roles across the different episode.

Other things

- We think this technique has its origins with Jonothan Neelands, though other claims are possible! Stories have been 'summoned' before, but the 'Whoosh!' command is such a brilliant innovation that makes the whole group animation of a full narrative manageable.
- As a group is introduced to the technique, you might begin by *directing* which pupils are to enter and take roles; perhaps in order around the circle – sometimes you might indicate an individual to take a part; sometimes a whole swathe of people might become, for example, the forest.
- As the group progresses, you might move towards a situation where pupils freely enter the circle and take roles themselves in a fair and reasonable manner. This kind of democratic 'turn-taking' is an emblem of a group with mature and positive social health.
- Feel free to introduce the spoken word into the 'Whoosh!' Particularly in these Shakespeare schemes, it is a good way of introducing text while in the flow of activity. You can speak the text yourself within the narrative and gesture for the pupil playing the part to repeat after you, or, indeed, the whole group to repeat key lines.
- At the end of each scheme we have produced a 'Story Whoosh!' sheet. This contains a simple version of the story written specifically to be spoken, and offering opportunities for object- and place-building as well as characterisation. Feel free to embellish at will.

Movement work

> **How?** Pupils are invited to become completely involved in the physical activity or physical expression of a character. This might follow on from the creation of a tableau and be signalled by a simple clap.

> **Why?** Understanding the physical make-up of a character can really help to develop empathy and identification. The physicality of the character suggests a whole set of attitudes and traits which might be explored orally or otherwise at a later stage. It is widely accessible to pupils and not mediated by their linguistic confidence or ability.

Other things

- Sometimes in movement work there may be an initial hesitation from pupils in becoming absorbed. It is important to let a sense of absorption 'settle' on the group; allow time for this to grow.
- During a sequence of movement work, feel free to freeze the action in order to pose new questions, pick out and share interesting practice; or even question individual characters.
- It is a subtle art to not let your interventions take away a sense of absorption, but to enhance it.

Construction tasks

> **How?** Pupils are invited to build the world of the drama using simple materials such as a variety of paper, cloth, masking tape, cardboard boxes, string, pipe cleaners, etc. – an equipment set sometimes referred to as 'junk modelling'.

Why? Once the narrative has been established, the construction of the world of the play becomes a way of capturing and summarising understanding. The finished product becomes a concrete representation of the narrative and the characters that aids full comprehension and might even be shared with the school community or parents.

Other things

- A great starting point for construction is the landscape of which the world is built. We first came across this technique in a workshop with Dorothy Heathcote. It involved laying an earth-coloured (brown, green, or even white for a colder climate) cloth on the floor, and putting other cloth or screwed-up paper underneath the cloth in order to make a relief of a landscape with hills, dips, outlines of pathways, rivers etc.

- This basic landscape must honour the realities of geography (which in itself is a useful cross-curricular link). For example, rivers must flow *down* and perhaps become wider as they flow; castles are situated on specific sites, such as on hills.

- The 'full-on' version of the activity involves building the site or *world* of the play and then populating it with the *characters* and giving the characters their key *text*. By using all three aspects, it becomes possible to make this an activity for a large group with clear demarcation of tasks.

- Scale can sometimes be a problem, particularly with the construction of characters. Indicate the scale size of a character – perhaps as big as a little finger. It will still in reality be out of proportion to the landscape, but at least it will be consistent.

- There can, of course, be multiple copies of the characters at different sites of the landscape world; for example, Macbeth at the witches' lair on the heath, and on the battlements, and murdering Duncan in his chamber.

- Your construction might be a temporary structure built in the hall, or a more permanent structure. It might be built quickly in a single afternoon, or take weeks of detailed construction. If it is temporary, you might consider creating a permanent map of the world the group has created (which is clearly easier to store), or you might make a video capturing the construction – when doing this, fun can be had with trying to create the impression of an aerial flight over the world which focuses in on specific events represented. You might then add music or spoken text onto the soundtrack – it's easier than it might sound. Really! Your pupils can probably show you the way.

Writing in-role (and for role)

How? Pupils are led through a variety of techniques and situations into identification with a specific character. The narrative is engineered to bring us to a point where the next decisive task is writing. For example, Friar Lawrence decides to write to the prince to make a confession and stop the terrible events around Romeo and Juliet from unfolding further. The pupils are therefore given an urgent reason for writing.

Why? Given an effective set-up of character and situation, writing in-role can be a very powerful way of enhancing children's writing. The drama allows them to develop a perspective, experience and build an extended vocabulary appropriate to the situation, and write from within a concrete emotional framework.

Other things

- The task can be enhanced by making available unfamiliar and compelling writing materials, such as quill pens and ink or aged paper.
- Writing *for* role is a slightly different task, in which the drama still demands that a literary document is created, but in which the pupils act at more of a distance and operate as script-writers supplying text or documents for a character or situation. The document is created out of the drama and then fed back in.
- When writing in-role, pupils might need to consider the language of the written expression carefully. For example, if it is one of Shakespeare's 'great lost...' scenes, we would expect 'antique' language, metaphor, image, blank verse, etc. This can give the task added interest.
- To support a writing in-role event, it might be useful to introduce a 'word bank' – as words occur, or later on reflection, they are written up for public view and individual use.
- It is sometimes useful to differentiate a writing task to allow for different levels of confidence and skill: what we don't want is for a writing task to switch off less confident writers. For example, in one scheme the situation demands that two letters might be written: one as a young child who has been stolen by fairies; and one from the child's grieving mother. In another, the letters can be generated by an expansive range of characters, from Bart Simpson to Florence Nightingale to Julius Caesar to Michelle Obama! If the situation demands that the writing be from a single character (as in the Friar example), your set-up of the situation might allow for varying levels of literary skill. For example, 'in his frantic state this excellent scribe... who is one of the few people of this city who *can* write... might struggle to get his words on paper... his hands are shaking, his mind is falling apart... but he must write'. Such a layer of detail might be viewed as needlessly anticipating struggle (in which case don't use it), but it simply aims to make plausible *within the drama* all levels of contribution. Of course, you know your children and whether this is necessary.

Sentence roots

How? Pupils are invited to create their own original text by completing a sentence root that gives structure and focus to their offering. For example, after a soundscape and elaboration of the ancient forest, they are invited to complete the sentence 'This is a forest of...'. Or elsewhere, after exploring the violent character of Verona, they are invited to complete the sentence root 'Verona, City of...'. Pupils are invited to supply a single word or phrase.

Why? This is a simple technique which enhances the pupil's response by allowing them to build on a structure that itself invites a focused and often 'lyrical' construction. It is a good way of summarising understanding and experience, which can be captured effortlessly as a whole group performance poem, or used as material for individual, drama-centred poetry-making.

Other things

- It is usually helpful to ask pupils to speak the sentence root themselves *before* adding their unique contribution; so *everyone* says, 'This is a forest of...'.
- Alternatively, *you* speak the sentence root each time and each pupil completes the sentence. It seems important that root and ending are heard together, rather than speaking the root once at the start of the process and assuming it to be in place thereafter.

- Value can be added to pupils' contributions by your repeating the whole line so that it is heard clearly by everyone.
- It is a simple step to make a copy of the contributions on paper. Pupils might do this individually and then you collate them together to make a whole, or the group might act to capture the text.
- The technique seems most effective when the initial expression of the pupil contributions are oral, and later captured as written text. This allows for continuity between the 'lived-through' drama experience and the imaginative statements of pupils.
- Having said that, other situations might call for a period of reflection and written text-creation before pupils present their offerings to the group.

Discussion

How? Pupils enter into a dialogue with each other and with you in order to discuss ideas that have arisen during the flow of the drama. Your role here is to *notice* and to *frame* the questions and to encourage your pupils to do the same.

Why? Because a good drama throws up important questions; the characters face dilemmas and situations; the stories point us to issues to be considered.

Other things

- Alongside the telling of stories, drama might be thought of as a compelling frame for important questions. Inasmuch as this is the case, the discussions that ensue from the fictional contexts are perhaps the real *point* of your work. Among the welter of educational opportunities presented in the schemes, the educational benefits of mature, committed group discussions are perhaps the most significant, taking us back to early schooling under the cypress trees of Athens! Your role is Socrates' role – to question, to challenge, to focus, to be awkward, to reflect back, to seek clarification, to engineer conclusion and consensus, or to leave problems hanging for another day.
- Children are inveterate questioners. 'Why? Why? Why?' One of the glorious things about using texts as rich as Shakespeare's is the opportunity, within the safety of the fiction, to allow children the opportunity to ask and grapple with sometimes big and sometimes genuinely pressing questions. A selection comes to mind from these schemes: Can words break scientific rules? Can a spell make a storm? What power do words *really* have? Are ghosts real? What is magic? What is a witch? Where does the idea of a dangerous old lady come from? What is it like for a child living in a war zone? If you'd never seen another human being before, what would you think about them when you discovered them? Why do fairies steal human children? What would it be like to lose a child? To be stolen? How do conflicts between people begin? How can they be ended? What happens when we die? What makes a person do 'evil' things? What is it like to be trapped in a world that you didn't create and doesn't let you feel at home? How does it feel to grieve? What makes a person kill? These are tough questions for anybody; our drama makes them askable.
- A further concept derived from Edward Bond's theoretical work is the idea of 'the gap'. For us at this point it is important to understand the nature of a good question. You might recognise the distinction between a *closed* and an *open* question – a closed question being one to which there is probably a single correct answer and which requires *convergent* thinking; an open question being one which invites diverse responses and requires *divergent* thinking. To go further here, we propose that the most educationally significant questions are those that are

not simply *open*, but which contain a yawning '*gap*'. These will be questions to which *you* don't know the answer… and, indeed, you probably *couldn't* know the definitive answer. For example, 'Are some people just evil?' Or 'What happens when a person dies?' When the question is posed (and especially when it 'falls out' of a compelling moment of drama), the most appropriate response is an empty silence. We stand in the gap created by the question. We don't know immediately how to respond. There is something a little like vertigo; 'the terror of the blank canvas', as Van Gogh reported. Then we start talking and our dialogue begins.

- Such questions do need to 'fall out' of the drama. Your key task is to *get the drama right*. This involves creating enjoyable, compelling, joy-filled, pulsing, human dramatic experiences for your children. Which we all hope will be the outcome of your use of this book.

Choral or 'choir' speaking*

How? Groups speak text as a group through the application of techniques for breaking the text down and demonstrating emphasis and rhythm.

Why? Speaking in chorus in this way offers an accessible introduction to the speaking of Shakespeare. It allows us to distribute the attention of speaking among the group, and draws our attention to the rhythm, metre and emphasis of the lines. It is also a great task for building a group's sense of itself. It facilitates the learning and retention of key text and can form the basis of exquisite performances.

Our introductory technique is as follows.

- Display the text on the walls (or floor) of the space in which you are working; perhaps on a screen, but ideally prepared on paper. In this way, pupils remain unencumbered by rustling sheets of paper.
- Ask the class to repeat after you the line you have chosen – simple call-and-response.
- Repeat it several times in rhythm, adding varieties of tone and volume, from whisper to shout. Indicate your hand as a volume control.
- Now discuss briefly the meaning of the line; in order to speak the lines, even as a group, we need to think about what we are saying and what the words mean. Attend to unusual words or allusions.
- Now place the line firmly in the context of the play. Again, this is important for the group to know when speaking the lines. Who says the line? In what circumstances? Why?
- Ask the group: Would you like to have some fun with the line? And learn about a special and dramatic way of talking *all together*? Explain that it is a difficult task and needs everyone to work together. It's hard, but if we manage it, it will sound fantastic. (We might even record it!)
- Divide the group, in a circle, into four quadrants or sections. Give them numbers from one to four. We find it helpful to make a sign for each section with its name on as a way of remembering and underlining each group's identity.
- Each section has a different job.
  Section 1: You are the *Living Pulse* – you are going to say the whole line calmly and steadily, and repeat it when you get to the end. You are also going to beat out the pulse of the line with your fist. Try. Everyone try. Section alone try.

---

* Although not strictly a drama convention, the schemes make much use of speaking Shakespeare's lines as a group, in chorus. The simple technique here has been devised for its simplicity and repeatability.

Section 2: You are the *Ghost Whisperers* – you are going to repeat the key word or phrase (you decide which) in a ghostly whisper over and over again. Sometimes it might be loud (but never a shout), and sometimes quiet. You are also going to make a ghostly hand gesture all together as you repeat each time. (Perhaps give one of the group the 'volume-control hand' as demonstrated earlier.) Try. Everyone try. Section alone try.

Section 3: You are the *Haunting Echoers* – you echo the last word of each line (or another word you select as appropriate) and repeat it, as an echo, until the next 'last' word, or the end of the line. Just like an echo, you start loud and fade out. You also give a hand gesture, which starts with you stretching your hand high and then drops until you touch the floor and are silent. All try. Section alone try.

Section 4: You are the *Word Punchers* – you say the 'punch' words as they come up. Listen to the lines and you can *hear* which are the strong words; you are adding emphasis. As you come in with each punch word, you all punch the air in front of you with a fist. These are the most important, the strongest words, and by emphasising them we are helping people to understand the meaning of the line.

- Now try them all together, bringing them in one at a time as a conductor; once established, try a range of volumes and speeds.

Other things

- Once you have given time to developing this activity, you might introduce a simple gaming element; for example, only the sections you call out can continue to speak – try them individually, then in combinations.
- Develop the challenge: 'That's all very well while you're standing still... and standing next to your group... but can you still do it if I mix you up? Everyone run around until I say stop... but remember your section name. Find a space. Try the speaking again.'
- Again: 'That's all right while you're standing still, but can you do it when you're actually moving around? Let's try.'
- Finally, try calling out the section names so that only those you call can move and speak. End on everybody moving and speaking, and raise the volume.
- You will need to think through (and probably speak) the line you are going to use with the group before embarking; become comfortable with the rhythm, the emphasis.
- There are many elements to 'choral' speaking, and we claim no special expertise. Once you have developed an ear for it through experience, you will be able to develop your own more sophisticated processes and research other techniques
- The above works easily with a pairing of lines, but you might attempt something more complex and spectacular with a much longer speech. In these circumstances, you might need to develop a notation for marking choral techniques on the text itself.

Story jigsaw*

How? A story jigsaw is a sorting activity, which involves pupils reading and then ordering the narrative of the play into the correct order. You will have printed off several copies of the jigsaw. Saving one for yourself that retains the numbering, cut the numbers off the pupils' sheets and then cut up the pieces of the story jigsaw. Jumble each set and place them in envelopes.

---

* Again, not strictly a drama convention, but an activity we use several times throughout the schemes and therefore worth some special attention here.

You might explain the task like as follows.

'A jigsaw is where we take a complete picture and cut it into pieces. We then try to put it back together again to make the complete picture. We're going to do a story jigsaw. We've taken the story of the play and broken it up into a number of pieces. We've cut each piece up and jumbled up the bits. We've then placed the bits for each piece in separate envelopes. In this game, your group has to try and put the bits back together again in the right order to form the pieces.'

Now form the pupils into five or six fairly large groups, and give out the jigsaw envelopes. Each group discusses and sorts the bits in the envelopes.

Make completion of the piece a timed activity, or make it a race; a little gentle, good-humoured pressure sharpens the task.

When complete, check each group's sorting.

Into performance

When each group has its correctly ordered pieces, tell the pupils that together as a group we are now going to tell the whole story. We have made six (or so) groups, and each group is now given responsibility for one section of the story; two adjacent pieces of the jigsaw, for example. Their job is to make two frozen pictures or tableaux (see above) to show the story in each piece. When they have made the two tableaux, they have to work out slow-motion movement which will take them from one picture to the next. When all groups have created their tableaux sequences, you can put the pieces back together again in the correct order. The whole story will be told by moving around the room in a continuous, complete flow; you have a simple performance of the whole play, ready to go.

You could enhance the performance as follows.

- Read the written jigsaw text yourself to accompany the performance; use a declamatory voice.
- Add appropriate music to accompany the piece.
- Begin the sequence formally with an announcement of the full title of the play, such as 'The Most Excellent and Lamentable Tragedy of Romeo and Juliet'.
- If Shakespeare's text has a striking end speech (such as Puck's end to *A Midsummer Night's Dream* or the prince's end to *Romeo and Juliet*), have this text to hand and be prepared to end the sequence with it.

This concludes our analysis of drama conventions.

Within the schemes, you will find a host of other activities which we have not isolated for particular attention, but which are useful and important approaches. The twenty conventions and techniques described above serve as a powerful arsenal out of which the schemes here are constructed, and out of which we hope you will soon feel able to construct your own.

Once you have begun to grasp the techniques, you might like to consider the following selection of other practical ideas relating to the application of drama and the creation and management of compelling experiences for your children.

3 Working with drama – practical advice

Before you begin...

The following short collection of ideas has emerged from practice over many years. This isn't a comprehensive or even a coherent list, but experience has delivered these ideas to us and we hope they will be of some use. We are sure you will soon be able to offer the fruits of your own reflections on your developing practice.

Gaming

Often in the early stages of a drama it is helpful to utilise the draw of gaming as a way of introducing work. But a game in drama is never *just* a game... for the teacher it always has an ulterior motive: it might be engineering the atmosphere of the group, releasing energy or gathering it in. Games are preparation for the next stage of work. In our schemes, games usually introduce characters or themes – they are *games-in-context*.

Your mock-innocent enquiry: 'Would you like to play a game?' is always met with a vibrant 'Yes!', enthusiastic whoops and high expectations. When the game is at the start of a scheme or session, it is a moment when the group freely chooses to join you in your work, and you are able to begin the journey that leads them into the worlds of the drama.

A nice 'trick' we like to play within these schemes is to use the basic form of a game, for example the form of 'Grandmother's footsteps' in *The Tempest* scheme, and build elements of the play onto this sub-structure. The game is both familiar and new at the same time. This allows pupils' enthusiasm for gaming to lead directly to more detailed exploration. It is *purposeful* gaming.

Playfulness

Following on from gaming, it is clearly important for teachers engaged in drama to retain a sense of playfulness about their work. You are always the teacher in the room, always the expeditionary leader, but you are also a full participant in the pretence. Children take their play seriously, whether it is tiddlywinks, a game of football or absorbed, imaginative play. You have to take your drama as seriously. You also need to demonstrate your commitment and your sheer enjoyment of the process of drama. Drama is a journey into play that you make together, and in which you need each other.

Role

It is commonplace to say that teaching is a performance. A teacher plays many roles in the school day, all making different demands on your presentation, your voice and the character you portray; on duty in the playground, taking the register, leading the netball team, teaching maths, getting the paints out for art, dealing with the fighting pair, meeting parents at the door.

The development of this range of roles for yourself is an important element in your professionalism and, indeed, in the maintenance of a healthy mental equilibrium. It isn't a matter of roles to 'hide behind', but of roles to 'work through'.

The role of drama practitioner is an extension of all of these, plus the ability to allow yourself to enter into fiction both in all seriousness and in all playfulness. It is a collection of roles in which you are more conscious of the effect and impact of your role. It is a specialised role, but one that is accessible to all effective teachers, given the prerequisite of developing a diversity of roles that is inherent in teaching itself.

You may find it important to find ways to signal to your children that you are entering a 'drama mode' and that you need them to allow you to enter a different teacher role. 'I may behave differently, speak differently, ask you to do different kinds of things… You need to allow me to play this different role… Or we will have to stop.'

Drama and your voice

Dorothy Heathcote uses the term 'subtle tongue' to describe teachers' complex manipulation of their voice during a drama encounter; great (and interesting) demands are made on your use of register, pitch, tone, emphasis, and even the very character of your voice. But far beyond this, you might be required to challenge your use of language itself (as your children might also be); to cajole, tease, trick, force, convince, demand, befriend, put at ease, lie. You may need to clearly say one thing and mean another. You may be a narrator, an emperor wizard, a spirit of mischief, a humble servant, a malevolent imp, a murderous lord, a manipulating wife, a fleeing child.

All of these things make demands on your use of voice; it is your most immediate and your most important tool. Test it. Challenge it. Rehearse its uses in private. Look after it.

Ritual

Our approach to drama utilises the human response to both story and ritual – two things we seem to find irresistible. By 'ritual' we mean the formal arrangement of elements in order to create a sense of significance. Your pupils enter a darkened hall, objects are laid out on a cloth in the centre of the room, evocative music is playing, they must enter in a formal line and in silence, you are already in the space to receive them, you gesture for the group to continue the line to make a circle, then when the circle is complete and we are all standing with focus, you begin to speak. This is the simple, repeatable use of ritual to create a spirit of serious endeavour. Of course, in a moment playfulness may burst through and we will be playing 'Ticky-it', but the sense of ritual can always be recaptured. We propose that you make such an entry a routine in opening your drama sessions for this work.

'Give me five'

In Chapter 2 we spoke about the importance of discussion and questioning in our drama. There are also many occasions when lower-level discussions are required, for example, when you are asking for suggestions, or for information in response to a specific question. On these occasions you might think about the very simple 'Give me five' technique as a way of helping to manage responses. It goes like this: on posing the question, hold up one hand and say that you are looking for five answers (one for each finger). As answers come in, put down a finger. The fingers are a good visual aid, and as they reduce in number there is some dramatic tension in moving to the final one. If answers come quickly, you can easily continue with 'Give me another five!'; 'On your other hand!'. The real beauty of the approach is that it helps to maintain the dynamism and pace of the session; you can 'Take five' and move on. As you use the technique habitually with a group, they come to understand that only five answers will be taken and begin to choose their answers more carefully. We often underline this sense of prioritising by leaving clear thinking time and saying, 'Who needs one of these five this time?'.

Using text

In these schemes we regularly use the original Shakespeare text, often in an edited form. In using text, experience tells us that the *last* thing you want to do is hand out to children flat, white, A4, photocopied texts (unless it can't be avoided). The texts we use are often so simple that it becomes a fairly straightforward matter to *display* them about the working space rather than distributing paper copies; and it also saves paper. You might consider the following ways of displaying text.

- Write the text on strips of cheap decorator's lining paper in black ink or black paint. Half a width of the role will be adequate to write quite large letters.
- Tear the paper, rather than cutting it, for an antiquated feel.
- Look up online a simple Elizabethan font, such as the free 'Illshakefest' font which is based on the print of the early Folio editions of Shakespeare's plays. You don't need to give a beautiful calligraphic rendition of the font, but a general sense of authenticity is useful. The impression created is one of 'original' text ripped from mammoth, agèd books. The time invested in preparation is more than worth it. As you become familiar with the handwriting style you develop, the preparation becomes a readily achievable task.
- Display the text on different walls so that, during rehearsals and performance, (by way of prompt) pupils can position themselves more naturally and see the text over the other character's shoulder, rather than all needing to look in one direction.

Circles and huddles

Making a circle in drama seems to have become something of a tradition. Of course, a circle is an important way of formalising the start of a session, and many gaming activities needs a circle. In a circle, we are all symbolically equidistant from the centre and therefore equal, and in a circle we can all see each other's faces and we are 'open' to each other physically, both of which encourage the group to communicate positively. Circles are good.

However, we would like to put in a strong word for 'the huddle'! Often in this work with primary-aged children we want to gather ourselves together without the formality of the circle, but with the intimacy of sharing a close space. The huddle promotes more immediate eye contact, and our voices can be softer and more nuanced. In a huddle, the sense can be generated of 'sharing a secret' together. Pupils are much closer together and need to be respectful and sensitive towards other people's sense of comfort. In a huddle, we are able to build focus on a moment, a significant object or, indeed, on you, the leader of this drama expedition.

Time in drama

There are a few things to consider in terms of the use of time in drama.

- In the management of drama, time is often elastic and under your control. If, for example, you have set a task for small-group work, the amount of time you indicate for completion might be, say, one minute. You have chosen this seemingly short period so as to underline the urgency of the task and add the gentle pressure of time. In fact, you are watching the progress of the groups very carefully and noting how they are moving towards completion. You are not necessarily *counting* that minute. Time here is elastic and under your control.
- Similarly, if you wish to indicate the end of a period of preparation, you might count down from ten to zero in order to indicate the coming end; however, the pace of your counting is not dictated by 'clock-time' but the time required by the group. Again, you are watching the progress of the whole group carefully, contracting the seconds to drive onwards, or expanding the seconds to allow for a fuller completion of the task. Some 'ten seconds' last a minute. It is time under the authority of human need!

- Of course, time in a narrative can go backwards as well as forwards. Shakespeare's plays are written in linear time – the story progresses relentlessly towards the inevitably destructive or celebratory end. In our drama, the purpose is different, it is educational, it is discursive and exploratory. It needs to know why? How? It can jump forward to explore implications and consequences, and backward to enquire into the 'why's' of character and action.
- When we become absorbed in a moment, time is distorted in a unique way; we lose a sense of the objective passage of time. Time flies.

Drama and control

In our experience, the most common response from teachers to the question 'What might hold you back in doing more drama?' is 'The threat of losing control'. This is worth pondering for a moment. On the surface, drama often involves working in relatively unstructured spaces and situations. If your daily routines involve classrooms, desks, pens, paper, books, etc., your entry into the flat, empty nothingness of the school hall might feel, at the very least, like an interesting challenge; or perhaps it's Van Gogh's terrifying blank canvas again. But the truth is that drama is actually a very structured activity that is bounded by both implicit and explicit rules about behaviour, technique and approach. When you have hooked the class's imagination by offering a compelling experience that they have freely chosen to enter, and if you keep the momentum rolling and the modes (see below) well structured and adaptive, your children are most likely to be *with* you and the issues of control are all but eliminated.

Of course, we'd prefer not to use the language of 'control' at all. Drama is a collaborative activity, and at its best you are operating as a fellow-traveller, a guiding spirit. Groups involved in heightened activity often need management in order to stay focused and on-task. Drama offers you a range of possibilities for how to maintain focus. You might like to consider the following.

- In dealing with a large, empty space (the hall, for example), consider changing the character of the space with simple alterations to the light. A large, familiar space can be made more intimate and unfamiliar by closing the curtains/blinds and adding an angle-poised lamp or other light source. (A good effect has been generated with a coloured carrier bag on the screen of an overhead projector.) If your hall has stage lights trained routinely on the stage area used for public performances, suggest that the lights might instead be routinely trained on the hall floor (and then re-angled for your infrequent performances) so that they become an option for transforming the hall into a more dramatised space.
- The addition of a focal point to a large space can draw the attention of groups together. This might be a compelling object laid on a simple cloth spread on the floor; or a striking image projected onto the available screen or (our personal favourite) angled to project onto the ceiling or a large, blank wall.
- Some teachers find it useful to hold a pre-drama discussion with their class in order to agree a 'drama contract'. The contract lays down conditions which we must honour in order to *do good drama*. It can be displayed in the classroom or working space.
- It is always better to do *no* drama than to do drama badly. Bad drama can easily crush confidence, destroying positive relationships between you and the class, and between class members themselves; it can undermine learning and create a negative climate. Bad drama is a public defeat for all involved. It would have been better not to have begun. This understanding should be considered and explored with your class; bad drama makes you feel smaller; all that's allowed is drama that makes us feel bigger. If we think our drama is not going well, we will stop and discuss why. If it continues to not be 'good', we will stop completely. This is your extreme sanction. Once children have gained experience of 'good drama' they will *want* to be involved – they will self-regulate.

Part Two: The schemes

4 Shakespeare – the man and his world

We launch ourselves straight into the world of Shakespeare and the world of drama with an introductory workshop, some simple and some fascinating facts, and an original verse play for reading and performing with your group.

Introductory workshop

This first workshop is offered as a free-wheeling introduction to Shakespeare: his work, his significance and his person. It also sets up some ways of working through drama which will be of use throughout this book. It looks to build a bridge between the child's perception of a gulf between work and play – it is serious fun; playful work.

Its aims are to:

- build commitment to the idea of exploring Shakespeare
- develop experience and understanding of the drama approach
- explore the power and significance of language – with Shakespeare's texts as the prime example.

Preparations

- Consider ritualising the working space appropriately: use lighting, music, a collection of props displayed centrally (such as quills and old paper, wooden daggers, a theatrical crown). This might also involve finding appropriate images for projection and music suggestive of the period, or perhaps learning the song 'Rose' yourself for a live rendition! (See 'Ritual' in Chapter 3.)
- Consider learning the first ten lines of Hamlet's 'To be' soliloquy and the 'Enter a murderer' extract (from *Macbeth* and *Hamlet* combined). (They *could* happily be read.)
- For the Shakespearean word shower, print, enlarge and cut up the sheets 'Words and phrases Shakespeare coined' (Figure 2) found at the end of this chapter.

Opening up

Setting the scene

Having ritualised the space, ask the group to enter in a 'ritual stance'.

Elizabethan music is playing, or you are singing the Elizabethan round 'Rose'. You can find renditions of this famous song via a simple online search. Although other versions can be slightly different, our version of the lyric is:

> *Rose, rose, rose, rose*
> *Shall I ever see thee wed?*
> *I marry that I shall*
> *When thou art dead*

You might just sing and repeat the first line. Although recorded music is an option, we challenge you to sing the song live yourself. There is nothing quite as powerful as a solo human voice in an atmospheric space. Your singing expresses your confidence, your commitment and, perhaps, your willingness to test the edges of your own comfort zone. All of which is useful modelling of the behaviour you will be asking of your pupils.

Discussion

Indicate for the group to form either a circle or a huddle (see 'Circles and huddles' in Chapter 3).

> **Question: What are the most famous six words in the whole world?**

Hold up one hand. You'd like five answers – one for each finger (see 'Give me five' in Chapter 3). This is a good 'gap-question' – a genuinely problematic but creatively interesting question that isn't even quite clear in its intention, but engages the mind.

> I wonder if it might be these... '*To be or not to be*'? Do you recognise these words? What's the next line? Does anyone know anything about these words? Where they came from? Who says them? Who wrote them? Most importantly, what do they mean? Discuss.

> Of course, they are spoken by Hamlet in Shakespeare's play called? ('*Hamlet*, of course'). Hamlet is a young man outraged by the fact that his father has died (perhaps murdered) and his mother has married his dad's brother almost immediately after the funeral. He feels so bad that he's thinking about killing himself, and he looks us, the audience, straight in the eye and says, '*To be or not to be, that is the question*'. He is asking us, should I carry on living? 'To *live* or not to live, that is the question. Listen to this:

> *To be or not to be, that is the question*
> *Whether it is nobler in the mind*
> *To suffer the slings and arrows of outrageous fortune*
> *Or to take arms against a sea of troubles*
> *And by opposing, end them. To die, to sleep...* [edit]
> *To sleep, perchance to dream: Ay, there's the rub*
> *For in such sleep of death what dreams might come*
> *When we have shuffled off this mortal coil,*
> *Must give us pause.*

You might not be in a position to learn all of this... but give yourself a realistic target. As with the singing a little earlier, your ability to deliver the lines 'live' will be deeply impressive and raise your stock in the credibility stakes. Of course, it is an iconic slice of English literature that is just satisfying to *know*. We challenge you to learn it!

You continue:

> What's special here is that Shakespeare is talking about the real, ordinary things of life: family members dying, stepfathers, falling out with mum, losing your girlfriend, feeling the need for revenge. But he finds such brilliant, beautiful, memorable ways to express the thought. He's talking about us. Today, we're going to be talking about Shakespeare. Everybody stand and repeat after me:

> *To be or not to be, that is the question.*

Repeat the line several times, inviting the group to take a step in a new direction with each repetition. Build the volume each time and build to a final, glorious declamation.

> *To be or not to be? That is the question.*

Indicate that you are going to move on quickly with…

> **Would you like to play a game?**

In this opening discussion, we have engaged the mind, set up ideas and issues, introduced and raised the status of the language, and suggested our personal ownership of the work. Now we need to change the mode; we have been sitting and talking, we need to move – to attend to the body and different kinds of energy.

The Shakespeare stage game

> We call this game 'The most glorious Shakespearean stage game'. It might be like another game you know. Here's how we play it… Everybody go and stand around the edges of the room.
>
> Imagine this is a stage… Shakespeare's stage… and the audience are there [gesturing to one side of the room]. The back of the stage, where normally the actors enter from, is here [gesturing to the opposite side]. *This* is upstage [away from the audience] and this is downstage [towards the audience]. Just to confuse the issue more, stage-left and stage-right are always from the point of view of the *audience* – so, the opposite to the actors facing out to the audience!

You might consider it useful to make simple signs for the walls to indicate the four key sites (up-stage, down-stage, stage-left and stage-right).

> Your first task is a task of memory. You have to remember all these things… my fellow actors… And go where I tell you to. Let's check. [Now you move to each area.] Where am I now? [e.g. stage-left] And now? And now?

If you are feeling ambitious, or if you feel your group would appreciate the challenge you might try the added complication of…

> And if I tell you that this is 'upstage centre', this is 'downstage right' and this is 'upstage left' – then what is this? [e.g. downstage left] Do you think you know where everywhere is? OK. Everybody. Go to…

Then freely improvise different positions as you see fit.

> Now that's the easy part. You know that if I tell you where to go, you go. But I might also shout out one of five instructions for you to do something particular when you get there. These are the instructions… Everyone spread out across the stage. I might shout one of these:

Now demonstrate each call and give pupils a chance to try them one at a time.

> - **'Hamlet!'** – at which you all instantly shout 'To be or not to be!' and strike *this* pose [straight-backed, one hand raised aloft – we're sure you can imagine!]. Then freeze in the pose.
> - *'Juliet!'* – a 'maidenly' shape, both hands on heart, and exclaim 'O, Romeo, Romeo! wherefore art thou Romeo?'. Then freeze in the pose.
> - *'Witches!'* – a lower, stooped pose, and shout 'Double, double toil and trouble!'. Freeze.
> - *'Bottom!'* – a foolish, clown shape and a shout of 'Eeyore!' – Bottom is a weaver who is turned into a donkey in *A Midsummer Night's Dream.* Freeze.
> - *'Macbeth!'* – saying 'Macbeth' is a curse in a theatre, so once you've said it you're terrified the roof might fall in, so you throw yourself on the floor and cover your head shouting 'Curses!'
>
> So now we're ready to play the game. If I've not shouted any of these directions, you're just coolly walking around in 'actors' neutral' position. Here we go…

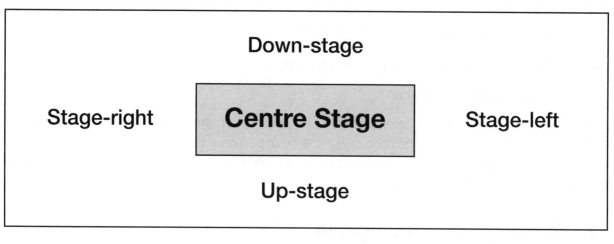

Figure 1 The areas of a traditional stage

This is quite a complex game of memory, which might require you relying on the 'wisdom of the group' (pupils will usually remember the sites better than we do). The game now continues for as long as it is enjoyable. The game can become extraordinarily complicated ('Witches at downstage left!'), but because of the combination of intellectual and physical challenge, it can also be exhilarating. Of course, through the game we have also placed participants in a simple theatrical landscape and introduced simple pieces of text, character and suggestions of narrative. There are three versions of the game for you to consider.

- You can play the game in a 'knockout' version, where the last person or people to reach each place, or to make each character shape, has to leave the game and stand at the edge of the space (off-stage).
- You can play the game without the knockout element, but just for the sheer joy of quick reaction and movement as a group. In this version you might add a little competitive spice by indicating individuals who are last to the correct space, or who are particularly 'theatrical' in their performance of the roles, but without sending anyone out.
- If your group is large, you can play the game with the group split into two halves – cast one and cast two. At any time, one cast is on-stage playing the game, and the other is 'in the wings' enjoying the spectacle.

Following the game, we can reasonably change tack again and return to activity that is more stationary and contemplative.

Shakespeare's words

Teacher-led discussion

What do people leave behind them when they die? Give me five. Perhaps another five – a body, family, things they've made? What if you left behind not only a set of plays that, 400 years later, are still performed *all the time*, and stories that people know and remember in every corner of the world – but what if you actually changed the way *that half the world actually speak!* Shakespeare lives in the very words that we speak.

Choose three pupils who you think could cope with and enjoy the attention that follows. Take each pupil in turn.

> If I were to say about X: 'That X, s/he has a *heart of gold* but s/he is eating me *out of house and home*'... I'd be speaking Shakespeare's words.

> If I were to say about Y: 'It's *as plain as the nose on your face*... s/he has made me *a laughing stock*'... I'd be speaking Shakespeare's words, or

> if I were to say about Z: '*Knock, Knock...*' And s/he would say in reply '*...Who's there?*' we'd *both* be speaking Shakespeare's words.

> Sometimes he makes completely *new* words, but sometimes he simply changes the *use* of words, for example by changing verbs into nouns and nouns into verbs. It's said that Shakespeare invented or introduced over 1700 new words and many phrases. Would you like to take a 'Shakespearean word shower'?

Shakespearean word shower

Preparation: you will need to have cut up the sheet 'Words and phrases Shakespeare coined' (Figure 2) and make sure there are enough pieces for your group. Toss them into the air at the centre of the circle you are sitting in, and let the words shower down – a much more dramatic moment than simply handing out the sheet.

Whereas most of the phrases are original to Shakespeare, many of the 'new words' are inventions in as much as they are new grammatical uses (such as 'nurse' used as a noun to mean 'a person who cares for', as distinct from someone looking after baby in a nursery). Some might simply have been Shakespeare being in tune with the new uses of words around him and being the first to *record* (or coin) them as words. Either way, it's a remarkable achievement to have had such an impact on the language.

So. Scatter the words and allow them to fall, then invite pupils to come and take one. They should sit down in the space where they have found the words and prepare to read them out. There are three stages. At each stage, pupils will move from the centre of the circle to remake the circle edge.

- Stage 1: if a pupil has a *single* word, at your signal they should stand, say the word loudly and clearly, and go back to the circle edge.
- Stage 2: if a pupil has a phrase with *no* string of full-stops (dots) before or after it, again, they should say the word on your signal and then join the circle. These are the complete phrases.
- Stage 3: if a pupil has a phrase with a string of full-stops at either the beginning or end, it means their phrase is not complete and someone else has the other half. Some of the phrases (the ones we think pupils *might* know) have been split. Now let's play 'Find the phrase'.

We now have just the pupils with split phrases in the middle of our circle.

- If their phrase starts with a capital and ends with a string of full-stops, they should stand up. These are the first halves of the phrases...
- One at a time, they call out their phrases.

> **Listen hard. Does anyone know the second part of the saying? It might be something you've heard an adult say. Think hard.**

- If not, ask those sitting in the middle (with the second halves of phrases) to call them out until someone thinks a whole phrase sounds right.
- Continue until the words are matched. The pair holding the words should then go and sit together in the circle.

● Once the phrases are all reunited, we can go around the whole circle and hear all the words/phrases that Shakespeare gave us.

> Imagine if we didn't have these words. Do you find it amazing that before this man, Shakespeare, sat down with his quill pen one day 400 years ago and wrote these words and phrases, they just didn't exist. And if he *hadn't* done, we wouldn't be saying these things everyday. The power of the pen!

Enter a murderer: words are power

In this section we move to look at the dramatic power of Shakespeare's words and to explore this as a model for pupils' own dramatic writing.

> These words aren't special just because they are remembered over hundreds of years... they're special because they capture the thoughts of a person, often at an extreme moment, in a powerful, sometimes miraculous way.

Now prepare to act out the following as you describe an actor entering the stage.

> Imagine this: a man enters onto an empty stage. He has a dagger drawn. He has decided to kill... To murder... To murder a king, here, tonight, in this cold, dark castle. He looks straight at the audience and opens his mouth to speak. What does he say? What would you give him to say? What would Shakespeare give him to say?

> In Shakespeare's time, his plays were performed at three o'clock in the afternoon. In reality, it's just an actor on a stage in broad daylight. We've got to make the audience *feel* that it's the middle of the night; that I (the character) am deadly serious about the murder and make the audience *believe* that I am going to carry it out. And all we've got are words... We want to paint a picture of the moment and terrify the audience with the idea of murder.

> What words would *you* give the actor to say? Let's write some words for the actor.

In pairs or small groups, pupils have five minutes to write the words that the character says when he walks on stage. One or more pupils from each pair/group must then prepare to act it out for us. Tell the group that later you will tell them the words that Shakespeare wrote for his characters at this moment in two different plays. Pupils then prepare their scripts. Encourage them to think about writing with a 'Shakespearean' voice.

> What would you expect to hear if it was a Shakespeare script? 'Old' words? (thou, 'tis, countless, etc.) Images? ('The stars blacken') and perhaps unusual word orders (instead of 'Do not hear me' – 'Hear me not'). As you write, think about using these things. They might add impact to your script.

Once written, each pair needs to decide how to perform their lines: together, or will one person take the role?

After sufficient time for writing and rehearsing, watch each performance. Offer some supportive directorial notes before they begin.

> The walk onto the stage is as important as the words. Take your time. Look at the dagger? Listen to the castle and the night. Move slowly. Murderously. Raise your face slowly and look straight at the audience before speaking. Wait a moment. Now speak your chilling lines.

After watching all the pieces, discuss how the 'moments' made an impact. Think about the actors' performances. Think about the words spoken. Which were particularly effective? Exciting? Powerful?

Shakespeare's turn!

Explain that you are going to take a few lines of *Macbeth* and a few lines of *Hamlet* and run them together. These are the words Shakespeare gives to his characters at approximately the same moment.

Exit the stage and re-enter with the dagger in your hand.

> *'Tis now the very witching time of night*
> *When churchyards yawn and hell itself breathes out*
> *Contagion to this world: Now could I drink hot blood,*
> *And do such bitter business, as the day*
> *Would quake to look on.*
> *I go, and it is done.* **(Dong! Dong!)** *The bell invites me.*
> *Hear it not, (my king), for it is a knell*
> *That summons thee to heaven or to hell.*

Do you think these are powerful words? It's important for all of us to learn to use words to say what we think and feel, and to try and imagine ourselves inside someone else's mind and express how they think and feel. Words can change the world!

Shakespeare's life

The following short, 'ham' script can be read or performed by your class. It contains a simple account of the facts of Shakespeare's life. These facts will need to be uncovered from the text in a way that offers a simple introduction to textual analysis of the sort needed when approaching the plays. There are several options that you might consider.

● Simply read the script around the class. This is likely to have the least impact.
● Prepare a 'rehearsed reading' of the script. This will involve looking more closely at the text for meaning and performance opportunities. To raise the value of this level of activity, we recommend making a simple recording of the reading. This could involve making a 'radio play' of the script. The clear advantage here is that the script would be realised with some completeness but without the need for lines to be learned or costumes considered. If you have the facility, you might think about making your radio play available on your school's website so that parents and friends can share in it.
● You could give the script a full staging. It is only a fifteen-minute piece; ideal as a class assembly piece, which would also be curriculum-linked and help to spread the word about the great bard. Such an event might draw your class together in a high-visibility performance opportunity, and also bring them status as young people with a special interest in, and a special commitment to, Shakespeare and his work. As you shall see, the piece is shamelessly celebratory.

You might note (if it is not obvious) that an attempt has been made to write in something approaching *blank verse* – Shakespeare's natural poetic idiom.

Fifteen-minute Will

The Poetical History of William Shaking Spear

Will is sitting at a simple desk with paper, ink and quill pens. His head is down as if he were writing… But the pen is still.

The chorus are humming the famous Elizabethan actor's song 'Rose'. Will looks up. The chorus are silent. Then he looks back to the page. Again. Again. Over the humming we hear, as if coming in and out of his mind…

CHORUS:	*Put out the light and then, put out the light…*
	…life is a walking Shadow…
	…a player who struts and frets his hour upon the stage…
	…and then is heard no more…
	…Ay, but to die, and go we know not where…
	…eyes without feeling, feeling without sight…
WILL:	*I am haunted by all I create.*

He gets up and walks to the window that the chorus have simply made. He pulls back a cloth curtain and looks out.

CHORUS:	*On London's filthy streets life bubbles on.*

The chorus break into new positions representing the street in a whole group tableau and create a soundscape: the sound of the Tudor street below – hawkers, hooves, blade-grinders, children, feet, shouts of 'watch out below'… splash!'… the hubbub of crowds.

Someone sees Will at the window.

CHORUS 1:	*Master Shakespeare!*
CHORUS 2:	*What light from yonder grubby window breaks?*

They all find this hilarious. They begin shouting famous comic lines.

CHORUS 3:	*Thou clay-brained guts…*
CHORUS 4:	*…thou knotty, pated fool…*
CHORUS 5:	*…thou whoresome, obscene, greasy tallow-catch…*
CHORUS 6:	*I'll tickle your catastrophe!*
CHORUS 2:	*Peace, ye fat guts!*
CHORUS 7:	*Mr Shakespeare, give us a verse…*
CHORUS 8:	*Sing us a sonnet!*
CHORUS 9:	*Shall I compare thee to a donkey's ass?*

Will withdraws from the curtain. The chorus return to their places…

CHORUS:	*On London's filthy street life bubbles on*
	The poet, playwright, Will, must write, must write
	The actor, theatre helmsman, Will, must write

> *The husband, father, working far away*
> *Four days' walk from home and family fires*
> *Must work, must write, must work while daylight burns.*

WILL:
> *Life gathers in me tight, I know not why*
> *Must work, must work, must work while daylight burns*
> *Night's candle wax has thickly run to ground*
> *And does my tiresome eyes seem to surround*
> *It is the light of day my pen does need*
> *But silence too. A silent mind,*
> *Is lost in a hungry city's noisy greed.*
> *Silence I need. But, no. My pen is dry.*

CHORUS:
> *The pen is dry. The ink undipped. And paper?*
> *Paper fresh and white and clear and blank*

WILL:
> *And blank.*

Enter a servant.

SERVANT:
> *Master Shakespeare…*

WILL:
> *Yes, Mary?*

MARY:
> *Your caller, calls again.*

WILL:
> *I will not budge.*

MARY:
> *No. You haven't eaten, Sir, for two days straight.*

WILL:
> *I am working, Mary.*

MARY:
> *I see Master Shakespeare.*

WILL:
> *I will eat when my mind comes free.*

MARY:
> *A little ale?*

WILL:
> *Thank you, Mary. You may bring me bread and cheese.*

MARY:
> *And a little ale, sir?*

WILL:
> *And a little ale, Mary. But send the caller away.*

Mary goes. Will tries to work.

CHORUS:
> *The glove-maker's son, from four days north*
> *Here in the city of flies, where gutters hum,*
> *The scarab throngs do hack the sticky mass*
> *Of potted human bee-skin. Undaunted.*
> *He writes. From this day till the end of days*
> *These scratchings on the rag-cut paper roll*
> *Will speak to all. To comfort, shock, cajole*
> *To find the words that all of us might speak.*

Mary brings in a tray of bread and cheese and a flagon of ale. Will takes a drink of ale.

WILL:
> *Haunted by the people we once were.*

CHORUS:
> *He sees and thinks and dreams and calls them here*
> *'The Several Days of William Shaking Spear'.*

The chorus step forward to animate each piece.

CHORUS: *Guessing at so many distant dates.*
                        St George's Day, a nation's ever pride
                        For John and Mary Arden, Stratford born.

FATHER: *The boy shall make white gloves, at father's side!*

MARY ARDEN: *But wait, good John, the boy is good with ink*
                        A gift with words, see how he speaks, with pen
                        Would write – a precious gift these peasant days.

Step forward a school-boy, Will.

CHORUS: *A King's School Latin learning calls him on.*

SCHOOL-BOY WILL: *School-boy creeps like snail unwillingly to school.*

CHORUS: *But come those Holy Days so distant spread*
                        The travelling players' troupes will call the sky
                        To fall and beckon out young Will's great task.

ACTORS: *Alack and wow and wow and thrice more wow!*
                        Our daggers of wood, our cloaks, our crowns
                        Our tales of glory, tragedy and love
                        Hook young eyes, spark young minds, land our greatest prize.

YOUNG WILL: *I am all this theatre's very all. Lead on.*

ACTOR: *Young moth, your eyes are singed and wedded firm.*

CHORUS: *But no, Young Will, you must for now remain.*
                        A comely Anne, does hath-a-way to reel
                        This young fish in.

Enter Anne Hathaway.

ANNE: *Am I that Anne, they say is years advanced*
                        A man at seventeen, junior by eight.

Enter young dad Will with baby.

                        Will Shakespeare, teenage dad. Let us be wed!

CHORUS: *Though London theatre worlds do wait your name.*

YOUNG WILL: *My Stratford line, my family are where*
                        I store and house and propagate my wealth.

CHORUS: *Though London calls, this place is always home.*

ANNE: *Be well, be strong and grow the gift of times.*

Will leaves for London.

CHORUS: *Your life a question, Will, of when and why*
                        And who and where and what and how and if.

Will enters the city. Soundscape.

CHORUS: *Through which gate did you pass that honoured day*

> *When the bustling streets of London Town*
> *Welcomed her greatest son to be, awash*
> *With hawking cads in pick-pock narrow lanes?*
> *London Bridge, not fallen yet, but hanging*
> *Staggering tight with swarming, raucous life*
> *And plague still lurking on the deadly pounce.*
> *Behold, the men of theatre are now primed…*

Enter Burbage and Heminges.

BURBAGE: *We shall build, we shall write, London shall hail*
All life shall see all life enacted here.

Enter bearded writer Will.

HEMINGES: *The bearded Stratford bard shall be the man*
To fill our double-thousand playhouse full.

CHORUS: *A business man, an actor, writer – 'Deal'*
So write, so write, so write, our stage is dark
And needs the light from words as yet to come
He writes. He writes. He writes. He writes.

WILL: *[at desk] I borrow people, stories, ancient tales*
And when the words are ended, as they will,
I build a new word, give it breath and life
It seems to flow elsewhere, through my own pen
But lightening strikes and channels slip and flow
I am bewildered by the gift I find…

Knocking.

MARY: *They are knocking at the door. Your actors all.*

Actors enter: Phillips, Pope and clown-Kemp.

PHILIPS: *Queen Bess, her majesty, demands new play.*

POPE: *We need it now, good Shakespeare, very now.*

KEMP: *And don't forget to learn your part as well.*

PHILIP: *On stage at three, my merry, brainsome Sir.*

They go.

WILL: *On stage at three and no words yet to speak…*

The three children enter together.

HAMNET: *Daddy, dear?*

WILL: *Yes, my precious Hamnet son.*

HAMNET: *When come home? [The others echo him.]*

WILL: *When plague cuts, theatres close, I may leave.*

SUSANNE: *We must pray for plague to have you home?*

WILL: *I must write, strong Susanna child, while lightening strikes.*

HAMNET:	*But Judith coughs. [She does so.]*
WILL:	*Where is your mother?*
HAMNET:	*A hacking cough.*
WILL:	*Susanna now, attend, you know my work* *This family's history will not build itself.*
HAMNET:	*One push upon the apple swing, one push.*
WILL:	*Be gone.*

He waves them away.

CHORUS:	*But think on this, my friends, it may be so* *That Shakespeare's name may as yet disappear* *The rush of life, of business, acting too* *Means Shakespeare's plays are lived and seen but not* *Set down on faithful, clear and honest leaves* *And may as yet full vanish from the world* *And we would not now know this treasure filled* *But, hark, a caller does appear...*

Enter Jaggard.

WILL:	*I said no visitors... Ah, you...*
JAGGARD:	*Apologies, Master Shakespeare, I come on an urgent task.*
WILL:	*I know it...*
JAGGARD:	*Your sonnets, Sir, are everywhere. A hit, sir we might say. Your poems,* *Venus and Adonis and your Lucrece are in every gentle-woman's cask. I* *must speak frank. You are London's brightest, noble star.* *The literate classes crave to read your plays.* *To hold them in their very hands. Your plays.* *Not the foul and feeble stealings of vagrant hands...* *but as you, my master-craftsman scribe, would have them shown.*
WILL:	*Again, Sir Printer...*
JAGGARD:	*I do beseech you brave William, my Sir. Time is too, too short. Give me* *leave to publish before your name is muddied by the horrid, liar's copies* *of your heaven's plays.*
WILL:	*My friend, you have my nod... When a day's peace comes.*
JAGGARD:	*When a...*
WILL:	*Enough!*

He waves him away.

WILL:	*Mary!*
MARY:	*Yes, Sir?*
WILL:	*No more!*

He writes.

CHORUS:	*In days when plays were only staged, not kept*
	For pleasure sure, nor studied hard as book
	To write them down for keeping made no sense
	But wealthy, learned folk would read them still.
WILL:	*My plays are for the people, all who need them.*
CHORUS:	*Does he know (he must) that all of history*
	Waits? No. He writes. He writes.
	Consider now what surely will be lost.
	If all the names and titles, words and all
	Were pulled from every ear and mind and heart.

The chorus step forward for each.

ROMEO:	*I, Romeo and she, my Juliet*
CHORUS:	*What light through yonder window breaks?*
ROMEO:	*It is the east, and Juliet is the sun*
JULIET:	*O Romeo, Romeo…*
ALL:	*…wherefore art thou, Romeo?*
CHORUS:	*Come, King Macbeth, whose witches do torment thus*
WITCHES:	*Double, double toil and trouble…*
ALL:	*Fire burn and cauldron bubble*
MACBETH:	*She should have died hereafter*
ALL:	*…there would have been a time for such a word*
MACBETH:	*Tomorrow and tomorrow and tomorrow*
ALL:	*…Creeps in this petty pace from day to day*
MACBETH:	*And all our yesterdays have lighted fools*
ALL:	*The way to dusty death.*
CHORUS:	*Step forward Caesar, Julius is slain!*
ANTHONY:	*Friends, Romans, countrymen…*
ALL:	*…lend me your ears!*
CHORUS:	*And Prospero the wizard king, his daughter fair…*
MIRANDA:	*O brave new world, that has such people in't*
PROSPERO:	*We are such stuff as dreams are made on*
CHORUS:	*We are such stuff as dreams are made on*
PROSPERO:	*And our little life is rounded with a sleep*
HAMLET:	*Alas, poor Yorick…*
ALL:	*I knew him well!*
JACQUES:	*All the world's a stage*

CHORUS:	*And all the men and women merely players*
MARY:	*Master Shakespeare, write, so all may know your name.*
HAMLET:	*To be or not to be…*
ALL:	*That is the question!*

They move forward as they repeat…

ALL:	*To be or not to be… that is the question!*
	To be or not to be, that is the question!
	To be or not to be, that is all our question…

Pause.

WILL:	*There is no time.*

Mary takes the uneaten food away. The chorus return to their places. They hum 'Rose' as at the beginning.

CHORUS:	*Our Will, will die and never find the time*
	To capture this great work for all mankind
	Not knowing all the treasures he had stored
	For all who come in years unnumbered yet.

Quiet.

JAGGARD:	*Our final heroes, friends of Will,*
	Who walked the stage beside him all the years.
	Hemminges and Condell.

The chorus repeat their names.

HEMINGES:	*From memory and scraps and little else.*
CONDELL:	*We give you all*
HEMINGES:	*The truest cast*
CONDELL:	*Of friend, Will's work*
HEMINGES:	*It must not pass.*
CHORUS:	*It must not pass. It must not pass.*

The chorus begin to repeat the famous lines heard earlier. Over and again. Building in volume.

CHILD:	*Good Will Shaking Spear is ours.*
	We want him back!

THE END

Words Shakespeare 'coined'

Premeditated	Advertising	Cater	Varied
Bump	Fixture	Epileptic	Generous
Flawed	Hint	Lonely	Negotiate
Torture	Worthless	Summit	Amazement
Obscene	Blanket	Bedroom	Mimic
Beached	Champion	Countless	Bandit
Addiction	Assassination	Rant	Arouse
Puke	Bump	Accused	Household
Summit	Obscene	Worthless	Premeditated
A Nurse	Fixture	Housewife	Zany

Phrases (idioms) Shakespeare

All that glitters…	…is not gold	Working-day	What's done is done
All's well that…	…ends well	Be-all…	…and the end-all
Brave new….	…world	Break the…	…ice
Budge an…	…inch	Dead as a…	…doornail
Eaten me out of…	…house and home	Fancy-free	Fool's paradise
Elbow room	Faint hearted	Forever and…	…day
For goodness' sake	Full circle	Heart of gold	It was Greek to me
The game is up	Good riddance	high time	Laughing stock
In a pickle	my heart of hearts	my mind's eye	Infinite space
so-so	It smells to heaven	Knock knock!…	…Who's there?
Kill with kindness	Knit brow	Laid on with a trowel	Laugh yourself into stitches
Lie low	thin air	Naked truth	Not slept one wink
(Plain) as a nose on a man's face	One fell swoop	Own flesh…	…and blood
Play fast and loose	Seen better days	Snail paced	A sorry sight
Stony hearted	The short and the long of it	Set my teeth on edge	Tell truth and shame the devil
Too much of a…	…good thing	Wild-goose…	…chase

Figure 2 Words and phrases Shakespeare coined

Shakespeare's life: a teacher's crib sheet

Even though he is very famous today, we actually know very little about Shakespeare's life. The 'facts' we do know for sure are taken from official records such as church records, financial accounts and law court records. Other information has been gleaned from secondary sources such as foreign visitors to London or comments from rivals, or has been assumed from the plays themselves.

- Born: 23 April 1564. William Shakespeare was baptised in Stratford-on-Avon on 26 April 1564. It is generally agreed that he was probably born three days earlier (as was the custom) and his birthday is accepted as 23 April. Which is also St George's Day... two national heroes for one day!
- Died: 23 April 1616. It is generally accepted that he also died on St George's Day.
- His parents were John and Mary Shakespeare. He had eight brothers and sisters. Three of them died in childhood. One of them, Edmund, was an actor.
- His father, John Shakespeare, was an important person in the town of Stratford – an Alderman, though later he seems to have lost all of his money and been in trouble with the law.
- Although the records of the Stratford school ('King's') are lost, because William was the son of an important local man, it is safe to assume he would have gone to that school. Here he would have learned much Latin – the language spoken by the Romans – which would have included ancient stories and plays, poetry, speech-making; all of which would surface in his writing in later life.
- In 1582, at the age of eighteen, he married Anne Hathaway, who was (perhaps scandalously!) eight years older than him. They had a child within a year so perhaps she was already pregnant.
- He had three children: Susanna (1583) and the twins Hamnet and Judith (1585).
- We know nothing about Shakespeare between 1585 (when the twins were born) and 1592, when he is mentioned in London theatres. These are described as his 'lost years'. Some say he was a school teacher in Lancashire; some that he travelled to Italy; some that he joined a travelling troupe of actors; some that he had to flee Stratford after poaching a deer from a local lord's land – all exciting stories, but we just don't know.
- He wrote thirty-seven plays. Though there is argument about whether some of these are co-authored, and whether he co-authored more.
- He first became famous for a long poem called *Venus and Adonis*.
- His first plays were probably performed at 'The Theatre', managed by Richard Burbage.
- Later (and more famously) his plays were performed at 'The Globe', of which he was part-owner as well as chief playwright.
- Shakespeare was also an actor, and probably played smaller parts such as the ghost of Hamlet's father.
- When Queen Elizabeth I died and James I came to the throne, Shakespeare's theatre company was so popular it became 'The King's Men' in 1603.
- None of his plays was published properly while he was alive. Some *bad* versions were sold... from people taking notes in the audience or from actors' prompt copies. If it wasn't for Shakespeare's friends and actor-colleagues Heminges and Condell, we might never have known the plays as we do. These two men assembled the first full versions of the plays in a huge collection called *The First Folio*.
- Shakespeare is buried in Stratford. He has no direct descendants.

The secret life of
William Shakespeare
gossip, hearsay and legend

Papers were said to be found in the loft of Shakespeare's family home, in which the family declared itself Catholic – a serious crime at the time

Shakespeare was the only major playwright of his time not to be imprisoned, however...

Members of Shakespeare's theatre company were nearly all hung for treason for taking part in a revolt against the king – by performing a Shakespeare play in which a king is executed

Shakespeare seems to have gone missing for seven years – some say he was on the run after being caught poaching deer in Stratford – some say he went travelling in Italy

Shakespeare was a teenage dad – marrying an older woman when he was eighteen (and she – Anne Hathaway – was twenty-six)

One legend says Shakespeare died after a massive binge-drinking session with fellow playwright Ben Johnson

All of Shakespeare's family line died out – he has no living descendants

When Shakespeare died, he left his wife Anne just 'the second best bed' – was this an insult?

Some people think his original manuscripts (the plays in his own hand-writing) are hidden under his bust* in the church where he is buried in Stratford

Some people say Shakespeare didn't even write the plays – that they were written by someone else – though other people say that they say this just because they believe somebody so clever and talented must have been highly educated and probably royal, not a glove-maker's son from somewhere up north!
(well, the midlands anyway)

*A bust is a statue of just a head.

Before 1564	John Shakespeare is a glove-maker in Stratford-on-Avon and an important local man. One of his jobs is 'beer-taster', making sure the pubs don't water down the beer. He and his wife Mary Arden have a son and call him William.
1564	The baby William was baptised on 26 April... from this we guess that he was born on 23 April – St George's Day.
About 1571	Will probably went to school at King's New School, where he learned to read, write and recite lots of Latin... the ancient language of the Romans.
1582	Aged 18, William marries Anne Hathaway, who is eight years older than him and already pregnant. A teenage dad! Within a year, his first daughter Susanna was born. Two years later, twins Hamnet and Judith were born.
Sometime in 1580s	A legend says that Shakespeare was caught 'poaching' deer – stealing – from Sir Thomas Lucy's land and had to run away to escape prosecution – and so left for London. Others say he might have joined a travelling actor's troupe that visited Stratford frequently.
1592	Shakespeare is spoken of as an actor and writer for the very first time by Robert Greene... Who calls him an 'upstart crow' – and obviously doesn't like his success.
1593	Published a very successful long poem called Venus and Adonis, making him very famous.
1594/95	Romeo and Juliet first performed – 'O Romeo, Romeo, wherefore art though, Romeo!'
1595	A Midsummer Night's Dream first performed.
1590s	Shakespeare joins The Lord Chamberlain's Men – he acts, writes for them and owns part of the company. Their first theatre is called 'The Theatre'!
1598	The actors tear down The Theatre and use the wood to build the famous 'Globe Theatre' – one story says they did it all in one night!
1600/01	Hamlet first performed – 'To be or not to be...'
1605	Macbeth first performed – 'Double, double, toil and trouble...'
1611	The Tempest first performed – 'We are such stuff as dreams are made on' – probably the first play in the new indoor theatre, Blackfriars.
1616	Shakespeare died in Stratford on his birthday – 23 April – St George's day. He left his wife just 'the second best bed' – which seems a bit mean!

Figure 3 Shakespeare's life: a story jigsaw

5 The Tempest – scheme

'O Braue New World'

To the island

A shape game

A simple, physical activity that starts in game mode and moves us directly to the heart of the initiating moment of the story – *The Tempest*.

> Walk around the room. Fill the room like a gas – spreading out until the room is full and you are as far from others as you can be, so there is a space around you that you try to keep. Walk so that you are walking no faster and no slower than anyone else.
>
> Now you're on your own, in your own space. Isolated. But in a moment we're going to play a game that involves asking you to work as one large group… one unit… and it's going to need you to solve some simple… and then more difficult… problems by working as a team: acting as if you were <u>one</u>. Keep walking. Freeze. Walk. Freeze. Here we go.
>
> I'm going to call out a shape and you will have just 10 seconds to make that shape. You can only use your body. You might be standing or lying. Decide what's best for each one. Starting with an easy shape… Make a square! 10, 9, 8… Freeze! [*Check, referring perhaps to the properties of squares*]. Make a parallelogram! 10, 9, 8… Freeze! [*Check, referring to the properties of parallelograms!*] Make a five-pointed star! The points as sharp as possible. 10, 9, 8… Freeze! [*Check.*] Now. I have a picture in my head. It's a ship. An old ship. A sailing ship. With a mast. A 'pointy-end' (what's that called? The bow). [*Indicate where this might be in the space.*] and a 'flat' end (What's that called? The stern). [*Indicate where that might be in the space.*] Make a ship-shape! (it must have a thick, strong mast) 10, 9, 8… Freeze! See the ship.

You now move from gaming mode to narrative mode. The group has freely entered into the drama experience. They have demonstrated the capability of 'the group' and successfully completed a fairly complex group problem-solving task. They are now at the initiating moment of Shakespeare's narrative.

At sea: George's ship

You narrate.

> Imagine this ship is at sea. It's a ship made of wood. At the centre of the ship, running front to back, is a single, central hull – the shaped and moulded trunk of an ancient oak tree. Cut into this are the ribs of the ship: the structure or skeleton that make its shape. [*Draw these things in the space as you describe them.*] To this are attached planks that have been sealed with black pitch and ship's varnish to make this vessel worthy of travelling the seas and oceans of the world.
>
> It's night. The sea is calm. The sky is clear. The wind is low. It's a gentle night. Most of the crew and all the passengers are below decks. The night watchman… who we will call George… is alone on deck. Would one of the people making the mask like to play Old George? He's sitting with his back to the mast and listening. What can he hear?

Take five answers ('Give me five'). As each one is suggested, model that sound quickly yourself, making the sound subdued. Expect: the sea, wind, the creaking bones of the boat, the sails flapping, gulls, the rigging tip-tapping...

> George has been at sea since he was a child of eight. When he stands on the land, it feels wrong... it's too still... he needs to feel himself being carried by the sea. It's where he feels at home. He has sea salt in his blood. From ship's boy to bosun, he's done all jobs on ships... and travelled to all of the known world... but now he is old and can't heave ropes, scale rigging, lift barrels. But the captain keeps him on board... to watch... George is the ship's night-watchman, and here he is this calm night... watching... and listening.

Now, with a gesture of gentle summoning, invite pupils to join you in the sounds of the ship. Summon the sea, the wind, the tap-tapping rigging...

George isn't a Shakespearean character. He is ours. Shakespeare has several sailors and a bosun... and George may be one of them. But it is useful here to build an empathy and allow the coming tempest to be seen through the eyes of a character we are free to imagine for ourselves.

At sea: the tempest

This first part of the session has been controlled, stationary and reflective. You are now about to move to a highly energetic and physical activity. Ariel's tempest approaches...

Tell the class that you are going to narrate the next part of the story, and everything that you say, they are going to do. It is going to be important that they listen carefully. The action starts with George. You narrate.

> George looks out to the horizon. He looks in all directions. He watches the sea and feels it under the ship. He's looking for other vessels... for pirates perhaps... and he's looking for changes in the weather...
>
> A soft wind suddenly brushes him from out of the west. He looks to the west. Nothing to fear. He looks away. He looks again. He sees the tiniest dot [*point to it*]. A 'something', maybe a small boat in the water, a large sea-bird in the sky. Nothing to fear. He looks away. He looks again. A wind brushes his face. He sits up. His back creaks. The tiny dot has become something more. A ball of 'something'. As he watches, it grows and moves in this direction. In all his days at sea, he has never seen anything like it. It is like a swirling cloud... Growing and growing as he watches. He feels the sea beneath the ship swell, and the ship begins to rise up and down, up and down... Rain begins to fall out of the clear night sky. A storm is coming. Out of nowhere. As if by magic, a storm is coming... George is spell-bound, he watches this swirling ball of cloud as it moves, faster and faster... Until it's above the ship... He screams... 'Awake! Awake! Awake!'
>
> Below deck, the crew and passengers are quickly awake and on deck as the ship is tossed higher and lower. Like a child's toy. The ship is carrying important passengers: a king, a duke, a prince. Will they survive this cold night? This now icy sea?

Tell pupils that you are now going to narrate the story in a series of steps. You will describe the action of each step, and then count down from 5 to 1 as they move into a completely frozen, still image of the action you have just described. Tell pupils they need to move quickly, and freeze when you shout 'freeze'. Here are the steps.

- George's alarm cry again: 'Awake! Awake! Awake!'. Emerging from below deck... the crew, the king, the duke, the prince. Just woken. Coming to see. Looking to the sky. 5, 4, 3, 2, 1... Freeze!
- Sailors run to their posts. The passengers panic. 5, 4, 3...
- The sailors need to get the sails down or they'll be blown over and into the raging sea. 'All hands to the deck!' 5, 4, 3... Freeze! Now, 'Heave! Heave!...' Freeze!

- The sails are down. The rain is beating down... The ship is thrown up to heaven... and down inside the mountainous waves. Drive the passengers back below decks. 5, 4, 3... Freeze!
- To survive a tempest, a storm such as this, to make sure they are not swept overboard and into the raging water, the crew must find ropes and must find something solid on the ship that they can tie themselves to... the crew lash themselves to the ship. 5, 4, 3... Freeze! Now, if the ship goes down, *they* go down!
- George has tied himself to the mast and, in this terrible storm... George is listening. Listening for the sounds of the ship... The other sailors watch Old George... What can he hear? 5, 4, 3... Freeze!
- George hears a terrible sound: an almighty cracking. The mighty, solid oak beam that runs the whole length of the ship [*indicate it again in the space*] is splitting... and in all this noise, George hears it. He screams, 'We split! We split!' and when George shouts this, *everybody* shouts it. 'We split! We split!'
- The ship splits in two. It's going down. You're tied to it! Unleashing yourselves! 5, 4, 3... Freeze!
- Stop.
- The ship sinks. The crew jump into the water. The passengers... king, duke, prince and all... jump into the water. 5, 4, 3...
- They swim to anything that has floated clear of the ship; to wood, to barrels, to the furniture from below decks. 5, 4, 3...
- Here they are... Afloat on an empty sea – clinging to debris. They look up to the stormy sky... They are amazed... The swirling circle of cloud is gathering itself together... Swirling smaller and smaller... into a hard ball of cloud and then into a dot of nothing. George knows how quickly the storm came... and just as quickly, as the ship is taken below the waves... he sees it vanish.
- It's the middle of the night. There is no light. As you float here in the water, you can't see anybody else. It is as if *you* are the only survivor! Show this... 5, 4, 3...
- As the sun begins to rise, something new and terrifying happens. You find yourself only miles away from an island. An island that shouldn't be there. An island that isn't on any maps. An island that seems to have emerged from the sea. 5, 4, 3...
- You paddle towards this mysterious island. It's your only chance.
- You climb onto the beach. Weary, terrified, you collapse and sleep.

[*A period of relaxation. Music introduced.*] What dreams might come...? Think back over all that has happened: the sudden storm, waking in the night, the ship being tossed on high waves, the ship splitting, jumping into the raging sea, clinging to wreckage for your life.

Waking and seeing

Having arrived on the island – which they don't yet know is magic – the crew and passengers are separated from each other. Each thinks he may be the only survivor. We begin to 'imagineer' the physical world of the play: Prospero's Island. We start with a soundscape.

The sun wakes you. Before you open your eyes, you listen to the sounds of the island. Keep your eyes closed. What do you think you might hear? We're going to make a soundscape. Imagine – if we were to paint a landscape of the island, we would stand and look and paint everything we could see in front of us. In a soundscape we will create everything we can *hear*. And, just like a landscape, some things are close by and look bigger (or sound louder); some are more distant (or quieter). Now. Decide on one sound that you can hear lying here on the beach. It might be a large sound that's close (the sea, for example) or a small sound that's more distant. You're going to make this sound with your voice. And you are *all* going to be part of the soundscape. Keep your eyes closed so the sounds you hear can bring pictures into your head, but raise your hand when you have decided on the sound you wish to add...

As the children raise their hands, move around the room and invite them to join the sound one at a time by touching their raised hands. It might be worth noting that once they have begun their sound, they should continue it so that the soundscape builds and builds. Also, point out that some sounds are continuous – the sea, for example; while others are intermittent (they come and go) – such as a parrot squawking up in the trees.

Build the soundscape. Give yourself the power to turn the sound on and off at will. You might give yourself a large, mimed volume dial – the fading up and down will help with management of the moment.

Once the full soundscape is established, turn it off and ask children what they can hear elsewhere (the sounds that other people are making). Turn the soundscape back on. Introduce your own, more threatening sound. Turn off the soundscape. Tell them of the threatening sound: a grunt, a howl, a beast – is it a wild animal, is it a monster? This will be picked up later when we talk about Caliban.

Turn the soundscape on. Off again. Ask again for images. Build a list of the elements of the island and the life of the island.

Finally, the survivors will wake. They may be kings, or dukes, or princes, or servants of sailors. Each person can decide who they are . . . but we don't need to know that yet.

Move the whole class to one end of the room so that there is a clear, empty space – this is the island. One at a time, pupils walk or crawl into the main space; exhausted, traumatised, desperate. They walk onto the island, mime an object that they find, and then say its name. Model this process yourself. Build a whole group tableau of the arrival on the island.

So. We have survived the mysterious storm, the murderous shipwreck. We find ourselves on the island. We don't know that anyone else has survived. Do you think this is an island you can survive on? Why? Discuss?

> Suddenly. You stand. [*Do so.*] You hear something. In the trees. On the beach. In the air. The sound of strange, magical music – 'a thousand twanging instruments . . . and voices' . . . out of the air. You feel like someone is always watching you . . . Turn around quickly to see who it is. There's no-one there. The truth is . . . this isn't an ordinary island . . . It's thick with spirits. They are everywhere. Watching. Invisible. Ready to control you, as they controlled the storm that brought you here. Not only that – the spirits have a lord, a king. You've been stranded on the island of Prospero, the Wizard King. He has brought some of you here on purpose . . . to take his revenge!

On Prospero's Island

You need: A drum. An old book that might pass for a 'book of spells'. Perhaps a staff and simple cloak. A recording of appropriate 'storm music' – perhaps good old 'Carmina Burana' by Carl Orff.

The spirits

The pupils lie down. They close their eyes. Call up the island soundscape again briefly. Ask the pupils to call up all they know, and can picture, about the island, about the survivors – kings, dukes, princes, servants, sailors.

> Remember: this island is not uninhabited! It is populated with many hundreds of invisible spirits. Led by the spirit Ariel. We are going to be these spirits. All stand. When I bang this drum, you may move. If I'm not banging it, you must be still. Let's try.

'Test' the group for quick reactions and stillness. Begin a pulsing rhythm that allows pupils to maintain more continuous movement. Now. State: 'You are this island's spirit army!' Develop the movement quickly by questioning: How does a spirit walk? Light? Heavy? What expression is on a spirit's face? What do hands that cast spells look like? Spirits might touch the sky [*stretch*] and touch the earth.[s*oop]. Model flowing movements that sweep from high to low. Freeze the group with a final heavy beat. Pick out unusual and committed movement. Continue. Repeat. The whole class is finally moving like spirits.

Prospero – teacher in-role

Freeze the action. The spirits have a master. He is the mighty Prospero. Ask the pupils to repeat his name with reverence: 'Prospero!' When he calls, they must obey. He is a powerful wizard. You (the teacher) are going to play Prospero in a moment and the spirits must obey you.

You take up your position with your spell book in front of you on a chair. Turn their movement on with a drumbeat. You call your spirits to you.

> I, your mighty ruler, Prospero, command the presence of my spirit league. Come to me! My spirits! Come to me!

Beat the drum to cover their coming to you. Indicate with a gesture that they should sit at your feet. Lay the drum aside, take up your book. Appear grave and perhaps irritated. As Prospero, you tell the spirits your story.

- You once were the Duke of Milan. You became obsessed with study, with learning, with your books.
- Your brother, Antonio, plotted against you, turned your palace, your servants, your people against you and took your duke's crown.
- He set you adrift on a rotting boat to die at sea. He put your daughter, Miranda, who was only a young child, with you in the boat.
- A kind servant smuggled food and your precious books onto the boat. But for this, you and your daughter would have died on that rotting craft.
- The boat drifted and you found yourself on *this* island. The spell book allowed you to take control of the spirits and creatures of the island.
- Now you want revenge on your evil brother!
- Your brother is setting sail to cross the sea. Your spirits must raise a storm to bring the ship here and then wreck it. Once Antonio is here on the island, you will torment him and take your revenge!
- You instruct the spirits to create a spell to raise a storm. Is this a task they can accomplish? Of course. They will obey.

Conjuring storms

Out of role, provoke a discussion: is it possible for words/spells/magic to change the weather? What can words do? Are words powerful? *How* are they? What is magic? Do you believe in magic?

Out of role, explain Prospero's task again. The spell has two parts: the movement and the words. First, we are going to create the movement. What different kinds of movement might we have? Take suggestions and demonstrate: sharp gesture (arms), turning around on the spot, movements reaching high and low, in and out and round and round. In small groups, pupils invent and prepare their repeatable sequence of spell movements.

TIP If each pupil invents one move and teaches it to their group, they will quickly build up the sequence, and everyone will have ownership of the full piece. You might decide that writing the spells should be a continuation of the workshop 'in-role', or a separate 'out of drama time' writing task.

Again, the words need to be powerful, strong, clear. These words are going to change the weather! Show that there are many blank pages in Prospero's spell book. When the spells have been created, they need to be presented as new pages in the book. This might involve ageing the paper, writing with quills, or using illuminated text. Even if completed outside 'drama time', there needs to be full understanding of the importance of the successful completion of this task once we return to Prospero's Island. Here, the completed spell book will be presented to him for his approval. He is sometimes difficult to please!

The groups are given sufficient time to complete this 'out of role' writing task. They will need to write the final text for Prospero's spell book, as well as retaining a copy to support them in their rehearsals.

Once the writing task is complete, tell the groups that the spirits need to prepare to *perform* the movement pieces now combined with the words they have created.

On completion of the spells and the book, gather the group at Prospero's feet as before.

> Have you done my bidding? The ship has left its harbour. It approaches only two leagues west of this very island. Present your powerful spells for conjuring storms. Ariel, come forward!

Choose someone who can bear this attention, and gesture for them to bring you the newly fashioned book of spells.

> You have served me well, Ariel and this spirit army. You have been my servants for many years. The time is coming when I shall set you free! But first, the storm! The ship must be wrecked. But let not one hair of the people of the ship, passengers or crew, be lost or harmed. Bring me my evil brother!

With this, send the spirits to their groups, to find their own space and to prepare to perform the movement and word pieces they have created. Explain that their sequences will be 'looped' so that, once they get to the end, they start again at the beginning.

Orchestrate the performance so that it becomes a continuous, accumulative piece; gesture (as Prospero, with magic staff, if you like!) for groups to begin and repeat their sequences one at a time. When all have been given individual attention, summon them again, but this time ask them to continue once they have started so that they join the almighty storm-summoning, one group at a time, and we build to a crescendo. At the peak of the crescendo you narrate:

> The waves rise, the wind blows, the ship is tossed to the heavens, George shouts 'We split! We split!' and *everybody* shouts 'We split! We split!'. And Prospero shouts, 'Bring me my evil brother and I shall have my revenge!'
>
> Freeze!
>
> Prospero has brought his brother to this island. What will happen next?

Discuss widely without giving the definitive textual answer; leave the next stages as an imaginative problem for the moment.

The survivors and the evil brother

The creeping spirits game

This game is a version of the old playground favourite, Grandmother's footsteps (aka Sly fox or Peep behind the curtain). The basic activity is simply this: the person who is on ('*it*') stands with their back to the group; the group try to creep forward to touch *it* on the back; *it* turns around sharply to try and catch them moving – the group freeze, anyone caught moving by *it* has to return to the starting line. If *it* is touched, the 'toucher' becomes *it* and the game starts again. In our version, the game model is placed into the narrative context of the play.

TIP It might be worth playing the straightforward version of the game with the group outside of the drama, so they have a shared understanding of the structure.

The aim of the game is to specify the interaction of the spirit and human worlds in the play and, quite simply, to introduce characters and have their names heard and spoken and their basic attitudes made concrete.

Here is the new version of the game, given through the teacher's voice.

> When the ship was sunk, who was on the ship and who survived? Kings, dukes, princes, servants and sailors. In Shakespeare's story, the sailors mysteriously vanish, and reappear only at the end of the story.
>
> So, on the island, we now have? Spirits, kings, dukes, princes, servants, Prospero. We also have Prospero's daughter, who was mentioned by him, she is called Miranda – and also ... the creature we heard howling in the woods!
>
> The spirits are watching the survivors ... Prospero has instructed them to do so. They are stalking them, following them. [*Model the sense and movement of these people as you describe them.*] The survivors can't help thinking that they are being watched. As they walk desperately around the island, looking for food, for water, for other survivors, they keep turning around sharply to see who is following them, who is watching them. Would you like to play a game about this? It's called the 'The creeping spirits game'. All show me the creeping spirits ... You have to freeze if you think you've been spotted! Now show me the desperate survivors ... as they creep through this mysterious island ... Good. Now I need to tell you who the survivors are. I will need some volunteers to play these characters in the game.

As you give each character's name and description, select a pupil and place him/her at the edge of the room with their back to the centre and the group. You might choose to make simple name cards, or to make versions of the names and text to display on the walls. These are useful because they allow the *spoken* name to be seen written down, and give the pupil–actor a visual aid to remind them who they are and what they will say on turning during the game.

The survivors, for the purposes of the game, are:

- **King Alfonso** – the powerful king of Naples, he says, 'My son is lost!'
- **Prince Ferdinand** – Alfonso's handsome son, he says, 'Where should this music be?'
- **Duke Antonio** – Prospero's evil brother, he says, 'Very foul!'
- **Stephano** – the drunken servant, he says, 'Have we devils here?'
- **Trinculo** – the king's jester, he says, 'What have we here? A man or a fish?'

Practise all these characters and their lines with the whole group. Ask the group to characterise each survivor physically. Repeat the text for each character so as to establish them widely.

Now the game is ready to be played.

Set the game space as in Figure 4.

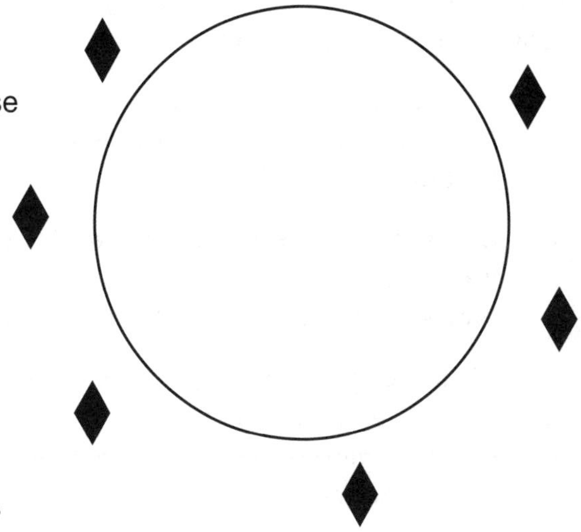

Figure 4 The creeping spirits game

♦ = surviving characters   circle = the creeping spirits

The survivors are now in place. They are miming a walk through the mysterious island, but staying on one the spot (model this). Explain again that they are searching for food, but also feel like they are being watched. When you call *their* name, they must turn around sharply to see who is following them. Meanwhile, the spirits (everybody else) are in 'stealth mode'. They are creeping airily through the island, watching (again, on the spot – demonstrate); sometimes *this* person, sometimes *this*. The rule is that spirits have to keep on moving... until the survivor turns around to catch them moving. They must then be stone-still. If they are spotted by a survivor, they have to leave the centre and sit by the wall – they are out! Check understanding of the game and answer any queries before beginning.

Play a 'no-penalty' practice version of the game with the spirits moving as in the earlier movement activity. Use the drum to provide a link with the earlier activity and to add dramatic tension. Call each character in turn. They turn and try to catch spirits moving. They then walk into the spirit group, saying their special line and looking for spirits who might react, giggle or move. If you spot someone moving, tap them on the shoulder, at which they will 'go to the wall'. When you bang your drum, the characters return to their starting spots.

For a final, dramatic complication: as well as shouting individual names, you might also shout 'Survivors!' at which point *all* the characters will turn around. Try this.

Once the practice run is complete:

> Are we ready to play the game? This time, if you're spotted moving... you're out! Good luck, my spirits!

TIP   It's useful to make the point that only *you* have the power to spot moving spirits. Spirits who are *out* don't need to worry about spotting others moving. They can just enjoy watching the game (and perhaps working out how to explain to Prospero that they have been caught out by the humans!).

Play the game until only one spirit survives. Or, if the feeling is that the group would like to play the game again... stop when there are five spirits left and allow them to swap places with the survivor characters. Then play the game again.

The evil brother – Antonio

Preparation: display Antonio's lines in large letters around the room. Simple but clear handwriting on pieces of sugar paper or lining paper is fine. It is best displayed on various walls surrounding the working space – so that, from the circle, the pupils will see at least one of them without needing to turn. Or you might consider using a whiteboard if you have one in the space. Make a circle.

Whole group discussion:

> What do you know about Antonio so far? What sort of person do you think he is? What do you think he thought about his brother when he decided to try and kill him? What does he think about his brother now?

> Shakespeare uses a lovely, old word to describe what he has done – he has 'usurped' Prospero. Which means he has removed him violently and taken his place. He is called the 'usurping brother'. All try and say it: 'The usurping brother'.

> Would you like to know just how evil Antonio is? Let us look at the very first scene in which we meet Antonio on the island. He has found some of the 'royal household': the king and the people travelling with him. Let's build the scene in the centre of this circle. We'll need some volunteers. Here is the scene.

Place a volunteer in the scene as you describe each element and build up a tableau of the scene (this is Act 2, Scene 1; see page 74).

> As well as those we know about, Duke Antonio (Prospero's evil brother) and Alonso the king, there are other survivors from the court. Let's place King Alonso first. He is very sad, 'distraught' over losing his son Ferdinand in the shipwreck. Ariel, Prospero's chief spirit, who has been following this group, has cast a spell to make the king fall into a deep sleep. With the king are Gonzalo (the kind servant who put food in Prospero's boat all those years ago) and other servants. They are all asleep.

> Wide awake and dangerous is Antonio. He is standing apart from the king and looking at him murderously... his hand on his dagger. Beside Antonio is someone else... the king's *own* brother, Sebastian.

> What do you think Antonio might be saying to Sebastian as they look at the sleeping king? Have a guess. [*Take five suggestions.*] Let's make him speak. If you know what he might be saying... here's your chance to be him. When I point to you, come into the circle, the scene, and place your hand on Antonio's shoulder. When you make contact, you will become him and speak his words. You will use 'I...', 'We...'. What is he plotting? What is he saying?

Now give a number of pupils the chance to enter and speak as Antonio.

> Fantastic! You are doing the work of playwrights; of Shakespeare himself. You are making characters speak. Would you like to know what words Shakespeare gives Antonio to say?

Indicate the text around the walls (or on the whiteboard). Read the lines:

> Antonio says:

> 'What might, worthy Sebastian? O, what might?... me thinks I see it in thy face... What thou shouldst be... My strong imagination sees a crown dropping upon thy head...'

> 'Here lies your brother... Whom I, with this obedient steel, three inches of it, Can lay to bed forever'.

> And Sebastian says:

> 'As though got'st Milan, I'll come by Naples.'

> Let's think about what each of those things might mean. What are he and Sebastian saying? What is Antonio trying to do? Why might he be doing this?

Discuss and agree.

Now offer pupils the chance to try out the scene themselves. Because this is quite a challenging task – speaking Shakespeare – offer the differentiated task of working in groups of up to five, with some as the sleeping characters and only two with the speaking parts, the most confident playing Antonio. The sleeping characters can be encouraged to make an important contribution by helping to direct the scene in rehearsal. Maybe, in the performance, they could shift in their sleep and influence the speaking characters. Talk about what 'directors' do – they look at the scene from the audience's point of view and help the actors to make the scene clear and dramatic.

Allow time for rehearsal of the scene, and then invite each group to perform at the centre of the circle.

Talk about the performances.

> How did the actors find speaking Shakespeare's words? How about the audience? Did you understand the words? Do you think the words... the language... are interesting, exciting, good to speak and hear? Do you think it is 'special' language? Discuss it.

> What can you tell me about Antonio now?

Prospero and Antonio

The group is back in the circle. Explain.

> We know what Antonio is like from the scene; from the things he says himself. That's one way of knowing a person. Another is to hear what other people say about him. What might the brother he tried to kill (along with his young daughter) say about him? What does Prospero say?

> We need an Antonio. Should we have a new one? Who would like to play him?

Place Antonio in the centre of the circle. He is trapped. This is a 'mind trap' (see Chapter 2). He is trapped in here by all that people say about him. In particular, he is trapped by the things his brother says about him. He wants to escape, but every time he tries, the walls send him back into the circle with their words.

What do the walls of the 'mind trap' say to Antonio? What does Prospero say of him?

Antonio, try to escape! (...but don't touch the walls). The mind trap group are instructed to repeat after you Prospero's thoughts about his usurping brother...

- 'Thy false uncle!'
- 'My false brother... awaked an evil nature'
- '...(who) did believe he was indeed the duke...'
- '...tell me if this might be a brother!'
- 'Good wombs have borne bad sons'
- 'Mine enemies'
- 'I... justify you traitor!'
- 'Most wicked sir!'
- '...whom to call brother would infect my mouth'

And this:

'That a brother should be so...'

What do you think Shakespeare says next? Who can finish the sentence, 'That a brother should be so...'?

Take suggestions. The 'proposer' can step into the circle to speak, the group repeat the line with anger, and the proposer steps back to make room for the next.

Finally, reveal what Shakespeare actually gives Prospero to say...

'That a brother should be so perfidious!'

Repeat it several times. Louder and louder. The group might move forward in an intimidating fashion towards Antonio. Enter the circle yourself and gently force Antonio down to the ground.

> Ask: How does Antonio feel about what he has done? He looks like he feels guilty. Scared? Maybe he just enjoys the power? Now he is the duke? He wants Sebastian to do the same as he... to kill his brother (the king) and take his power. Why? Does he want him to share his guilt? Does he feel alone? Scared? Vulnerable? Discuss.

> What do you think Prospero will do when he gets his evil brother here on the island? Here, where he has absolute, terrible, magical power. What revenge will he take? Discuss. What is a fitting punishment?

> You might be surprised!

Miranda's lonely place

Fathers and daughters

Discuss.

> Have you noticed anything funny about his play? How many females are there on the island? How many women? How many girls? There is only one! (If we take it that spirits are not either gender!) Why has Shakespeare written a play with only one female part in it? Discuss. One thing is, the story he wishes to tell is about brothers and kings and dukes... All male... Do you think it would be any different if it were about sisters and queens and duchesses? Why? Another thing to consider perhaps is that women were not allowed on the stage in Shakespeare's time. The first woman to go on a stage in a public play in England was in 1660! The Tempest (this play) was written in about 1611. This was thought to be the last play that Shakespeare wrote on his own. Maybe he was just fed up of writing big parts for women that he knew would only be played by boys!

> Girls, would you like to be Miranda? The only girl on an island of men? Take opinions. Before the shipwreck and before the survivors climbed out of the sea onto Prospero's island, the only people on the island were Prospero and Miranda. Apart from these two, there were Ariel and the spirits... and the mysterious howling monster, the son of a witch, that we haven't met yet. I wonder what it was like for Miranda, here on the island before this story begins. Do you think she liked it on her own with just her dad? What would life be like if there was just you and your dad together all the time? Especially if your dad was someone like Prospero!

> Miranda is fifteen years old. Since she was three, she has only known one other human... her father.

> Alone on the island... her dad studying his books from morning 'til night. What does she do with herself?

> We've been sitting down for long enough. Everybody stand! Find a partner... perhaps boys and girls is best. Of course, just as in Shakespeare's time, boys can play girls! Decide who's going to be Prospero and who Miranda. Miranda, walk away from your Prospero... Here's the scene we're going to explore... As I describe it you, the actors, must act it.

> Prospero is in his 'cell'...

Discuss briefly as an aside: Shakespeare calls Prospero's own place a 'cell'. What might a cell look like? It's not a prison cell. It's interesting that often Shakespeare uses words that we understand... but are just not the word we would use for it. They are 'special' words... or 'specially chosen' words.

> ...he is reading. In fact, he is lost in his reading... concentrating so hard that if you spoke to him, he might not even hear you. (Aside: do you ever lose yourself in something like that? What?) [*Take five, perhaps.*] Prospero loves his books... show us that image; lost in his books.

> Miranda is watching him at a distance. She wants to speak to him; to *anybody*. She knows that he doesn't know she is even there. All Mirandas, show us that image. I wonder what she's thinking at this moment? He seems to have no time for her... Does he sometimes sound irritated by her? Prospero continues with his head down to his books. This is what Miranda *thought* but did not say: 'Father...' [*a simple 'sentence root' activity, see Chapter 2*].

Tell pupils that you are going to tap some of the Mirandas on the shoulder, at which they will speak her thoughts and complete the sentence. Give pupils a little time to compose the line they will say. By way of differentiation, if pupils have nothing else to say, they can just say gently under their breath with appropriate feeling, 'Father'.

Having heard suggestions, tell the group that, in a moment, you are going to bring the scene alive. When you clap your hands, Miranda will approach her father and speak to him. He is *so* lost in his books that he might not respond straight away... but she will insist. She is going mad with having no other human being to speak to. She *must* speak. I wonder if she has something important to say to him, or just wants to chat? I wonder what she might say... and I wonder how he will respond?

> Before we begin, think about this: how will they speak? They are Shakespeare's characters. Maybe you can think about experimenting with a different way of speaking; some different kinds of words. Decide what you think this means yourself. We shall see what happens. For a start, she only ever calls him 'Father'... not 'Dad'.

Clap your hands and allow the scene to happen; the children improvise freely. After a well judged period, freeze the action. Ask all the Prosperos to repeat the lines they said first when she disturbed them. Touch them on the shoulder quickly. Ask both to consider where the scene might end... what do the two characters *want*? Who is going to *get* what they want? Miranda, tell us what you *want*. (Shoulder-tap again.) Prospero, tell us what you *want*. (Shoulder-tap.) Continue the scene. When you get to the end... Freeze! And hold that important freeze. This should tell us how they both feel at the end.

> Now. How did you find acting the scene? What did you learn about these two people? Discuss.

> In your pairs, decide on the most important moment in the scene you have just completed. You are going to choose two lines... one for each character... which you would like to share with everybody else. Think and decide. Now. Put yourself in a freeze which is exactly where you are at that moment in the scene. We are going to 'spotlight' these scenes. As I move around the room, I will tell you where the spotlight is falling... [*with a gesture*] and where it falls, comes alive...

Watch the scenes.

> Who can finish off these sentence roots?
>
> 'Miranda, a girl who...'
>
> '...a daughter who...'
>
> 'Prospero, a father who...'

Miranda's place

Prospero has his own special place on the island; his cell. It is where he keeps his most precious things... his book; where he can be alone. Does Miranda have a place like this?

> Find yourself a space on your own. Those of you who have just been Prospero... give up that character. You are now *all* going to be Miranda.

She has been trying to speak to her father. Whatever it was you chose to make happen in your own scenes, let's say that Prospero's reply was simply... 'Not now, child. Later!' Miranda walks away from him. She decides to *do* something... Maybe it's some 'work', maybe something to entertain herself? Think about this... What *does* she spend her day doing? What does her *father* want her to do? To study? To do housework? What does *she* want to do? Is she making something? Building something? Does she have a favourite game? What things does she *have* to do? Does he give her chores? Tasks? Homework? Must she cook? Clean? Find food? Think now. What does Miranda go and do next? Now create a frozen picture of Miranda *doing* this thing. Ignore everybody else. There is *just* you here alone on the island. What are you doing?

> Great. Now when I give you a signal [*clap or drum*], you have to begin to *do* this thing. You act it out like Prospero reads his books; with complete concentration. If someone spoke to you, you wouldn't even hear them. You are completely absorbed in the *doing* of this thing.

[*Model the movement as you explain; it might involve moving a little, with fine, careful actions, or being very still.*] Are you ready? Begin!

> The children then begin this piece of isolated 'occupational mime'. They should become absorbed. Leave it to run for as long as pupils maintain focus. You might usefully fade in a sound effect or a piece of soft music. You might propose that they 'loop' the action, so if it is an action that has a natural end, it is repeated with even *more* concentration.
>
> Finally, give a countdown to the completion of Miranda's task. How does it end? Does she step back with satisfaction? Brush off her hands? Sit down with exhaustion? Pack away 'stuff'?

All continue to *be* Miranda and to *do* as I say. She looks up at the sun. This is how the time is told, here on the island. She looks at the sun and knows it is beginning to slide down the sky. It will, before too long, fade. Before it does so… every day… she must visit her own special place. Prospero has *his* – where he keeps his books; where on the island is Miranda's *own* special place? Near the sea? In a cave? On the hill that might be at the centre of the island? Where?

Once you've decided *that*, decide *this*… Do *you* have a special place yourself? Somewhere you feel at home, comfortable? Prospero keeps his most important and precious objects in his special place... his books; in Miranda's special place, she also keeps *her* most important and precious thing. What is it? Is it something from the past? Something she has found? Something that has been given to her? Something she has made? Decide as you make the journey to Miranda's special place. If she lost this thing, if it was taken, it would be as if the world had ended. What is it? Think about the journey she has to make; from where she *was*, doing the action, to where this special place is… does she have to cross a river, crawl inside something, climb a hill, walk over hot sand? Whatever it is… Make that journey… *Now* (again, you can't see any one else… they aren't here!)

> Give the children time to make the journey. Allow them to become absorbed. Narrate Miranda arriving at her special place; finding this most important object, taking it out, or unwrapping it, looking at it as she holds it in her hands. Look and see the tiny details of it. What marks might be on it from it being made or handled over the years? What is Miranda's most important, significant object? Now visit each and every child. Tap each on the shoulder and give each the chance to explain and describe what they have. Where a pupil seems particularly focused, ask further questions. Where did it come from? Who owned it before you? Why is *this* the most precious object you own?

I wonder what will happen when the fifteen-year-old Miranda sees another human being for the very first time, now they have arrived on the island? How do you think she will feel? What will she think?

Everybody stand. For one more minute, you are *all* still Miranda. Remember. The only other human being she ever remembers seeing is her father. When I clap my hands/bang my drum… she is going to *see* everybody else in the room. She is going to *see* and she is going to react [*model this*]… How will she react? Ready?

> Clap. The children show Miranda *seeing* and reacting. Freeze! Hold the freeze.

Remember we talked about Shakespeare choosing *special* words for his characters very carefully? Would you like to know (and learn) the line Shakespeare gives Miranda to say at this moment?
   She says,

'O brave new world, That has such people in't!'

What does that mean? Listen. 'O brave new world, That has such people in't'. What might it mean? Discuss briefly… Perhaps, 'How wonderful the world is to have such wonderful people in it!' Would you like to learn that line of Shakespeare's?

Repeat the line several times yourself, with the pupils repeating it each time. Continue until you think they have all learnt this wonderful line. Now try again the moment in which Miranda sees other people for the first time. This time, let her see, react and then speak the line. Practise, with the whole group acting the moment on your signal. Then give individual children the chance to act the moment and speak the line. End on a flourish. *'For the final time. Everybody!'*

> *'O brave new world, That has such people in't!'*

Challenge the group before finishing the session; ask them to find an opportunity to speak this whole line in their real lives; in the playground, at home, in the park. You might ask the group to report on their use of the line in the next session.

The 'monster' Caliban

By contrast with the previous section, we now introduce Caliban.

Caliban is called a monster (and much worse) by most of the human population of the play. His mother, Sycorax, a witch, was banished to this island before Prospero arrived. She died leaving Caliban alone and, in his mind, 'ruler' of the island. On arriving, Prospero taught him to speak and was kind to him, but because of the terrible things Caliban did (he tried to molest Miranda!) Prospero now keeps him as a slave and punishes him with boils on his skin and other torments. Caliban is vicious, resentful and bent on destroying his 'master'.

> When we first created this island by creating its *sound* (a soundscape, remember), we heard a sound far off that seemed to disrupt the peace of the island. It was a dangerous, scary sound; the sound of a beast howling in anger.

Summon up the soundscape. Introduce your 'monster' sound and invite pupils to join you in making this terrible noise. Turn the sound off.

> It's time to meet this new character, placed by Shakespeare on the magical island.

> His name is Caliban. Does that remind you of any other words you know? If you jumble up the letters... cannibal! No-one says he *is* a cannibal... but Shakespeare chooses his words carefully.

> Would you like to find out about Caliban?

Playing Caliban

You need: a recording of Sibelius' crazy 'tone poem' 'Prelude to The Tempest' (Opus 109). It is an evocative piece of music, which might make a perfect accompaniment to the physical movement work of this section. Also, quill pens, ink and agèd paper, and the prepared curse.

> Everybody here has Caliban in their bones. Imagine this terrible, dangerous, sad, twisted creature is trapped inside you. We're going to let him out. What do you think this creature looks like? Discuss.

> Start standing on your own, as still as a rock. Listen to this (begin the Sibelius track). What does it sound like? A storm? Imagine you are at the centre of a storm. Your feet are rooted to the floor... but your body, arms, legs can move... they are being blown... blown by the violent storm. Caliban is outside in the storm. Maybe howling up to the sky! Do it now! You are being blown, whipped by the wind and rain and thunder. Now you can move around the room. The storm is passing. You are Caliban, that we call 'vile monster'.

> Listen to what people say about him, and try to 'let him out' – see what your body does to make each thing seem true. [*Model this.*] How does Caliban move on his feet? How upright is his body? How rounded are his shoulders? Does he work evenly? Heavily? How does he breathe as he walks?

Listen. What do these things *mean* and how will your body *show* each one.

Caliban is:

> 'A freckled whelp, hag-born'
>
> 'Thou most lying slave'
>
> 'Filth as thou art'
>
> 'A thing most brutish'
>
> 'A thing of darkness!'
>
> 'Some monster of the isle'
>
> 'A howling monster'
>
> '...poisonous slave, got by the devil himself'

Take up your book and become Prospero again.

When the powerful Prospero passes close by you, Caliban, what do you do? How do you react? Enact this.

When Prospero came to the island and found the lonely, deformed creature Caliban, he started out being kind; he taught him to speak... perhaps to write; but not any more. Prospero thinks Caliban's evil can't be tamed, and controls him with torture; with pains of all descriptions.

[*With a gesture Prospero inflicts each torture and the children react as Caliban... perhaps writhing on the floor.*]

> '... tonight thou shalt have cramps...' *(terrible, terrible cramps all over)*
>
> 'Side-stiches that shall pen thy breath up'
>
> 'urchins (goblin hedgehogs!) shall exercise on thee... all night long'
>
> '...Thou shalt be pinched as thick as honeycomb...'
>
> '...each pinch more stinging Than bees that made 'em.'
>
> 'goblins grind (thy) joints'

Order Caliban (now perhaps in a heap on the floor) back to his cave. The pupils do so. And Freeze! Bring them out of role.

Do you think Prospero is fair to Caliban? Why does he treat him so badly? Is it just because he doesn't think he's human – just a savage? Be prepared to give further details of Caliban's story that might show why he is so angry with Prospero, and why Prospero is so angry with him. Will they ever be able to live together in some kind of peace? How can you ever sort out things like that when they have gone *so* far? What advice would you give them? Discuss.

When he is alone in his cave, Caliban writes curses about Prospero. He uses the writing skills Prospero taught him, and the paper he has stolen from him... to write terrible, terrible curses of revenge. I wonder what a monster's handwriting looks like. Here's one of them [*your modelled example*], but he writes one every day. He is so twisted with hatred. What curse does he write today?

Caliban's curse:

> 'A south-west (wind) blow on ye
>
> And blister you all over... All the charms
>
> Of Sycorax – toads, beetles, bats – light on you!'

The children now write their own curses for Caliban. This may take some time. Invite them to collect the resources they need and then return to their caves. The quills, ink and agèd paper will add real value to this writing task. Point out that, again, the words they use should be as carefully chosen as Shakespeare's.

TIP   At the end of the task, the children might like to share their curses with the group. Offer to read them out yourself – adding a suitably gruesome and dramatic voice will add further value to the children's writing and its reception. Make special note of interesting vocabulary... and the handwriting of a monster!

Caliban's story

Caliban's story in the play, on its own, is an exciting, dramatic and comic one. In this next, fairly straightforward section, we shall pull together Caliban's own story in the form of a 'Story Whoosh!' (see Chapter 3). We make a large circle.

> Would you like to help me to tell the story of Caliban, so we can see what happens to him? The simple rules are: any character or thing I mention, and anything that I say that happens to them, must be 'summoned' to the centre of this circle – our stage. You have to listen carefully and react quickly. If you are, for example, Caliban at the start, you don't need to be him all the way through... the parts swap around. If I say 'Whoosh!' and wave my hand over the stage, you have to clear the stage and go back to where you started for the story to carry on anew on the empty stage. Here we go.

The story of Caliban: a Story Whoosh!

- Once upon a time there was a witch... called Sycorax. She was banished by the king from her native land, Algiers, for weaving terrible spells.
- She was banished to a distant island, where she gave birth to a strange child – Caliban – whose father is said to be the devil himself!
- In time Sycorax, the old witch, died. Leaving Caliban alone with the spirits of the island. Whoosh!
- But look. Who approaches on a rotting, slowly sinking boat? It is Prospero, his three-year-old daughter, and his books.
- Prospero is kind to the strange, inhuman Caliban – teaching him to speak. Through the power of his books, Prospero takes command of the whole island and all its spirits – becoming its king and master. Caliban believes the island should be *his* and becomes angry and bitter.
- One day, Caliban attacks Miranda... and Prospero loses his patience. He turns Caliban into his slave and punishes him with terrible tortures. Caliban curses Prospero every day and plots to destroy him. Whoosh!
- One night, there is a terrible storm. Caliban dances in the wind and rain. He watches a ship sink out at sea.
- The following morning. Caliban meets two survivors of the shipwreck. A drunken servant, Stephano... and a foolish jester, Trinculo. They are terrified of Caliban – the monster – and he is terrified of them.
- Stephano and Trinculo get Caliban drunk and he comes to believe that they are royalty; that Stephano is the king. Caliban enlists their help in murdering Prospero. They hatch a plan to kill him as he sleeps in his cell.
- Ariel, Prospero's chief spirit, overhears their plot and tells Prospero. Prospero sends Ariel to torment them. To terrify and chase them.
- Finally, Caliban, Stephano and Trinculo are brought before Prospero. Caliban realises how stupid he has been to think Stephano a king. Caliban asks to be forgiven...

What do you think Prospero will do? Discuss.

Prospero's forgiveness

Prospero is a man much 'wronged'. Think about that word – 'wronged' – again, it's not how we would usually use the word ourselves; we might say 'it was wrong' rather than 'he was wronged'?... but we know what it means. It just takes a moment for our brains to work it out, and then we understand it perfectly well. It's good exercise for our brains! Prospero is a man much wronged.

In what way has he been 'wronged'? Discuss. Clearly, his brother has turned his people and servants against him, 'usurped' his crown, tried to kill him and his daughter; Caliban has tried to assault his daughter, and later to kill him in his sleep.

Prospero is a powerful man who controls spirits that can conjure storms: he can make things invisible, change their shape, send boils to torture a person. He could take all sorts of terrible revenge. But what does he do? He says (to the worst villain, Antonio):

> *'I do forgive thy rankest fault!'*

(Aside: what might 'rank' mean here?)

After all that, old Prospero forgives his brother, and he forgives Caliban.

Does anyone understand that? Discuss. When things have got so bad, why is forgiveness the best option?

Maybe Prospero feels he is getting old and closer to death... and he wants to put things straight. Or maybe it is this... 'the power of love'... listen...

For some half-cheesy fun, fade in John Paul Young's seventies classic, 'Love is in the Air'...

As the song builds, explain more about Miranda when she sees other human beings. The first person she sees is the young and handsome Ferdinand – son of the King of Naples. They fall deeply in love at first sight... and, seeing this new young love blossoming before him... maybe Prospero's vengeful heart melts... by forgiving, he perhaps makes the world a better and happier place for his daughter to live in.

Plus, finally, from Shakespeare's point of view... he knows he is writing a *comedy*. As well as this meaning that we can expect it to be funny (think about Stephano, Trinculo, drunken Caliban), it also means, in Shakespeare's time, that the play will end with people *coming together*; in *marriage*. The opposite of a 'comedy' is a 'tragedy' – a Shakespearean tragedy ends in things *falling apart*; in *death*, such as in *Romeo and Juliet* or *Hamlet* or *Macbeth*.

So, at the end of the play, a marriage is being planned for Miranda and Ferdinand; Antonio gives Prospero back his kingdom; Caliban, Ariel and the spirits are set free; everyone is forgiven... *and*... the ship that sank at the start of the story... is discovered safe and well in a harbour on the island, equipped and ready to take Prospero, Miranda and everyone else home. Hoorah!

The world of brothers and sisters

We have now explored the whole story of Shakespeare's *The Tempest*. Let us think about the story for a moment.

What other stories do we know about brothers and sisters? Discuss. Hansel and Gretel, Cain and Abel, Coronation Street, The Simpsons, Jacqueline Wilson. All these stories... and any others you can think of... belong to a special world: 'the world of brothers and sisters' [*gesture to draw a large circle – like a mathematical 'set' in the air*]. All these stories... as well as Shakespeare's story... belong in this world. It isn't some strange alien world... it is ours. Do you know who else belongs in 'the world of brothers and sisters'? You and me. How many of you have brothers or sisters... *or*, at least *know* someone who has brothers or sisters? Probably everybody. Well, we all belong inside 'the world of brothers and sisters', along with Prospero and Antonio. Shakespeare isn't just writing about old things and old people in old words... he's writing about *us*... about what it's like being a human being. I bet lots of you can think of a time when you felt just like Prospero or Antonio; a time when you felt bad towards your brother or sister and wanted to get revenge?

Pupils might like to tell their own simple stories.

Building new

Would you like to make a play that happens in *your* world, in *your* time, in *your* words? We're going to invent our own piece of drama, which follows the pattern of Shakespeare's story, but happens in our own world, in our own language.

Remember when we started out, and we drew the ship in the air? What held the ship together and in the right shape? The oak beams underneath; the thick, main beam and the wooden 'ribs' that made the shape. If the shape wasn't right, the ship would sink! A story is a little like that; although you might not notice while you're listening to it or watching it... Inside the story there is a structure... A pattern that holds it in place... One way people talk about this is when they say a story must have 'a beginning, a middle, and an end'. Do you recognise that? But *this* story is a little more complicated. It has five simple steps in the pattern.

Either on individual cards or on the board show/write the following pattern:

- Step 1: A brother/sister is 'wronged'.
- Step 2: The 'wronged' brother/sister plans to get revenge.
- Step 3: A sudden, unexpected, surprise event changes how they feel.
- Step 4: The wronged brother/sister forgives.
- Step 5: Peace returns.

Small groups are formed and pupils are asked to create a simple story, set in their own 'world'. It might be one of the stories they told a little earlier. Each story must stick to the pattern: the story structure. Insist that each step in the story can only last a maximum of ten seconds.

Give the groups time to create these pieces of drama. This is a piece of straightforward 'small group play-making' (see Chapter 2), which allows the children more direct ownership of the story. They are working on an original, improvised, contemporary 'text', but within Shakespeare's structure.

TIP   Before rehearsing on their feet, ask the groups to produce a plan for their drama that clearly shows the five steps. Ask each group to whisper their simple plan to you and, when you agree it is clear, they can begin to make their play.

After sufficient time, perform the pieces and reflect on the pattern of each one.

Reflect: you have just created *new* stories to sit alongside Shakespeare's inside 'the world of brothers and sisters'.

Rebuilding the world: a final task

Construction task

You need: large, light brown sheet of cloth, newspaper for scrunching and relief-making, coloured paper for tearing/cutting and modelling. Suggested colours – two shades of blue (river and sea), yellow (sand), green (for trees and other greenery), paper masking tape for use in modelling, coloured pens or markers, or paint, assorted cardboard tubes, small boxes, plasticine/play-dough, coloured tissue paper, any other 'junk modelling' materials that you think might be useful, video camera.

In this section, we return to dealing directly with *The Tempest*. The purpose of this activity is to summarise all we have explored and understood through a piece of whole group construction. By the end of the activity, pupils will have demonstrated a full knowledge of the play's narrative, characters and language.

The group's final task will be to create 'the world of Shakespeare's *Tempest*' – more specifically, we are going to build Prospero's Island. Our model will include all the locations of the play and our work together, and all the characters of the play. We will also devise a way of displaying the key lines spoken by the characters. (See 'Construction tasks' in Chapter 2.)

Of course, we can trust in the magnificent resourcefulness of primary school teaching staff, but a few notes might be of use.

- It might be necessary to spend some time creating a sense of equivalence between the three tasks. In particular, the text task should be explained as a construction task in its own right. As well as selecting text, the group needs to invent a way of displaying it and integrating it into the construction.
- We suggest that you begin with the raw island-building task first, so that the group is given a clear and concrete impression of how the whole project might be realised. Gather the group together in a close circle. Produce the brown cloth and ask a range of pupils to scrunch up a pile of newspaper. Demonstrate how the newspaper can be put under the cloth to make a relief – so it looks like an island. Having done this, show how the edges of the cloth can be 'shaped' to show something approaching a natural island. Very quickly it should be possible to create a simple island shape. Now step back from the model so it can be seen clearly, and describe the task as above.
- You might usefully use the language of commissioning, as in the following.

> I have a difficult task for you to complete. If you think it is a task you can complete successfully, you may accept the 'commission'. It is a commission to 'rebuild the world' – to rebuild Prospero's Island. You will build it here. If the commission is successful, we will invite the public – your family and friends – to visit this exhibition and to learn from you all about Shakespeare's *The Tempest*. We will also commit it to memory by making a video of the final piece (or photographing it in detail).

> **The world you create here must include:**

> - all the sites of the play (the site of Prospero's cell; the site where Miranda keeps her precious object; the site where Trinculo and Stephano are washed ashore...)
> - all the people of the play
> - the words spoken in the play.

The first task will be to produce comprehensive lists of these three elements. This planning task might be done as a whole group or, better, the three commissioning groups produce their lists as a first task and then report back to the whole group, who might suggest any omissions from the list.

The three groups now set about the task of creating their element of the whole construction.

The work begins. The conversations involved in completing the task will provide rich opportunities to remember and reflect upon the journey you and the group have been on.

We offer an alternative, less resource- and time-intensive summary activity below, but please do consider the first task.

Story jigsaw (alternative or additional)

You need: copies of the story jigsaw (provided at the end of this chapter), one jigsaw per group. For each jigsaw, the story is cut up into twelve pieces, which are mixed up and placed in an envelope. (See 'Story jigsaw' in Chapter 2.)

There are two parts to the task: the 'ordering' exercise, in which the stories are reassembled; and a simple whole group performance of the whole story.

> A jigsaw is where we take a complete picture and cut it into pieces. We then have to put it back together again. We are going to do a 'story jigsaw'. We have taken the story of *The Tempest* and cut it into twelve pieces. They have all been jumbled up. In this game, you and your group have to try and put the pieces back together again in the right order.

We form six groups and give each group a jigsaw envelope. The groups discuss and sort the pieces. We check the order of the pieces. Now we all have the full story.

> Together as a group we are going to tell the whole story. Each group is to be given responsibility for two pieces of the story. Their job is to make two frozen pictures or tableaux to show the events in each section. When you have made the two tableaux, you have to work out slow-motion movements that will take us from one picture to the next.

Groups work on this.

Suitable music plays. The class perform the whole story in the right order. Make a point of noting that this is *one* spectacular, continuous story; not six pieces. Use the music and speak so as to add value to the dramatic moment. Have all actors frozen in position at the very start of the sequence in their own spaces, so that performance can be smooth and continuous. Announce the performance:

'The Tempest, by William Shakespeare'

Addendum

> We have looked at all aspects of Shakespeare's play: the characters, the story and the language. We would like to leave every one of you with a gift! A gift of words that you will remember and take with you. You will remember it forever. Shakespeare is regarded as a genius partly because of the way he is able to sum up a thought and express that thought in beautiful and memorable words.
>
> If there was one line from this whole play that you think this class should learn, what would it be? Discuss.

Propose two lines that say how wonderful we human beings are (or could be). Consider these two lines:

1. Prospero: 'We are such stuff as dreams are made on ... (and our little life is rounded with a sleep).'
2. Miranda: 'O brave new world, That has such people in't!'

● Discuss again the meaning of the lines. They are both lines that celebrate human life:
  1. We are miraculous, wonderful, beautiful things. We are the stuff that 'dreams' are made of: magic, starshine, imagination. We are great.
  2. The world is lucky to have people as wonderful as *us* in it ... the future will be brave and ambitious and great.

Which shall we learn? Perhaps both.

TIP   Give each pupil a copy of the lines, and permanently display them in the classroom. You might even like to integrate it into your classroom procedures, as one school has done, by making the lines a declaration of brilliance made at the start of each school day.

A teacher's crib sheet

Background information

- Written around 1611 and probably performed straight away for King James I.
- Published in the First Folio in 1623 after Shakespeare's death.
- May have been inspired by a shipwreck that happened in Bermuda in 1609. The play, taking place on an unknown, 'foreign' island, perhaps reflects the age's interest in exploring the world in what is known as 'the age of exploration'.

Brief summary of story

- Prospero has been deposed as the Duke of Milan by his brother Antonio. He has been set adrift on a boat with his young daughter, Miranda. The pair survived and Prospero took control of a distant island through the power of his magic.
- Several years later, when Miranda is a young woman, Prospero uses magic and the spirits of the island to conjure a storm to drive his brother's ship onto the island.
- The spirits taunt the wicked Antonio, who has arrived with the King of Naples and tries to get *his* brother to kill him and take the crown.
- Miranda falls in love with the king's son, Ferdinand.
- The monster Caliban hatches a plot to depose Prospero, but chooses fools as partners.
- Finally, Prospero forgives Antonio and they all return to Milan.

Main characters

- Prospero: the deposed Duke of Milan, an accomplished magician.
- Antonio: Prospero's brother, who deposed him to become Duke of Milan.
- Miranda: Prospero's daughter.
- Alfonso: The King of Naples.
- Ferdinand: the King of Naples' son.
- Sebastian: the King of Naples' brother.
- Caliban: a half monster who Prospero controls, original inhabitant of the island.
- Trinculo and Stephano: a jester and a foolish cook.
- Ariel: Prospero's spirit servant.

Other things

- *The Tempest* is usually thought of as Shakespeare's last great play; probably the last one he wrote on his own.
- Some have said that Prospero's somewhat cruel treatment of Caliban mirrors the treatment of indigenous people by European colonists in Shakespeare's time.
- *The Tempest* might have been the first play performed after Shakespeare's company bought the Blackfriars Theatre – an indoor theatre that charged much more than the public theatres, which might have marked the start of an 'elite' theatre and a separation between popular and high theatre in England.

Facts and legends for pupils

Shakespeare may have been inspired to write **The Tempest** by a real shipwreck that happened in 1609 in Bermuda (in the 'magical' Bermuda Triangle?).

The play was written at a time of great exploration of the world – the magic island is like one of the faraway places that were being discovered.

The Tempest is usually thought of as **Shakespeare's** last great play – it was first performed in 1611 (he died in 1616). He may have written a few other plays afterwards with other people.

Some people say that Prospero is **Shakespeare** – his magic is his writing. When he gives up his magic, saying 'here I do o'er-through my books', it is **Shakespeare** giving up writing in his last play!

The Tempest was probably the first play to be performed in **Shakespeare's** new **Blackfriars Theatre** – which was inside rather than outdoors, and charged five or six times as much as **The Globe.**

When **Shakespeare's** company bought the **Blackfriars Theatre,** it already had musicians, which might be why there are so many songs in the play.

It could also be because it was performed at the **King's** court – and at **King James'** daughter's wedding – so is full of 'spectacle'.

Milan, where Prospero was Duke, and where they have sailed from and return to at the end, isn't even on the coast – **Shakespeare** obviously didn't know the city!

A page of famous lines

'We are such stuff as dreams are made on
And our little life is rounded with a sleep'

'Good wombs have borne bad sons'

'O brave new world,
That has such people in't!'

'We split! We split!'

'Misery acquaints a man with strange bedfellows'

'He that dies pays all debts'

'Our revels are now ended. These our actors,
As I foretold you, were all spirits, and
Are melted into air, into thin air.'

The Tempest: A Story *Whoosh!*

On a magic island, the magician-duke Prospero gathers with Ariel and his spirits. His daughter, Miranda, waits at a distance while the monster Caliban shifts heavy logs and curses his master, Prospero.

. . . Whoosh!

At sea, a ship is thrown into an almighty storm – a tempest – conjured by Prospero's spirits at his command. On the storm-torn ship, Prospero's brother and the court of the King of Naples: his son Ferdinand and his brother Sebastian. The ship is sunk, but all are spared and washed onto the island beach.

. . . Whoosh!

Prospero tells his daughter of her early life: how his wicked brother Antonio seized his crown as the Duke of Milan and set them both adrift on a rotten boat to die. How Prospero used his books to bring them here and take control of the island, its spirits and Caliban. Prospero has brought his evil brother here to take revenge!

. . . Whoosh!

The monster slave Caliban mistakes a jester and a cook for royalty and hatches a plan to murder his master Prospero. Ariel the spirit torments them and tricks them with disappearing food, monsters and silly clothes. Their plans are never going to work!

. . . Whoosh!

Over the sleeping King of Naples, evil Antonio talks Sebastian, the king's brother, into killing the king and taking the crown. Ariel thwarts the plan.

. . . Whoosh!

Meanwhile, Miranda comes across the king's son Ferdinand and they fall madly in love – going off to play chess! Is it their love that melts Prospero's heart? For, despite all that Antonio has done to him, Prospero forgives him! Antonio surrenders his crown to his brother.

. . . Whoosh!

Prospero gives up his magic, frees the spirits, and reveals the sunken ship safe and ready to sail. They all leave for Milan to restore Prospero as duke, Miranda and Ferdinand marry!

The End. Whoosh!

A story jigsaw

At sea, a ship is thrown into an almighty storm – a tempest – conjured by Prospero's spirits at his command. On the storm-torn ship are Prospero's brother and the court of the King of Naples: his son Ferdinand and the king's brother Sebastian.

The ship is sunk but all are spared and washed onto the island beach.

Prospero tells his daughter of her early life: how his wicked brother Antonio seized his crown as the Duke of Milan and set them both adrift on a rotten boat to die.

Prospero has brought his evil brother here to take revenge!

The monster slave Caliban mistakes a jester and a cook for royalty and hatches a plan to murder his master Prospero. Ariel the spirit torments them.

Over the sleeping King of Naples, evil Antonio talks Sebastian, the king's brother, into killing the king and taking the crown. Ariel thwarts the plan.

Prospero's daughter Miranda comes across the king's son Ferdinand and they fall madly in love – going off to play chess!

Their love melts Prospero's heart.

Despite all that Antonio has done to him, Prospero forgives him! Antonio surrenders his crown to his brother.

Caliban and his foolish assassins are brought before Prospero terrified.

Prospero gives up his magic, frees the spirits, and reveals the sunken ship safe and ready to sail.

They all leave for Milan to restore Prospero as duke, and Miranda and Ferdinand marry!

© 2012, *Shakespeare for the Primary School*, John Doona, Routledge

The Tempest scheme structure map

Section	Drama approaches	Possible curriculum opportunities
To the island		
A shape game	Gaming in context	Maths (shape); PE in context
George's ship	Teacher narration; whole group enactment	History; literacy: literary narrative, understanding narrative, building context and belief
The tempest	As above, with whole group tableaux	PE in context; literacy: building tension, dramatic language
Waking and seeing	Soundscape; characterisation	Geography (environments); literacy: sense of place, character empathy
On Prospero's Island		
The spirits	Movement work for character	PE in context
Prospero	Teacher in-role; story-telling; hot-seating	Oracy; personal and moral education; literacy: character understanding and empathy
Conjuring storms	Small-group writing and performing; writing in-role; teacher in-role	Oracy; science (magic); RE; literacy: performance poetry (spells)
The survivors and the evil brother		
The creeping spirits game	Gaming in context	PE in context; literacy: narrative understanding
Evil Antonio	Using text; discussion; performance	Literacy: textual analysis, character development; personal and moral education
Prospero and Antonio	'Mind trap'; characterisation; use of text	Literacy: developing new text from the old, character development; oracy
Miranda's lonely place		
Fathers and daughters	Discussion; pair improvisation	Literacy: script-making, character delineation and empathy; PHSE
Miranda's place	Absorbed solo work; character development; occupational mime	Literacy: character insight, empathy
The 'monster' Caliban		
Playing Caliban	Character-based movement work; using text; teacher in-role; discussion	PE in context; literacy: writing in-role, character empathy
Caliban's story	Story whoosh!	Literacy: narrative understanding, individual character role in whole text
Prospero's forgiveness	Discussion; use of text	RE; PHSE: moral and personal education
The world of brothers and sisters		
Discussion	Discussion	Literacy: understanding and developing structure
Building new	Extended small-group play-making; performance	
Rebuilding the world		
Construction task	Construction task (used summatively); whole group construction	Design and technology; art (3D models); literacy: understanding narrative, character and language
Story jigsaw	Story jigsaw; performance	Literacy: narrative understanding; problem-solving (sorting)

Resources needed	Teachers Notes
Setting of space for drama	
Props: cloak and ancient books	
Paper, pens	
Game rules and instructions to hand	
Text displayed or copied	
Appropriate music	
Appropriate music	
Story Whoosh! sheet	
Paper and pens	
Junk modelling materials; paper and pens and pens	
Prepared story jigsaws	

We offer the chart above as a starting point. There are a whole host of learning opportunities in a rich drama experience that would have been exhausting to list: developing positive groups, expanding language opportunities and vocabulary, developing self-image and confidence, fostering imaginative responses, to name a few. Also, as you translate the work into your own classroom you will, we hope, create for yourself a whole unanticipated flood of new opportunities for learning. The heart of such learning is the rich experience we all hope to build.

Resources – Act 2, Scene 1

A poster-style page declaring:

'O brave new world, That has such people in't!'

And another saying:

'We are such stuff as dreams are made on
And our little life is rounded with a sleep'

The edited scene used in the scheme, with this text:

Antonio says:

'What might,
Worthy Sebastian? O, what might?
…me thinks I see it in thy face,
What thou shouldst be…
My strong imagination sees a crown
Dropping upon thy head…'

'Here lies your brother…
Whom I, with this obedient steel, three inches of it,
Can lay to bed for ever'.

And Sebastian says:

'…as thou got'st Milan,
I'll come by Naples.'

6 Macbeth – scheme

'Something Wicked this Way Comes'

In this exploration of one of Shakespeare's bloodiest and most powerful dramas, we make the most of the 'ghostly' elements of the text before entering the physical world of the play, Castle Dunsinane, and going on to imagine new dramatic possibilities through the eyes of the children of this martial community. We consider the character of Lady Macbeth and the final, climactic assault on the castle.

A story of blood: a ghost story

Story-telling

Preparation: darken the room, light a candle, place a single chair; perhaps play music (or a radio mistuned to produce static) to cover the group's entry.

Pre-session: alert the group to the fact that, in the drama you are about to begin, you will be asking them to enter into another kind of world. In this world, you are going to behave differently... less like yourself as a teacher, and more like a magical story-teller. They will need to allow you to do this properly, or the drama session will have to end.

Place yourself in the darkened space behind the candle. As the class enters, welcome them with a gesture and indicate for them to sit on the floor in front of you.

Begin 'The story of blood': Macbeth's story.

TIP It is important to *know* the main points of the story well enough to be able to recount them without hesitation. This isn't as difficult as it might seem, particularly as you may rely on the story-teller's characteristic use of the dramatic pause. Enjoy the telling and enjoy your own embellishments of detail. If you do make a mistake in the central narrative – wait until later to correct it... outside the 'story-teller's trance'.

The key story-telling skills to demonstrate are –
Physical:

- showing control; allowing the story to rise out of stillness
- using a suitably agile face and expressive voice
- gesturing clearly, sparingly and with definition
- tying the group together with inclusive gestures and careful eye contact
- 'seeing' events before you and gesturing accordingly.

Language use:

- allowing silences to 'hang'
- demonstrating contrasts in pace, volume and tone; supporting these with gestures
- painting a linguistic picture by referring to sensory details.

The important points of the story are as follows.

- On returning from a bloody battle, victorious, the general Macbeth and his best friend Banquo cross a dark moor and see three witches conjuring spells.
- The witches call Macbeth by his name and tell him that he will be king.
- They tell Banquo that he will not be king himself, but that his children will be.
- The two soldiers return to Macbeth's castle. Macbeth tells his wife, Lady Macbeth, about the witches' prediction. They agree that he must kill the king.
- The king is due to arrive at the castle to celebrate Macbeth's victory.
- Macbeth murders the sleeping king. Lady Macbeth smears the king's blood on his guards' knives so they will be blamed.
- When the king's body is found, Macbeth slays the guards to indicate their guilt and hide his own crime.
- The king's sons flee in terror to England with a nobleman, Macduff.
- Macbeth, the hero-general, is made king.
- Afraid of the witches' prophecy that Banquo's children will become kings, Macbeth hires assassins to kill Banquo and his son, Fleance. Fleance escapes.
- At a feast, Banquo's ghost appears to Macbeth and terrifies him. Guests think he is becoming insane.
- Macbeth visits the witches again. They tell him to be afraid of Macduff... but also that Macbeth need not worry because he will be king until 'the woods come to the castle' and that 'no man born of woman can harm him'. Macbeth returns home feeling invincible.
- He orders Macduff's wife and children to be murdered brutally.
- Lady Macbeth is driven mad by guilt and takes her own life.
- Macduff has raised an army in England to attack Macbeth. They attack, holding branches stripped from the woods above their heads for protection – the woods are coming to Dunsinane!
- Macbeth is cornered by Macduff. They fight hand-to-hand, Macbeth says he is safe because 'no man born of woman' can harm him. Macduff says that he wasn't 'born of woman' but 'untimely ripp'd' from his mother's womb.
- Macduff kills Macbeth. The witches' predictions have all come true. They have tricked Macbeth.

TIP   As an aid to remembering the story, you may find it helpful to visualise Macbeth's journey through the narrative as you might in a mnemonic 'memory palace'. As you visualise each event, place a striking image at this 'site' in the journey. Visualise yourself moving through the journey.

At the end of the story-telling, discuss the story – gather the pupils' responses. Is it possible actually to predict the future? What is a witch? Did the people of Shakespeare's time really believe in the supernatural? Whose fault was Macbeth's downfall: his own, the witches', Lady Macbeth's? Discuss.

Story Whoosh!

The group will be becoming uncomfortable on the floor by now. A shift in activity mode is necessary.

The group is invited to stand. They creep around the room, avoiding the candles, perhaps looking at the shadows they are making on the walls.

As they walk, give the characters you would like them to be: witches, soldiers, kings, ladies. The pupils move in-role and freeze in clear, definitive 'statues' of the characters.

If necessary, explain the rules of a 'Story Whoosh!' (see Chapter 2). As the story has just been heard in some detail, you can now tell it again in a less detailed version. Tell it quickly, focusing on the characters and their key actions. You will find a 'Story Whoosh!' sheet at the end of this chapter.

TIP   For the climactic fight scene, you might find 'in slow motion' a useful instruction.

Do you feel you *know* this story now? How do you feel about it? What questions do you have about the story, or any of the characters? For example, why does Macbeth believe the witches so easily? Why do they want to do this to him?

Reflection

When I was telling the story to you before, what did I *do* to make you listen, to make the story feel spooky, to make it dramatic?

Tell me five things I did with my body

Tell me five things I did with my voice, and the words I used

Discuss these performance techniques... Do you think *you* could do these things? Try to remember the story – practise your own telling of it; tell each other the story, tell someone who doesn't yet know it. Later, you will be asked to tell your own version.

The witches

You need: text displayed on the walls (see 'Using text' in Chapter 3).

Do you believe in ghosts, in witches? Do you think Shakespeare did? Do you have to believe in things to make use of them in a story? Do you think the people of Shakespeare's time believed in ghosts and witches? Let me tell you, King James, who became king at the time this play was written, and who adopted Shakespeare's company as his own so that they would be called 'The King's Men'; this king, who was already King of Scotland and came down to rule England and Wales on the death of Queen Elizabeth; this king wrote a whole large book about the supernatural called *Daemonologie*. To King James, and most ordinary people of his time, witches were real and dangerous things!

Today we're going to think about what a witch, is and how to *be* a witch (or, rather, how to *act like* a witch in our drama). Then we're going to look at Shakespeare's witches in Macbeth. We're also going to try and learn, and then perform, Shakespeare's own words. We will do this in three stages, building up to a full scene from early in the play, in which the witches start their plot against Macbeth. (Aside: I wonder why they do?). We will *all* be witches, and then *some* will choose to play Macbeth and his friend, Banquo. Are we ready for this challenge?

Using your body

- Walk around the room. Stretch high, bend low, touch the sky, touch the floor, stop.
- Stretch like a witch's cat: in all directions, all joints, all muscles. Yawn, meow, like the witch's cat.
- Walk again.
- How does a witch move? Are they always old women? Can't they change shape? Perhaps they're light on their feet? Show me.
- Now. How does a witch move when casting a spell and making a potion? There are movements up and down, round and round, in and out.
- Small groups of five (or so) create the witch's spell movement – their 'magical dance'. It has at least three different movements that then repeat.
- Groups prepare.

Development into text

As the groups prepare, stop them and draw their attention to the words you have now displayed on the walls. These are the words Shakespeare gave to the witches at this point. Try and learn them, and use them as you move. Think about how to speak them in order to *add* to the dramatic or spooky effect.

> *Fair is foul and foul is fair*
> *Hover through the fog and filthy air*

And, from later in the play, the famous lines:

> *Double, double toil and trouble*
> *Fire burn and cauldron bubble.*

We want to avoid having copies of the script around the classroom, which will limit pupils' work and performance. Make large copies of the text for wall display (again see 'Using text' in Chapter 3). It shouldn't be too hard to learn these words, particularly as learning will be a *group* task in this situation; offer an instruction for the words to be learned as a group.

After the required amount of time, prepare for the 'interim' performance. If possible, isolate and enhance the performance space with lighting. Explain that we haven't finished with the scene yet; there is more to do.

Watch the groups perform, and reflect upon the work. How did pupils find speaking the lines? What do they feel about language like this? Did they understand it clearly? Explain that we are now going to add further characters and further text.

Development into the whole scene

Let's move on to the rest of the scene. The witches are on the heath, making spells and summoning Macbeth to them.

Macbeth and Banquo enter. Here are some more lines – the lines that Shakespeare gives Macbeth, Banquo and the witches to say at this moment.

The lines are displayed here on the walls around the room.

Ask the group to repeat the lines a few times together... and check understanding.

Here are the lines:

Witch 1:   *A drum, a drum!*
                 Macbeth doth come.

Banquo: *What are these,*
                 So withered and so wild…?

Macbeth: *Speak if you can: What are you?*

Witch 2:   *All hail Macbeth*
                 That shalt be king hereafter

Banquo: *Speak to me…*

Witch 3:   *Your children shall be kings*

The witches vanish.

Macbeth: *Whither are they vanished?*

The groups now choose who will be Macbeth and Banquo. Other pupils remain as witches. The groups practise the scenes: thinking about movement, use of the stage space, voices appropriate to each character. The witches' spell-making and then Macbeth's entrance are put together. Again, challenge the pupils to try and learn the simple lines from the displays on the walls.

- -

TIP Anticipate that some groups might not have been in fives; a group of four can have only two witches, with Witch 3's lines spoken by them both. A group of six or more can have more witches, with lines spoken together. Explain that two voices speaking the same lines together can be very dramatic.

- -

Perform the scenes in full. Reflect on the scenes at the end of the sequence of performances:

- What did you see that really made it feel spooky/dramatic?
- How did the actors make the scenes feel dramatic and enjoyable?
- Did you find it easy/hard to learn and to speak Shakespeare's words?
- What's special about Shakespeare's words?

- -

TIP There has been substantial preparation for these scenes, and it might be worth considering capturing the pupils' work by making simple video recordings of the scenes, or (often our preferred option) digital audio recordings. These could be watched, shared and considered at a later date outside your drama time.

- -

The castle

You need: 'junk modelling' materials, including a large box to form the basis of the castle, pipe-cleaners or soft wire, paint, coloured pens, masking tape, string, cloth, newspaper, coloured paper, modelling clay, a light source, appropriate background music. (See 'Construction tasks' in Chapter 2.)

You might choose to do some preliminary work on castles in Britain and Scotland during the eleventh and twelfth centuries. Or the work can be completed as a completely *imaginative* task, with your direction feeding in the necessary information.

Your introduction:

> So far, we have looked at the story of *Macbeth* and at one of the important scenes. Today we're going to look at the place where the play takes place: Macbeth's castle – Dunsinane. We'll also look at how a playwright (Shakespeare or *you*) might go about choosing special language to paint a 'picture in words' of the place where your story happens.

- What do you imagine Macbeth's castle is like? Tell me about it.
- Think about all the things that happen there.
- Where is it?
- When in *history* is it? (The 'real' Macbeth lived in the eleventh to twelfth centuries.) What will this mean? What will provide light? Heat?
- What is the castle made of?
- What do we know about the surrounding land? (Desolate heath and dark wood.)

Visualisation

Ask pupils to lie comfortably on the floor. Tell them you are going to describe, and they are going to imagine, entering the castle. Sometimes you will ask a question and tap a pupil on the shoulder to provide an answer; they should answer straight away or shake their head so you know to choose someone else.

- We're going to go there. Before we do, let's imagine ourselves into the place.
- Lie down and relax (having stood and stretched first).
- Imagine yourself in a dark wood. The trees close together, the branches pressing against you, the smell of dead leaves, the taste of dew in your mouth. You're moving forward along a faint path. Through the trees, you can see some flickering lights. Off in the distance, you hear what sounds like a mad cackle, an evil laugh, you move quickly away from the noise towards the lights. As you come to the edge of the trees, you can see where the lights are coming from – a castle. Huge, thick walls, grey, cold stone. You go towards it . . .
- How do you get in? A bridge across a moat? Imagine the door. How do you get in?
- Inside, there is a courtyard full of different kinds of people. See these people. Who is the most important person you see? What is he/she doing? Who is the least important? What are they doing?
- The courtyard is full of different smells. What smells?
- As you look around, you can see narrow corridors going off to different areas and different rooms. What rooms? Kitchen, banquet hall, chapel, armoury, barracks (for soldiers), bedroom chambers, king's chamber, dungeon, courtyard – animals, stables). You make your way to one room. Which room? Where is it? Imagine yourself walking there. What have you gone there to do? Now stop.

Characters: the people of Dunsinane

- Stand, imagine yourself as one of the people in the castle – king, servant, soldier, lord, peasant, cook, stable boy, etc. (Try and think of someone who perhaps no-one else will think of.)
- Take up a shape that indicates your character; a definite *action*. Give it a title – a noun and a verb: A soldier trains; A jester dances. Tell us.
- When I clap my hands, we want to see the activity come alive here. You will *be* this person and live through the actions you have decided on. It is work you will do *on your own*. Think what you will do. Think about what you will have in your hands: your 'tools'. Forget about everyone else and lose yourself in these actions. Think.

Clap. Allow the pupils to become absorbed in the task (see 'Movement work' in Chapter 2). Once established, prepare to stop and start the actions with a call of 'Freeze!' and then question certain characters about their actions and their roles within the castle. In particular, ask questions about the social structure of the castle and the character's place within it. For example, when you see the king approaching, how do you react? When you see a humble kitchen maid approach, how do you behave? Ask the group to recap the title of their actions ('A cook mixes'; 'A soldier trains'...) then ask them to look around the space and notice who is higher than they are in the social order of the castle, and who is lower; and to give them a look that shows how you feel about them. Invite the group to move around the space for a few moments and share those looks. Return to the origin shapes of the characters.

Clay modelling

At this point, produce the clay and ask pupils to come out of character. Ask the group to silently create a model of either the character they have created *holding* the object or tool they have been using, or the object itself; this object now represents them. Find some appropriate music to cover this period of individual clay modelling. Once the task is complete, spread a large cloth on the floor and invite pupils one at a time to lay their models on the cloth, with some ritual and a restatement of the name–verb around the candle.

Building the castle world

> These people need a place to *be*. We're going to build the landscape of Dunsinane – Macbeth's Castle. We're going to build it out of this pile of junk. When it's complete, we will put our people in it.

> What do we know about the castle so far? In the story there is a wood, heath and the castle. Where do people build castles? Perhaps on a hill, in which case we will need a hill. What else would you expect to see? A river? A well? Pathways leading to the doors? flags? A moat and drawbridge? Outlying houses? A village?

After discussion about building the castle and the assignment of tasks, the group building begins.

TIP Depending upon the size of your group, you might choose to divide the group and make more than one model. However, by the allocation of tasks as described in the notes on 'Construction tasks' (see Chapter 2) – building the set, making characters and adding text to the model – it is possible to make this a large group task.

When the model is complete, think about darkening the room and lighting the finished landscape from various angles to give it definition and create atmosphere: the castle at night.

When the model is complete, ask pupils to think about the person they imagined and created earlier; the clay representation of this person can now be placed carefully where you think they are at this precise moment. Invite pupils to retrieve their models one at a time, and to place them. The model is now complete: 'The World of Macbeth'.

TIP For added fun and effectiveness, use battery-operated imitation tea-lights placed inside cardboard models to give the impression of internal light.

Finally, as explored in Chapter 2, you might think about 'mapping' the landscape once complete; perhaps with pupils in role as twelfth-century cartographers. The mapping could be done individually or by a 'specialist' group working on a large sheet of paper.

Into descriptive writing

Having imagined, acted, modelled and now built the castle and its people, our heads must be full of images, words, thoughts, imaginings about this world. We need to let these out and we need to capture them for all time! We're going to write a dramatic 'performance poem' about the castle. A 'performance poem' is one that is written especially to be read (or learned and performed) out loud to an audience.

In Shakespeare's time, most of these plays were acted at 3 o'clock in the afternoon in the open air. There were no lights, elaborate sets, projections; there were just Shakespeare's words. Imagine now: we're going to step onto a stage and speak to the audience and *paint them a picture with words* of the place where all this terrible action is going to happen.

This is a task that could be achieved as a whole group. Individuals or pairs contribute a line each, and these are collected in sequence onto a single roll of lining paper so as to suggest a scroll. Alternatively, the task could be an individual, pair or small group task.

Once the pieces are complete, consider how they will be best performed. They might be performed individually or as pieces of 'choral or "choir" speaking' (see Chapter 2).

The Great Lost Scene: the children

Macbeth is full of children who live through this terrible time of war. Many of them don't survive; can you remember who they are? Fleance, Banquo's son, is one who does. I wonder what it would be like for children living in such a time? Are there children living through a time of war right now? Dare we say, are you living in a time of war? How does *that* feel? What about other places in the world? Other times? Your own families... grandparents? Great grandparents? Is it possible for us to imagine what it might be like for a child living right at the centre of a war? Right at the centre of this castle, and the murder and battles that happen here? Let's try.

Let us imagine that Shakespeare wrote scenes in which only the children appear. These scenes have been destroyed; lost. But today we're going to write them again on Shakespeare's behalf! Let's see just who the children might *be*.

Summoning the children of the castle

Ask the group to form a circle. You are going to summon this group of children into the centre of the circle. Ask for volunteers, and as you describe each of the child-characters below, invite the actors chosen to take on the description you give and create a 'statue' of the child. Each character remains in the circle so that when you have finished, we have a complete set in the centre of our 'stage'.

Here is the character group to describe.

- **Malcolm** – King Duncan's older son – heir to the throne – escapes when his father (the king) is murdered by Macbeth. Becomes king at the end.
- **Donalbain** – King Duncan's younger child (you can make them a boy or girl) – also escapes when his/her father (the king) is murdered.
- **Lulach** – a character not in the play – but we have discovered that the *real* Macbeths may have had a child from a previous marriage (you can make the child male or female).
- **Fleance** – the son of General Banquo – escapes when his father is murdered by Macbeth's assassins.
- **Macduff's children** – General Macduff's children have no names... there are a son and two younger children who may be daughters – give them names. They are murdered along with their mother by Macbeth's men. Macduff raises the army against Macbeth, and it is he who kills Macbeth in the end.

- **Child servants** – there must be servants in the castle who have children. These children will have jobs of their own. Give them names and jobs.

Once the full collection is 'summoned', invite the pupils still in the outer circle to think of questions they might like to ask one of these children. Invite the questioners to enter the circle, tap the character on the shoulder and ask the question. Either the character can be allowed to answer, or we can leave the questions 'hanging' in order to inform the next piece of work.

Ask the pupils to now choose which character they feel a connection to; which one they feel like they could *be*, or would *like* to be, in a drama. Ask the group to enter the circle one at a time and touch that person on the shoulder, and hold the touch. In this way, the pupils are freely choosing their parts for the next phase of work.

TIP There doesn't need to be an equal number of each, but you might find there are becoming a lot of high-status characters (the king's son or Macbeth's child). If you see this happening, it is your role to speak for the other characters and underline their importance and value; if your persuasion isn't working, move to 'I think we have enough kings!' When the process is finished, don't worry if the numbers are still not equal. This will mean that each group, when formed, will have a slightly different composition, which is fine. For example, if there is no Malcolm (the king's son), maybe his absence can become part of the story of the drama the pupils make; does he think he is too good to play with the others?

Finally, check that everyone is happy with their character choice. Last-minute wrangling and negotiation over underrepresented characters is sometimes a mucky business, but fine if accomplished with a smile!

Now quickly give out numbers to each character (Macbeth 1, 2, 3, 4, 5; Duncan 1, 2, 3, 4, 5, etc.) and assemble all the 'ones', 'twos', 'threes', etc. to form their working groups. Call the groups together for a moment.

Ask the group to make a very quick tableau together to show how they feel about each other. Demonstrate this very simply; use gesture, body language, orientation, height and attitude. Give a short amount of time for this to be completed. Count down from ten to zero. At zero, the tableaux must be held around the space.

Once the tableaux are held, examine each one yourself. Consider them. Try to 'read' them. Report what you see. But at this point, don't enter into big discussions. We need to press on.

Explain:

> When actors come to play a character on stage, television or in a film, they 'study' their character. This means finding out all they can about the character from the script (and sometimes there isn't much… with Lulach, for example, there is *nothing* in the script!) Often this is not enough for the actor, and they have to begin *imagining* the rest of the character's life and filling in the gaps the writer has left. The actors can't make up *anything*; the things they imagine have to fit in with the facts that are given by the writer. For example, an actor couldn't imagine that Macbeth was unmarried, because we know he's married to Lady Macbeth. But an actor could imagine that Macbeth has always been afraid of Banquo, because that might make sense in Shakespeare' story.

> So here we are. Soon you're going to *write* a scene for these characters and then perform it for us. Would you like to try and imagine the missing information about your character? Would you like to work as a professional actor might? Then let's begin.

Character maps

You need: paper and pens.

> We're going to invent details about each of the child-characters in a number of stages and *then* we are going to write them into 'The Great Lost Scene'.

Help each pupil to develop a character map for their character as follows.

- Ask pupils to think about the child-character they have chosen to be. Try and ensure there is an even spread of characters within the groups in order to facilitate the smaller working groups in a little while.
- Having given out paper and pens to each pupil, tell the group that they are going to work on their own for a little while. Ask them to write the character name in the centre of a blank page titled 'landscape'.
- Circle this and draw a number of 'spikes' or 'branches' off the circle (show or draw an example). Label these: Me/My life/My people/My castle/My feelings. Leave one or two other branches empty of a label – these can be completed at the pupil's individual discretion.
- Explain that it is important to concentrate very hard on building up these characters, and establish a 'ritual quiet' in the room.
- Ask pupils to fill in the spaces on the 'map' freely as you ask a series of questions to prompt their thinking. These will correspond to the branch-labels. With each new thought, they should add their answers to your questions on the most appropriate branch. Sometimes a new, large branch can split into a number of smaller branches (again, your example is key here).
- Ask your questions. Really, they can be anything that suggests an aspect of a person's life in a twelfth-century castle. Here are our suggestions:

> Do you have a favourite colour? What is it? Where will you sleep tonight? Do you like the castle? Who do you hate in the castle? What did you have for breakfast? What do you think you are good at? Have you ever seen a witch? When is your birthday? How do you celebrate it? When you are an adult, what will you be doing? What is the furthest you have ever been from this castle? Who makes you laugh? What's your favourite piece of clothing? What scares you most? Who is the most important person in your life? At 3 o'clock in the afternoon, what are you most likely to be doing? Who is your father? How do you feel about him? Who should be king? Have you ever seen a person killed? What is your most precious object? etc., etc. Improvise!

Once these character maps are complete, the pupils will have a compelling set of notes on the child-character. There are a number of ways in which you might use them.

You could:

- Explain that this is a piece of 'research' to try and imagine as much as we can about the character so that we can try and bring him/her to life in the scenes that follow. Then press on to the scene.
- Use the information the pupils have generated to create a hot-seating situation. You could hot-seat the characters one at a time, but this might prove a huge task. Alternatively, call the groups back together again now. One group at a time, invite them to form a circle with each character facing outwards. The rest of the class are given the chance to visit a number of the characters in a given, brief period of time. On your call of 'Change!' the questioners move to another character. We might call it a 'Hot-seat wheel'. After the allotted time, another group takes the hot-seats until all groups have been interviewed. In summary, ask the group to report on the interesting or surprising things they found out about Dunsinane's children.
- Invite the pupils to use the character map to improvise a 'soliloquy' about their character. This is an advanced task, but possible because there is so much information waiting to be used on

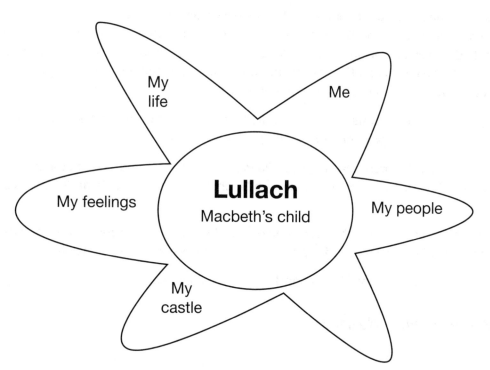

Figure 5 A sample character map – the basic outline

the character maps. If the pupils are triggered to begin improvising in character spontaneously, they are often able to assemble thoughts, narratives and characteristics out of the raw materials of the map with a flow that surprises even them! This has been seen to occur in wondrous ways! You might make a simple, single-shot video recording of each speech. This could prove great storable and sharable evidence of your drama work. A similar approach could be taken to create a written task.

Now we're ready to make 'The Great Lost Scene'.

Performing The Great Lost Scene

Explain:

> We're going to imagine a new scene that involves this group of children. Imagine this is a scene that Shakespeare wrote but was somehow lost... (perhaps in the Great Fire of London in 1666!) Lost, that is, until now! We have just discovered this Great Lost Scene, and this will be its very first performance since Shakespeare wrote it! 'The hand of history is on our shoulder!
>
> The script is going to look and feel like Shakespeare's manuscript: old paper, quill pens, real ink. It will be written in 'believable' handwriting.

TIP The only things we have in Shakespeare's handwriting are a few signatures, but we know what very early copies of his plays might have looked like.

At this point, you might show an example of an Elizabethan/Jacobean font, for example the freely downloadable 'Ilshakefest' font created by the Illinois Shakespeare Festival and based on the font of the *First Folio* edition of Shakespeare's plays.

> You have imagined much about the characters. Now, as a group, you need to think about the story of the play and decide just where your *new* scene is going to fit in. For example, the scene

might take place straight after the start of the play. Macbeth and Banquo have just been told that Macbeth will be king and Banquo's children will be kings after him. Macbeth has written to his wife, Lady Macbeth, telling her of the witches' prediction. Has Lulach seen and read the letter? Perhaps he has even told Fleance! What do they now say and do? Then King Duncan arrives in the castle with the young princes. What happens?

This is a good choice because all the children are still in the castle and alive! But there are alternatives, depending upon the composition of the groups.

Or (particularly if a group hasn't got a Fleance), the scene could take place at the time of the banquet, when Banquo's ghost appears to Macbeth. Maybe just outside the doors of the great hall?

Or, with some imagination, the scene could take place towards the end of the play when Malcolm returns with Macduff. Maybe Macduff's children could be in the scene as ghosts?

Ask the groups to discuss possibilities and announce their proposals.

To make the scene – 'devising'

Explain:

We are going to set up the scene you have decided to create and 'improvise' it. You will have a short time to discuss the steps in the action of your scene. Then we will set up the beginning of the scene as a freeze-frame and simply begin to act on my signal. It will be a spontaneous improvisation. We might try this a few times. This will help you to think about how real children (like you) might deal with being children at this time, in this place: what they might do, think, say. If we choose to try it a few times, something different might happen each time. When you improvise in this way, probably no-one will see your scene – it isn't for 'showing', it's for exploring. We will see the finished scene.

Explain that this is how some people make plays. Eventually, a script is written, but first the actors 'play around' with the characters and the possible stories; just as you are going to do. It is called 'devising'.

When the devising process has run through, you can think about using your ideas to create the final script. The groups will write their 'draft' scripts and then be ready to create the authentic document scripts with agèd paper and quills.

As an added level of stimulus to the writing process, and one that might help to generate the use of heightened dramatic language, consider offering the following.

From the fire which we think destroyed Shakespeare's text, we have recently discovered a few burnt scraps of his script: the words 'scared', 'intoxicate', 'henceforth', and this other scrap of dialogue: '...darkest night, owls scream...' must be put back into the scene.

Discuss these words and Shakespeare's language in general. If our script is meant to look and sound like Shakespeare actually wrote it... what would you expect to hear?

- 'Old' vocabulary – 'thee, thou, art, henceforth'.
- Unusual word orders – instead of 'Do you think he...?'; 'Think you he...?
- Images described carefully – night, witches, blood.
- 'Blank verse' – simply expressed – ten syllables on a line.

TIP Remember: the children 'know' the terrible time they are living in, with bloody battles, witch-craft, darkness, murders, etc... even as they play together... the scene helps to paint the picture of the world.

The groups now write and prepare their scripts. You offer support on language, plot and preparation of the script.

When the pieces are complete, you will have a number of 'products' to consider from each group: a performance (possibly 'script in hand') and a quill-written text ideal for display.

TIP The child-characters might each have a 'signifying object' which can usefully help to distinguish them in the scene. The soldier's children might have staves or toy swords; the princes might have simple paper crowns; a servant, a brush.

Lady Macbeth

Some people often think that it is Lady Macbeth, Macbeth's wife, who causes the trouble. When she hears the prediction the witches have made, she is desperate to make it come true and to be queen. Macbeth seems terrified of killing King Duncan, and it is his wife who encourages, even *forces*, him to do it; she taunts him, bullies him. Let's think about how she does this.

The Lady Macbeth mind trap

You need: the script written on thin strips of roughly torn lining paper to represent old manuscript, blu-tac (or stones) for fixing the text to the floor. A cloak for Macbeth, perhaps.

Gather the group together in a circle. Ask for a volunteer to play Macbeth, and place the volunteer in the centre of the circle in a kneeling position. Place the cloak over their shoulders. Explain that the person in the centre is Macbeth and everybody in the circle is Lady Macbeth. This is the 'Mind trap' (see Chapter 2) that Lady Macbeth creates with her words in order to control her husband and get him to do what she wants. (We might decide later that this is a harsh image of Lady Macbeth, but for the moment let's explore the idea.)

> Macbeth has his head down. He is not here until we call him. Lady Macbeth is alone and working herself up in excitement. She is waiting for Macbeth to return.

She says:

> *Come you spirits*
> *That tend on mortal things, unsex me here*
> *And fill me from the crown to the toe top-full*
> *Of direst cruelty! Make my blood thick.*
> *Come thick night!*

Discuss for a few moments what she means; she is asking for the dark spirits (like the witches) to give her the strength to do terrible things. 'unsex me here'? perhaps 'Stop me being a woman and more like a violent man.' (Discuss!)

Tell the group that when *you* speak Lady Macbeth's lines again, they should all repeat the line after you. Now do so.

Continue:

> Having called up evil to help here, she calls her husband with the name of the new title that the king has given him and that the witches predicted.

> *Great Glamis!* [Repeat after me. A whisper.] *Great Glamis!*

> Repeat, getting louder and louder until Macbeth raises his head. Hear now the things that Lady Macbeth says to her husband Macbeth to encourage or force him to kill the king!

Reveal each line one at a time. Read them, then stick them to the floor inside the circle on the edge facing out to the group, so that pupils can see and read them later. Here are the lines (feel free to choose as many as you think appropriate to your group).

Lady Macbeth tells him how to behave:

> *Your face is as a book where men may read strange things*

[She means, you are looking like you are up to no good... hiding your true feelings.]

> *Look like the innocent flower but be the serpent under it!*

Macbeth says:

> *We will go no further in this business*

[*Invite the actor playing Macbeth to repeat this line as s/he sees fit as the scene develops.*]

Lady Macbeth puts on the pressure:

> *[You are] too full of the milk of human kindness*
> *Was the hope drunk wherein you dressed yourself?*
> *[Were you drunk when you promised to kill the king?]*
> *What beast was it then*
> *That made you break this enterprise to me?*
> *When you durst do it, then you were a man*
> *Screw your courage to the sticking place*
> *What cannot you and I perform upon*
> *Th'ungaurded [king] Duncan*

Having shown and demonstrated the lines, ask the circle to repeat them after you. Remind the pupils that they are *all* Lady Macbeth and speaking to Macbeth in the middle of the circle. Say these things to him in anger, with venom. You *need* him to be strong, to kill the king so you can be queen!

Ask Macbeth to try and escape the mind trap; to break out. Remind Macbeth of the line learned earlier. This is the line he tries to escape with. But every time he moves to the edge of the circle, the pupils shout the line that is displayed closest to them and repel him back. Encourage his movement to become more frantic and the calling of the lines more powerful. Build to a crescendo, enter the circle, and as the volume increases gently force Macbeth back to the centre and down to the floor; crush him with the text!

Stop.

Discuss:

> What do you feel about this? Do you think Lady Macbeth has bullied her husband into the murder? Do you believe it? What do you think about Macbeth? Lady Macbeth? If she was here, what would you say to her? What would you like to ask her?

Explain that the group is going to get the chance to speak to her now. You are going to play Lady Macbeth yourself and try to answer their questions. She is in a dangerous state. The king is dead, they have been crowned king and queen and Macbeth has disappeared back to the heath. So you are talking to the queen, but at this moment she is in her own room; private, withdrawn. She will soon go mad. The following might help you to develop her basic attitude and tackle any questions that come.

Lady Macbeth is acting as if washing her hands. She speaks.

Out damned spot! Out! I would be clean again. Listen. Listen.

[She listens.]

It is done and I am queen. See this, my crown [she touches her head, the crown is gone] *gone. It is a thing of dreams. No. It is safe; safe in the guarded castle keep where no man shall have it.* [Wait.] *It is a fine thing to be queen. Do you know? A fine thing. All look to me with honour. All but… all but those who look to me with distaste… as if I were not born to this. My family have been kings before me. It is my blood.* [Wait.] *It is a terrible thing to be queen… When there is blood that will not wash. And a husband king who fears the shadow that is his own.* [Smiles at the group.] *My subjects. You come to my private chamber; where I am myself. I welcome you. What do you wish of me? What do you wish to know?*

From here, begin to take questions. In your responses, perhaps challenge the view given of Lady Macbeth in the mind trap. Perhaps she has been 'strong', but only because Macbeth is so weak. He needs her to cajole him. Or perhaps it is because she is a woman that she can not be ambitious *herself* at that time and needs to achieve through him. Build sympathy for her; whatever she has done, she now regrets it deeply. The guilt will drive her mad, and then to taking her own life. You know this will happen, and out of role you can let the pupils know this too. It will give an interesting colour to the hot-seat.

After the hot-seating, reflect with the pupils. How do they feel about Lady Macbeth now? What have they learned about her?

Extension task:

Imagine that Lady Macbeth has a sister or a very good friend who lives in a distant land. This is the only person who Lady Macbeth can truly confide in. She writes a private letter to her friend/sister. What would she say? Offer pupils quill pens or agèd paper to enhance the value of this task.

Do you know what happens to Lady Macbeth? Would you like to see the whole of her story… separate from the rest of the play?

Lady Macbeth's story

If you need to explain the rules of a Story Whoosh!, do so now (see Chapter 2).

We are going to summon *her* story here in the centre of the circle. You must create all the people and all the things that are mentioned in the story. This is The Lady Macbeth Story Whoosh!

The Lady Macbeth Story Whoosh!

- Lady Macbeth is in Dunsinane Castle. A letter arrives. It is from her husband Macbeth. It tells her of his encounter with three witches on the heath. The witches have foretold that Macbeth will become king. Whoosh!

- Lady Macbeth learns that the king, Duncan, is to visit their castle that night. When Macbeth returns to the castle, Lady Macbeth tells him that they must kill the king. Tonight. Whoosh!
- Macbeth is fearful of the murder, but Lady Macbeth insists on her plan. She will get the guards outside the king's bedroom drunk and take out their daggers ready for the murder.
- Macbeth will then take their weapons, enter the bedroom and kill the king. He will then smear the sleeping guards with blood so that they will be blamed.
- Perhaps reluctantly, Macbeth carries out the murder. Lady Macbeth waits close by. When Macbeth returns with the bloody daggers in his hand, she tries to send him back. He refuses and she takes them back herself. Whoosh!
- Following the king's death, Macbeth and Lady Macbeth are crowned king and queen. At a banquet, Macbeth seems to be becoming unhinged; seeing ghosts at the table. Lady Macbeth sends everybody away and scolds Macbeth. Whoosh!
- The next time we see her, she is sleep-walking: she has become mad with guilt. She constantly rubs her hands to remove blood, saying, 'Out damned spot!' As Macbeth prepares to fight the advancing army, he learns that Lady Macbeth is dead; she has killed herself. Whoosh!

Discuss:

> Why does she kill herself? Do you have any sympathy for her? She seems haunted by the terrible things she has done; is that how she is punished? What would you say to her now? [*Give me five. Another five.*]

She should have died hereafter: Macbeth's speech

> When Macbeth learns that his wife is dead, he knows his plans are crumbling at his feet. He makes a speech that has become famous. It is a beautiful and terrible speech. Would you like to hear and maybe learn some of it?

> *She should have died hereafter*
> *There would have been a time for such a word:*
> *Tomorrow and tomorrow and tomorrow*
> *Creeps in this petty pace from day to day*
> *To the last syllable of recorded time.*
> *And all our yesterdays have lighted fools*
> *The way to dusty death. Out, out brief candle*
> *Life's but a walking shadow, a poor player*
> *Who struts and frets his hour upon the stage,*
> *And then is heard no more. It is a tale*
> *Told by an idiot, full of sound and fury*
> *Signifying nothing.*

You might read through the speech again and paraphrase (clumsily) as follows:

> *I wish she had not died now.*
> *Life just creeps along so slowly*
> *We don't think about dying*
> *Just about playing our little silly part.*

Life feels to be full of important things
But really, in the end, it means nothing.

What a depressing thought!; but just perfect for Macbeth to say at this moment as his life falls apart. What do you think about the speech? [*You might like to consider initiating the following discussion if you feel it is appropriate*.] We all, as old or young as we are, sometimes have to face people close to us dying... and at those times people often feel hopeless, depressed, lost; like Macbeth seems to feel here. His wife dying makes him think about the whole of his life and the whole of life itself! What is he feeling?

A possible extension to this work might be to produce a simple piece of choral speaking in which the whole group will speak the speech together. The simple procedures we have developed for introducing some techniques of choral speaking can be found in Chapter 2.

TIP This speech is in three sets of four lines. For the purposes of the exercise introduced in Chapter 2, you might try one set of four at a time and build up to the whole piece, or just use one of the sets of four.

The speech is reproduced at the end of this chapter.

An army approaches

You need: a set of character cards (Figure 6); the constructed castle (if still available). Military music (such as the opening to Beethoven's Battle Symphony or similar) or the sound effect of a battle (for both of these, search online). Agèd paper and quill pens.

Exposition

And so we arrive at the climactic end of the play. Macbeth's Dunsinane Castle is under attack by Macduff (whose wife and children Macbeth has murdered) and the English army. They plan to take the castle, remove Macbeth as king, and make Duncan's son, Malcolm, the new king. In order to make a surprise attack, Macduff's army cut tree branches from the woods and hold them over their heads. They advance. This fulfils the witches' prophesy that Macbeth cannot be defeated until Burnham Wood comes to Dunsinane. The witches must be having a great time watching their plan unfold; they must think it hilarious to have tricked Macbeth and now to destroy him!

Imagine the scene: in the castle, the army, the servants, the children we met before are preparing to fight, or hide, or run. In the woods, the attacking army sharpens it swords, cuts branches, prepares for battle; Macduff, Duncan, ordinary soldiers, servants, perhaps wives and children of senior officers. Above, maybe the witches circle high in the air on their broomsticks. Maybe the people of the local village watch – waiting for their lords and masters to change again.

Close your eyes. Picture the castle. Picture the people of the castle. What might be the sounds *inside* the castle? Macbeth is shouting with supernatural confidence: 'Our castle's strength will laugh a siege to scorn.'

Dunsinane soundscape

Quickly, around the circle build the sound of the castle. Perhaps some panic, some urgency. Now the sound of the *attacking* army; they are trying to make a surprise attack. Perhaps just the sound of an army of feet marching on the forest floor. Moving forward. Let's make this sound: everybody stand and face one way towards the castle; march on the spot (demonstrate). Introduce the military music.

> **Let me see the look in your eye of an army marching to face the solid walls of Macbeth's mighty castle.**

Allow this action to continue. Then stop – Freeze! Continue the music or introduce the sound effects. Ask the group to lie down and close their eyes again. You are going to ask them to *think* about the story of the march on the castle and the battle between the two armies; to make it real by imagining it. Now:

- Either – spend a little time asking the pupils to think about one character from the story who they would like to live through the battle as. The character can be from either side, from high up the order of importance or right from the bottom: a soldier, a servant, a child, an observer, a witch. Ask pupils to picture the person they wish to be, and then slowly 'melt' into a statue of this person at the moment they choose – are they hiding in a cupboard, marching at the head of the line, standing on a battlement, flying high above on a broomstick, clinging to their mother in a corner of a room hoping to not be discovered?

- Or – allow pupils to choose one of the characters on the list (see 'An Army Approaches' at the end of this chapter), or distribute them randomly, perhaps picking from a hat. Ask the pupils to picture and then create a statue of their character as above.

Writing the battle

Tell the group that we are going to tell the story of the battle through many pairs of eyes.

> **Everyone's perspective or viewpoint is going to be different, but we are then going to put them all together to make one big picture. We want to know what it *feels* like, smells like, *tastes* like, *looks* like, *sounds* like. Only you can tell us about *your* character, because only you see through those eyes.**

If you still have your model of the castle, perhaps gather round it now; ask pupils to consider exactly where in this 'world' their character is . . . and what they can see/hear/feel from there. Now distribute quill pens, agèd paper. Ask pupils to consider what their character will say about the battle if they were to write to someone about it (which would entail writing in the first person, past tense); or as if they were experiencing the events as they happen now (first person, present tense), more as a playwright.

> **Listen to the music. Think about the real danger that your character is in; *everybody* is in danger here. Think carefully about the words you choose; like Shakespeare, you will choose the most *perfect* words to capture your character's thoughts. Describe the *details* of what your character experiences; the flicker of lights, the swish of arrows passing your ear, the pounding of a heart, the smell of smoke. This description of the battle is like an almighty jigsaw: every one of you will create a single piece in the jigsaw and then we will put it all together.**
>
> **Write well! On the back of your page, write your character's name now. Turn over and begin your account of the battle . . .**

Now, with lights dimmed and battle music playing, give the group time to write.

When complete, you will probably think about displaying them around a picture of the castle; but first, let's think about using them dramatically.

If you have your castle model, place it now in the centre of the circle. If you do not, think about creating a centrepiece for the circle – perhaps a picture of a castle, a cut-out castle shape or a few artefacts to represent it. Allow the music to continue in the background. One at a time, invite pupils to stand, read their character's name and then read their unique account of the battle. When finished, they can place their paper close to the castle on the floor; in a ritual mode we will have the pieces performed and the pieces of the jigsaw assembled.

An alternative to this is to make simple, 'close-face' digital video recordings of each piece and simply edit them together and add the music; if you are particularly ambitious, and ICT-literate (or have class members who are), you could use simple green-screen technology and add a background of a dark, northern castle. In the recording, your pupils could be encouraged to think about 'acting for the screen', in which the tiny details of the actor's performance are visible. Because it is a close-face shot (the face fills most of the screen), you needn't worry about costume unless you would like to; maybe 'dirtying' faces would be good, or having simple pieces of material to mask any visible signs of school uniform or the children's own clothes.

Testing the story

Campfire night: story-circle

As we come to the end of this scheme of work, we return to the beginning – to ghostly story-telling around a fire. There is always something satisfying about this kind of structural circularity. At the start, *you* were the story-teller who related the dark tale of the destruction of an ambitious general at the hands of supernatural forces. Now it is the pupils' turn to take on the 'mantle of the story-teller' and make it their own. Recall asking them to consider practising their own 'tellings' of the story. Recap the techniques you discussed, right at the start of the scheme, for how the story-teller creates impact: pace, body-language, eye contact, gesture, tone, etc.). This new story-telling event will happen in its own dramatic context . . .

We all sit in a circle around the candles. We imagine it is a dark night.

> It's many years after the battle of Dunsinane; there's nobody left who survived or witnessed the battle. We are soldiers sitting around a fire on the edge of the forest, next to the ruined castle of Macbeth. It is said that Lady Macbeth's ghost haunts the ruins; she wails through the night and searches the ruins for her lost husband, Macbeth. I am a young boy soldier who has just joined the army and has never heard of Macbeth. The group are my battalion; you are 'old-timers', experienced soldiers who have seen much. You are going to tell me the story of Macbeth and you are going to try and terrify me. It is a cold, dark, moonless night. Is that the sound of witches chanting in the forest?

Signal for the group to sit like a group of soldiers, as described above.

Introduce the idea of a 'get-out clause': when the story comes to you, if you are too scared of Lady Macbeth's ghost to speak, you may say 'I must be silent on these things'.

Around the circle, the group tell the whole story again from memory, trying to use the story-telling techniques discussed above. The story is addressed to you (as the boy soldier) and to the rest of the group.

The story jigsaw

Finally (or as an alternative to the above), make use of the 'Story jigsaw' sheet at the end of this chapter, and the notes on the technique in Chapter 1.

Both options offer a dramatic way of summarising and testing understanding of the story.

A teacher's crib sheet

Background information

- Written between 1603 and 1606, soon after the Scottish Stuart King James came to the English throne
- There were questions over who should be the monarch of England after Queen Elizabeth I died without children. King James, who was already King of Scotland, took the crown. One of Shakespeare's heroes in the play was believed to be a descendant of James – so, when the witches tell Banquo his 'children' shall be king – they mean James! Shakespeare liked to keep his monarchs happy!
- The story of the real Macbeth was probably taken from Holinshed's *Chronicles of England, Scotland and Ireland*, but Shakespeare, the master playwright, develops the story in dramatic ways and probably takes liberties with the truth; for example, it seems Macbeth (or his army) did kill Duncan, but in a battle – not in bed!
- Witches were real to Elizabethan audiences, especially in Scotland, where many women still died every year as witches.

Brief summary of story

- On their way back as victors from battle, Macbeth and Banquo meet three witches. They tell Macbeth that he will be king (and Banquo's heirs will be kings 'hereafter').
- Macbeth tells his wife, and she encourages him to kill the current king, Duncan, so as to realise the prediction.
- Macbeth kills the king, blames (and murders) the king's guards, and is made king himself. The king's son, Malcolm, escapes to England.
- Macbeth then hires murderers to kill his friend Banquo and his son, Fleance. Fleance escapes.
- At a banquet, Banquo's ghost taunts Macbeth in front of the assembled court.
- Macbeth returns to the witches, who tell him he is all but invincible; he won't be defeated until the woods come to his castle, and he can't be killed by any man born of a woman.
- Macduff works with Malcolm to attack Macbeth with the English army.
- Lady Macbeth kills herself.
- The English soldiers cut branches from the woods to disguise themselves (the wood is coming to the castle!). Macduff corners Macbeth and reveals that he was born by caesarean section ('untimely ripped'). The witches have tricked Macbeth. He is killed by Macduff.

Main characters

- Macbeth: a Scottish general, later king of Scotland.
- Lady Macbeth: his forceful wife, later driven mad and to suicide.
- Banquo: Macbeth's friend, later killed by him and returns to haunt him.
- Duncan: King of Scotland, killed by Macbeth.
- Malcolm: the king's son, flees to England and returns with an army.
- Fleance: Banquo's son, survives.
- Macduff: rival of Macbeth, his wife and children are killed by Macbeth, finally kills Macbeth.
- Siward: the general in charge of the advancing English army.
- Three witches: trigger the story with their predictions, engineer Macbeth's downfall.

Other things

- *Macbeth* is the shortest of Shakespeare's tragedies. It also vies with *Romeo and Juliet* to be considered the most performed Shakespeare play of all time!
- One story we have come across says that the play is cursed because, on the opening night, real swords were used instead of fake ones, resulting in real bloodshed!
- Another story is that witches cursed the play because Shakespeare stole their real spells! Stories, stories!

Facts and legends for pupils

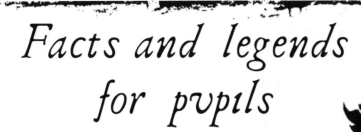

Shakespeare probably borrowed the basic story of Macbeth from a book called Holinshed's Chronicles of England, Scotland and Ireland.

There was a real king of Scotland called Macbeth and he was followed by another called Malcolm – but the story of the witches, and the murder of the king in his bed, are probably Shakespeare's own gruesome, dramatic inventions.

The real Macbeth is thought to have come to the throne in 1040 after defeating King Duncan on the battlefield – not murdering him in his bed!

Lady Macbeth's real name was 'Gruoch', and Macbeth was her second husband – she had a son called Lulach from her first marriage – neither is mentioned in the play.

Ghosts and witches were real to the people of Shakespeare's time; King James himself wrote a whole book about witches and the supernatural called Daemonologie, published in 1597. There were many trials for witches… particularly in Scotland, and many women were killed as witches.

Macbeth was written around the time that King James of Scotland became King of England; Banquo (whose children would become kings, as the witches predicted) was said to be an ancestor of King James. So the play celebrates the real king's relative as a hero.

Shakespeare liked to keep on good terms with the monarchs of his day. His company became the king's favourite and was renamed 'The King's Men' – this allowed them to wear clothing of a special colour.

Even today, it is meant to be very unlucky to say 'Macbeth' inside a theatre. Actors will call it 'The Scottish Play'. Some say this is because the play contains real witches' spells, others that the legend came about because struggling theatres often put on this popular play to try and bring in a good audience and save themselves – when this didn't work, the play became associated with failure… and therefore thought to be unlucky.

A page of famous lines

'When shall we three meet again
In thunder, lightening, or in rain?'

'Fair is foul and foul is fair
Hover through the fog and filthy air.'

'...too full o' the milk of human kindness.'

'Is this a dagger which I see before me?'

'Hear it not, Duncan, for it is a knell
That summons thee to heaven, or to hell.'

'Sleep no more! Macbeth does murder sleep.'

'...never shake thy gory locks at me.'

'blood will have blood'

'Double, double toil and trouble;
Fire burn and cauldron bubble'

'By the pricking of my thumbs,
Something wicked this way comes'

'Out, damned spot!'

'What's done cannot be undone.'

'Tomorrow, and tomorrow, and tomorrow
Creeps in this petty pace from day to day
To the last syllable of recorded time.'

'Life's but a walking shadow, a poor player
That struts and frets his hour upon the stage,
And then is heard no more. It is a tale
Told by an idiot, full of sound and fury,
Signifying nothing.'

A story jigsaw

On returning from a bloody battle, victorious, the general Macbeth and his best friend Banquo cross a dark moor and see three witches conjuring spells.

The witches call Macbeth by his name and tell him that he will be king.

They tell Banquo that he will not be king himself, but that his children will be.

Returning to Macbeth's castle, Macbeth tells his wife, Lady Macbeth, about the witches' prediction. They agree to kill the king, who is arriving that night.

Macbeth murders the sleeping king. Lady Macbeth smears the king's blood on his guards' knives so they will be blamed. Macbeth, the hero-general, is made king.

Afraid of the witches' prophesy that Banquo's sons will become kings, Macbeth hires assassins to kill Banquo and his son, Fleance. Fleance escapes.

At a feast, Banquo's ghost appears to Macbeth and terrifies him. Guests think Macbeth is becoming insane.

Macbeth visits the witches again. They tell him to be afraid of Macduff… but also that Macbeth will be king until 'the woods come to the castle' and that 'no man born of woman can harm him'. Macbeth returns home feeling invincible. He kills Macduff's wife and children.

Lady Macbeth is driven mad by guilt and kills herself.

Macduff has raised an army to attack Macbeth. They attack, holding branches stripped from the woods above their heads for protection.

Macbeth is cornered by Macduff. They fight hand-to-hand. Macduff says that he wasn't 'born of woman' but was 'untimely ripp'd' from his mother's womb… so he can kill Macbeth! And he does so.

Malcolm, King Duncan's son, is crowned king.

Resources

'She should have died hereafter;
There would have been time for such a word.
Tomorrow, and tomorrow, and tomorrow
Creeps in this petty pace from day to day
To the last syllable of recorded time;
And all our yesterdays have lighted fools
The way to dusty death. Out, out, brief candle!
Life's but a walking shadow, a poor player
That struts and frets his hour upon the stage,
And then is heard no more. It is a tale
Told by an idiot, full of sound and fury,
Signifying nothing.'

The following edited text:

THE WITCHES: *Fair is foul and foul is fair*
Hover through the fog and filthy air
*Double, double, toil and trouble
Fire burn and cauldron bubble.

WITCH 1:   *A drum, a drum!*
Macbeth doth come.

BANQUO: *What are these,*
So withered and so wild...

MACBETH: *Speak if you can: What are you?*

WITCH 2:   *All hail Macbeth*
That shalt be king hereafter

BANQUO: *Speak to me...*

WITCH 3:   *Your children shall be kings*

The witches vanish.

MACBETH: *Whither are they vanished?*

[*These two famous lines are from later in the play.]

Trader	Mercenary	Watchman	Macduff	Macbeth
You sell the castle meat. You were making a delivery when the battle began. Now you are trapped.	You are a paid soldier inside the castle. Do you care who wins?	Your job is to watch from the castle turret for danger. Are the trees of the forest really coming towards you!?	You have come to avenge your family's murder by Macbeth	Fighting for his life – thinking he is invincible because of the witches' words
Soldier's Child	**Nursemaid**	**Beggar**	**The Cook**	**Malcolm**
You are the child of a soldier who lives in the castle. You hope to see him again.	Your job in the castle is to look after the children. Where are they now as the castle is attacked?	You beg for scraps from the castle kitchens. You were once a soldier	You just want to make the king's banquets. But today there's a sword in your hand	A young man, marching on the castle to be made king, knowing that Macbeth murdered his father
English Soldier	**Foot Solider**	**Fleance**	**Witch 1**	**Soldier Boy**
You always try to keep to the middle of the line when you attach. You think it's safer.	You are an ordinary solder just doing his job. You've seen it all!	You are Banquo's son. You saw your father killed by Macbeth and are here with the army to attack.	You have tricked Macbeth and will soon destroy him. Is it funny?	A 13 year old boy who has recently joined the English army. This is his first battle charge
Soldier's Wife	**Minstrel**	**Witch 2**	**Piper**	**A young girl**
You have had a good life living in the castle, but you think it might be all over.	You travel with the army and sing songs for entertainment. How did you end up in the thick of battle?	You are flying high above the castle waiting for Macbeth's death – which you know will come.	You play the pipe to rouse your army; here you are leading the march on the mighty castle	Aged 9, hides in the castle with her little brother
Bowman	**Doctor**	**Old Soldier**	**Villager**	**The Castle's Jester**
You will fire your arrows from the slits in the castle walls. You are an expert archer.	You are the doctor who looked after Lady Macbeth before her death. You wish you could have escaped.	You have seen many battles. Now too old to fight and kept in the castle to clean the king's boots	You live in the village near the castle. You don't care who's king as long as they don't bother you.	Your job is to make us laugh, but not today
Stable boy	**King's Guard**	**Lullach**	**Priest**	**An English army officer**
You look after Macbeth's horses here in the castle. He is always kind to you.	Your job has always been to protect the king (Macbeth) but you are suspicious of him.	You are Macbeth's forgotten son. You want to run away.	You are the village priest. You think dark forces are at work here.	Not sure why you've been brought to wild Scotland to fight

Figure 6 An army approaches: a set of character cards

Macbeth scheme structure map

Section	Drama approaches	Possible curriculum opportunities
A story of blood: a ghost story		
Story-telling	Teacher as story-teller	Literacy: literary style; performance technique; history
Story Whoosh!	Story Whoosh!; whole group enactment	Literacy: narrative understanding
Reflection	Whole group discussion	Oracy; narrative understanding; RE; history
The witches		
Using your body	Discussion; movement work	Literacy: developing character and empathy
Development into text	Using edited text; performance	Literacy: textual understanding; historical language
The castle		
Discussion	Focused discussion	History; oracy
Visualisation	Dramatic visualisation of place	Literacy: developing place, character, empathy
Characters: the people of Dunsinane	Characterisation in social context	Literacy: developing vocabulary, language, empathy
Clay modelling	Modelling	Design and technology (tools), art (3D sculpture)
Building the castle world	Group construction	Design and technology; art; literacy: narrative understanding
Into descriptive writing	Writing from role	Literacy: developing sense of place, descriptive vocabulary
The Great Lost Scene: the children		
Summoning the children of the castle	Teacher exposition; group tableaux	Literacy: character development, empathy
Character maps	Technique for character development	Literacy: character development in depth
Performing The Great Lost Scene	Group script-writing; rehearsal process; performance	Literacy: script work, specialised language; history
Lady Macbeth		
The Lady Macbeth mind trap		
Lady Macbeth's story		
She should have died hereafter: Macbeth's speech		
An army approaches		
Exposition	Teacher exposition	
Dunsinane soundscape	Soundscape; visualisation	Literacy: sense of place; history
Writing the battle	Whole group writing in-role process	Literacy: multiple perspectives, narrative 'epic' style; ICT (extension task)
Testing the story		
Campfire night: story-circle	Whole group drama; pupil as story-teller	Oracy; literature: narrative understanding
The story jigsaw	Story jigsaw exercise	Literacy: narrative understanding; problem-solving;

We offer the chart above as a starting point. There are a whole host of learning opportunities in a rich drama experience that would have been exhausting to list: developing positive groups, expanding language opportunities and vocabulary, developing self-image and confidence, fostering imaginative responses, to name

Resources needed	Teachers Notes
Setting of space for drama	
Safe candles	
Story Whoosh! sheet	
Appropriate music	
Plasticine/clay	
'Junk modelling' materials; the text available; paper, pens	
Paper, pens	
Paper, pens	
Agèd paper, quill pens	
Character sheet copied and cut; pens, paper; appropriate music	
Safe candles	
Prepared story jigsaws; appropriate music	

a few. Also, as you translate the work into your own classroom you will, we hope, create for yourself a whole unanticipated flood of new opportunities for learning. The heart of such learning is the rich experience we all hope to build.

7   A Midsummer Night's Dream – scheme

'Ill Met By Moonlight'

The forest waits

Establishing the setting

Preparation: darken the room, light a candle, play music or a drum to cover the group's entry. Props on display on a cloth in the centre of the room: a heart, a simple model of a mother and child, forest branches and lights, a lump of plasticine, the spirit king's pendant, a red nose.

Begin the following discussion.

> If you could travel in time, and go back 10,000 years, what would you see *here*, where we are right now? If you were standing here, and looked out on the landscape (if you could see very far), what would you see? [*Take ideas*.] Here in northern Europe, you would see forest: tree upon tree upon tree. Before there were people on this land, there was forest; before people came and cleared the land to make space for homes, for farms, and then for roads, towns, cities; before humans came and took control, there was forest. Forest is the natural environment of this place. And listen... if all the people in this place; if all of *us* disappeared... and you waited just a 1000 years... what would you see *here*? Forest! Forest before and forest after; we live in a space, a gap between forests. In our stories, the woods or the forests are places *outside* our cities; places of strangeness, places where our human rules don't always apply. Wild places!

TIP   You could discuss: Is a forest the same as a wood? There seems to be some disagreement about the difference, and in normal life the words are often used interchangeably. Shakespeare says the play is set in 'Athens and a wood near it', but Theseus the Duke also refers to 'foresters'. Let's agree that either can be used. A forest and a wood are both places 'outside' the city, where anything is possible.

Soundscape

> What might we hear in such a forest? As yet, there are no people. What sounds would we hear? We're going to make a soundscape of this place and summon up all of those sounds.

(See 'Soundscaping' in Chapter 2.) Once the soundscape is established, pause the effect and ask individual pupils what they can hear; identify animal and plant life.

> What stories do you know that include forests/woods/jungles? List ten. [*Expect mention of traditional stories: Hansel and Gretel, Red Riding Hood and others*.] Why are there so many stories about forests? Perhaps it's because stories sometimes need their characters to be taken away from their home place, because it's away from home that unusual and exciting things can happen. Think of *Little Red Riding Hood*: the story starts when she leaves the security of home.

> Would you like to go there?

Now, imagine it's *you* entering this forest – how would you feel? Keep the soundscape going – now, on my signal, all enter together. You are alone; you can't see any of the other people. But you have a feeling that someone is watching you – you turn sharply. There's no one there. You move on. Allow the sense of being lost in this place to develop. Then stop.

We're going to be looking at another story that takes place in a forest; a forest inhabited by spirits, a forest into which humans from the nearby city enter to escape for many reasons. It is a play by Shakespeare, one of his most famous comedies. It is called *A Midsummer Night's Dream*. Who does Shakespeare put into his forest? Come and gather around this cloth in the centre of the room, and find some clues.

The clues you show are simple props that represent the key character-sets in Shakespeare's play. They are:

- a heart – representing the escaping lovers who have come into the forest to escape the demands of their families, and possible exile
- a shiny pendant – representing the royal house of the fairy kingdom
- a simple representation of a mother and child – representing the child-stealing spirits
- red clowns' noses – representing the mechanicals, who are 'clowns who don't know they are clowns'
- a lump of plasticine/clay – representing the mischievous 'shape-shifting' hobgoblin (Puck), who is servant to the king of the fairies.

Ask the group if they would like to look at one of these characters right now. Get agreement for looking at the shape-shifter.

Ask the group to get back on their feet. Enquire:

> If you were a shape-shifting hobgoblin, what would you turn into? You think humans are stupid, and you like nothing more than tricking them and causing them problems. You're famous for it. You were alive even before Shakespeare took you and placed you in his play. You have been known to enter human houses, pretend to be objects in their houses (a chair, a pan, a spoon…) and then to change again and terrify the foolish humans. Always skipping away laughing, 'Ho! Ho! Ho!'

Shape-shifter game

> Let's play the shape-shifter game. Now quickly demonstrate the characters and ask pupils to copy you. There is a shape for the *forest* – ('make like a tree and do the soundscape'); the *clown* (a wide-eyed, buffoon shape); the *escaping lovers* (perhaps finding a partner, clinging together and looking behind you nervously); The *King and Queen of the fairies* (a regal, high-status shape); and *Puck* – on this call, pupils can be anything you want – he is the shape-shifter. It should be something different every time! Once you have demonstrated and established the shape for each character, the game is simply for the group to walk around neutrally, waiting for your call. Pupils will then need to react very quickly and make the correct shape.
>
> Anticipate your call of 'Puck!' by suggesting different scenarios, for example: he's hiding from the king in the forest – what does he change into? Or, he's hiding in a human house in order to trick the people – In this case, once the objects' shapes have been demonstrated, you might *be* the human in a few of these houses. Make use of the objects made, and improvise their change (for example, a sweeping brush might become a snake). After each one, we hear Puck's refrain 'Ho! Ho! Ho!'

Questions to ponder with the group:

- What are clowns doing in the forest (remember, they don't know they are clowns, they think they are *proper* men).
- What are the lovers escaping from?
- Why have the spirits stolen a child? Why are they arguing about it?
- What mischief will Puck get up to tonight? On this magical Midsummer's night?

Again, ask the pupils to spring to their feet – a drama activity that reflects the game played earlier.

> Shhh! Someone's coming... it's Shakespeare's characters... Who's coming? As I say them, you are invited to *be* each one:
>
> - someone seeking... a place to escape
> - someone seeking... a place to hide the child they have stolen
> - someone seeking... a place to make magical mischief
> - someone seeking... a place to play
> - someone seeking... a place to be together with the one they love.
>
> This forest is teeming with life. Before we forget and before we move on, let's capture this place and keep it...

'This is the forest of...' – an all-senses performance poem

You need: small, roughly torn pieces of paper, a roll of lining paper, coloured pens.

> Think of this sentence root: 'This is the forest of...' (see 'Sentence roots' in Chapter 2). Thinking of all we have spoken of, how would you complete this sentence? Think about it. Decide. Share it with a partner. Imagine if this was going to be a line in a poem that's spoken out loud. Is there anything you'd do to it to make it sound more poetic, more dramatic, or to make it interesting to say? What kind of things might I mean?

Give pupils time to prepare their lines in pairs or small groups. Ask them to then write their line on a small piece of paper so that it is captured precisely.

On a roll of lining paper, write the sentence root: 'This is the forest of...'.

Roll out the lining paper across the room, and invite pairs to take a range of pens and come to a section of paper. Pupils then write down their lines in big, readable letters, with 'This is the forest of...' in smaller text above each line. Ask pupils to try and make their section of the paper interesting and attractive in its own right; suggest that the finished roll-poem itself will be displayed. The group then gather along the roll of paper and complete their work.

When the poem is complete, suggest that it is performed straight away, with pupils speaking their own lines together as a group, with a little preparation. As a development, you might try the performance without a rhythm initially, and then with a rhythm.

So now we know something of the *setting* of Shakespeare's play – but what occurs here? Would you like to know the whole of the story of Shakespeare's play, *A Midsummer Night's Dream*? Let's hear the whole story...

The whole story – a Story Whoosh!

(See 'A Story Whoosh!' at the end of this chapter, and notes on the 'Story Whoosh!' in Chapter 2.) In brief, a 'Story Whoosh!' is a technique for enacting stories in a compelling, physical way that involves the whole group. It is especially useful with longer or more elaborate stories. As you tell the story, pupils are invited to make tableaux of the objects, characters and settings as you mention them. You might invite selected pupils to act certain moments in action or even words.

At the end of each section, you call 'Whoosh!', and the 'stage' is cleared for the next one. Different people can play the same character at different times.

Ideally, you should try to 'know' the story, to internalise it yourself, before doing the 'Story Whoosh!' This allows you to give your full attention to the 'Whoosh!', to be spontaneous and to show confidence.

The animals who saw...

We immediately reinforce the narrative now with an opportunity to 'own' and reiterate the story and to consider it from different points of view.

> **What animals did you say you heard before in the forest? Where do they live in this forest? High in the trees, in burrows in the ground, in the roots of trees, on the banks of rivers? These wild forest animals are witnesses to the story of humans and fairies that we have just heard. What would they have to say? How do they feel about the humans who sometimes come here, to their home? How do they feel about the spirits, the fairies? We're going to imagine the story as *seen* and then *retold* from their point of view.**

Invite the pupils to make small groups, then to decide which animals they will be, and where they might live. Ask them to think about creating a tableau of the animals at home. Some members of the family group have just returned from a day in the woods. Now, before beginning the spontaneous improvisation, ask the returning character(s) to decide which part of the story they have witnessed, and perhaps which character they have followed or tracked today. Finally, what is the character's attitude to the humans or fairies they have seen? They might find them hilarious, ridiculous, annoying, upsetting, or something else.

Having prepared these ideas, ask pupils in groups to devise tableaux of the animals 'at home'. What do they occupy themselves with domestically? They can't believe what these people/spirits get up to! They should be tableaux of the moment the returning character(s) come through the door in an excited or agitated state. Create the tableaux around the space. Now, on your signal, the scene is to come to life; propose that the first line of reportage is something like, 'You won't believe this...'. Now each group improvises, telling the story of an aspect of the play from this character's unique perspective. Let the story-telling continue unhindered for a time and then 'spotlight' each group; after you have determined the content of each group's tableau, you might suggest retelling all the episodes in the order in which they appear in the play.

Extension task

From where we are now, it is a simple step to create a very interesting writing in-role task (see 'Writing in-role' in Chapter 2). Suggest the idea of these animals keeping diaries of the life of the wood. Or propose that the forest has an authority figure among the animals (an owl, perhaps?) who keeps the ancient 'Annals of the Forest' in which the animals must record all events that occur here. You could introduce this character with a simple moment of 'Teacher in-role' (see Chapter 2). In either case, the final moment of the section becomes an opportunity for pupils to write in-role and reiterate the story of the play. This might be a task that is completed outside your drama time in the classroom, or as homework.

Puck

Exposition and text

You need: a set of name cards (provided at the end of this chapter), the text about Puck displayed around the room, simple period music as Puck's theme, (perhaps a jig on a tin-whistle), a drum, the farmer's monstrous-looking stick.

In this section, we look at the character of Puck. If it were possible to say who the main character of the play is, it would probably be Puck. He makes much of the dramatic action happen, and he is also a great character to explore with children. Explain this to the group and ask:

> What do we know about him already? His other name? Robin Goodfellow. Why would he have another, 'ordinary' name? Shakespeare didn't make him up... he used him... He's an ancient character in English, British and European folklore. [*Show other names*] 'Puki' – Old Norse, 'Puke' – Old Swedish, 'Pwca' – Welsh, 'Pùca' – Irish, etc.

What does Shakespeare say of him? Come and look around the walls [*where quotes are displayed*]:

> *'that shrewd and knavish sprite'*
>
> *'That frights the maidens of the villagery'*
>
> *'that merry wanderer of the night'*
>
> *'Misleads night-wanderers, laughing at their harm'*
>
> *'And sometime lurk in a gossip's bowl*
> *In very likeness of a roasted crab'*

and Puck says...

> *'Lord, what fools these mortals be!'*

Discuss the meaning of each line and what it tells us about Puck.
In a number of stages, we look into and experience the character.

Puck laughing and moving

> Puck enjoys himself. He laughs. You can tell a lot about a person by how they laugh. How does Puck laugh? Try around the circle. All join in and copy each suggestion. What do the different laughs tell you?
>
> How might a sprite, a hobgoblin, a mischievous spirit move? Let's try.
>
> What music might be his theme tune? [*Play your suggestion – a jig on a tin whistle?*]

Ask pupils to listen to the music and use it to decide how they might move as Puck. Pupils are given time to explore 'being Puck'; offer suggestions of what he might be doing – collecting herbs for potions, looking for opportunities for mischief, hiding from his master the king, following a foolish human. Feel free to freeze the action with a bang on your drum to celebrate 'good practice'.

The irate farmer: teacher in-role

Having brought the pupils into role, prepare now to step into role yourself (or invite another amenable adult to take the role) as an irate farmer wielding a monstrous-looking stick, who has been tracking Puck to exact revenge!

Ha, found you, Robin Goodfellow! I knew if I looked long enough in these woods I'd come across you. The villagers said a sprite couldn't be caught. I'll show them. I'll catch you... and more! It's time for your comeuppance. Your last trick on me and my wife was the final straw. They'll make me king of the village when I rid them of you. But how come there's so many of you? You've multiplied before my eyes. What is this further trickery? Only one of you can be Robin Goodfellow. Who is it? Or has he given himself the power of multiplication! Everything's possible with you, Puck! And don't even think about shape-shifting into something else... I've got my eye on you... What have you got to say for yourself? Which one of you is Puck? Or are you other sprites of a similar kind?

Now have a free dialogue with the group. They may trick or deceive you. They will certainly invent ingenious ways to distract and confuse you. As the farmer, grow impatient and angered:

'Enough, tittle-tattle, I didn't come here to be run fairy-rings around... I came here to *kill* Robin Goodfellow!'

Freeze!

Come out of role at this threatening and dramatic moment. Question the group about the farmer (they can come out of role too). Why is he so angry? What has happened? Discuss. He seems to know a lot about the 'fairy-world', to be something of an expert. What questions would you like to ask him? Ask the group if they would like the chance to question him. Then prepare to re-enter the role yourself (or 'unfreeze' your adult assistant). Pupils are now given the chance to 'Hot-seat' the farmer (see Chapter 2). The farmer will talk generally about Puck, giving a suggestion of his ancient history, and might give his *own* story about the mischief Puck has been up to with him and his wife. He *won't* tell the stories of the others in the village, but he will allude to these in preparation for the next step in the work. A good rendition of the farmer will open up delicious gaps about Puck and the villagers, which pupils will fill in a few moments.

End the in-role interview along the lines: 'This village has had enough of his mischievous spirit. Some people think he's fun... like a naughty child... I think he's got an evil side! He's dangerous. You just ask the people of my village...'

In a village home

You need: masking tape.

We now move to an exploration of villager life, and visit the homes of a set of characters who turn out to be Shakespeare's 'mechanicals', who appear as the cast of Peter Quince's terrible and hilarious play.

Ask the group to form up to six family-sized groups and assign themselves a space to serve as their home. Each house is then given a character, as follows.

- Quince the *carpenter*
- Bottom the *weaver*
- Flute the *bellows-mender*
- Snout the *tinker*
- Starveling the *tailor*
- Snug the *joiner*

In the house, there will be the named person, their wife, and family members. Establish the houses around the room, marking the walls and doors of each house with masking-tape lines on the floor.

Now, stop to discuss the work of the houses. What are the jobs mentioned? Tinker? Joiner? Bellows-mender? This could be an interesting historical discussion. The houses are the places where their work happens: part-workshop, part-home. So, in the corner of each single-roomed house, Bottom is weaving or Flute is mending bellows. Perhaps other members of the household help in this work. Others are doing other kinds of work – sewing, cooking, etc. Ask pupils to prepare to show the work of each house; insist that each piece of work entails its own unique sounds: the squeak of screws turned, bellows squeezed, wood shaved – the person using a tool must make the noise. The first time we enter the houses, no-one will speak (unless they need to as part of their work), but everyone will work. After a short time for preparation, ask for a tableau from each family of 'The house at work'. On your signal, the houses come to life and we see and hear their focused, detailed labour; this is an 'occupational mime'. After allowing the pupils to become absorbed in their work, spotlight each group. Bring the homes alive again for a moment, and indicate that discussion can now happen. Suggest what might be discussed: the man of the house is part of an amateur dramatic group that his wife objects to ('a waste of time!') and his children are embarrassed about; or the discussion might be about Puck's recent antics, or the Duke's coming wedding. Finally, as part of the action, instruct one person to leave the scene (they are going to come back in as Puck!).

Having established the nature of each family, we now move to a simple piece of 'Small group play-making' (see Chapter 2). Discuss: what mischievous and highly irritating trick is Puck going to play on this family now? Remember, he is a shape-shifter and likes nothing more than making humans looking foolish. Puck gives some examples in the play, he says:

> 'Sometimes lurk I in a gossip's bowl
> In the very likeness of a roasted crab
> And when she drinks, against her lips I bob': and

> 'The wisest aunt, telling her saddest tale,
> Sometimes for a three-foot stool mistakest me
> Then slip I from her bum. Down topples she'

Check pupils' understanding of the text. Now each family group is to decide on some inventive and thrilling trick. Then they should firstly make three tableaux to tell the story. Once these have been seen, they can develop the tableaux into full scenes. You might suggest that pupils think about finding a voice that is appropriate to the characters, noting that Shakespeare's 'mechanicals' are generally slow-witted, lower- or working-class people with 'common' accents. Later, we find out that Flute has a high voice and Snug can't read; maybe everyone has a funny voice. Think about comic voices, *and* about old-sounding language such as 'thy' and 'thou'. This will lend some authenticity and comedy to the scenes. Once complete, the scenes can be performed and enjoyed.

Puck captured!

You need: plasticine (or other art materials); music: a slow-air lament (again, perhaps on a tin-whistle).

As the last scene finishes, re-enter the space as the irate farmer.

> [*Shouting:*] **People of the village come quick! I've cornered Puck – the imp Robin Goodfellow! You must come now… I can't hold him long.**

Call them by their surnames, as above. The people of the village all gather. Instruct the group to form a circle and hold hands. Announce that there is a magical chant to say, to imprison the sprite in this circle… Who knows it? Some-one quickly improvises a spell… or you step in with your own. Everyone chants the spell. The Farmer shouts,

> **'Ha! We have you now Robin Goodfellow! He has made himself invisible to us!**

Instruct the group to turn their back on him in case he should look us in our eyes and bewitch us in his desperation.

> **Turn your backs, but keep the circle complete. Close your eyes. Summon a picture of Puck into your mind. That's him. Can you see him? When I say, all turn around and look at him. We've captured him in the centre of our magic circle! Repeat the chant now. Louder, Ready? Everybody turn!**

> **What can you see? What has he shape-shifted into? How do you feel, looking at him? Give me some words... one, two or three words... no more...**

> **Stop. Before this image vanishes, we need to capture it. To capture Puck for ever!**

Now indicate to pupils the chunks of plasticine you have prepared for them. Each person is to take their plasticine and silently model the Puck they saw in the centre of the circle*. Play the musical lament as pupils work.

As an alternative idea, you could ask pupils to paint or draw the Puck they saw; but clay modelling has a solidity and accessibility that we find of great value.

When the modelling is complete, present them all in the centre of the circle, each pupil bringing their Puck and laying it down with ceremony. When they are all assembled, continue in-role with some tenderness:

> **We have captured you now, ancient Puck – Robin Goodfellow! You have played your last trick...** (wielding weapon)... **'Will we kill him, people of the village?'**

Now Puck is captured, we return to the farmer's unnerving proclamation: we are here to capture and kill him. Will the people of the village wish to carry this out? Has this spirit a right to life? What are the consequences of killing a supernatural being? Discuss.

Now let him speak for himself. We move to a 'Distributed hot-seat' (see Chapter 2). Place three squares of paper on the floor inside the circle. We are going to allow Puck to plead his case before the people of the village. Any pupil can stand/crouch/sit on the papers, and when they do so, they will speak as Puck. If another pupil wants to change places with Puck, they will gently touch him on the shoulder and 'Whoosh!' him away. Allow the moment to take its course.

Can he save himself... with words? (Yes, we hope he probably can!) Puck is the play's singer of songs; perhaps you might bewitch the villagers yourself with your singing. To the tune of 'Rose, Rose' (see Chapter 8 or search online), sing Puck's song from Act 5, Scene 1: 'Now the hungry lion roars...'. Alternatively, think about using or paraphrasing Puck's apology from the end of the play:

> *If we shadows have offended,*
> *Think but this and all is mended*
> *That you have but slumbered here*
> *While these visions did appear.*
> *Gentle, do not reprehend*
> *If you pardon, we will mend...*
> *Give me your hand if we be friends*
> *And Robin shall restore amends.*

---

*   I am indebted to Allan Owens for the kernel of this idea.

Additional idea

Our researches have uncovered a poem (actually a song lyric) that may even have been written by Shakespeare's contemporary and friend Ben Johnson. It is a rollicking, bawdy tale of Robin Goodfellow's mischief-making among the human world. It has a tub-thumping metre and would be excellent (perhaps with a little editing) as a whole group reading. It also has a laughing refrain. The structure, metre and rhyme scheme could be offered as a model for pupils to copy to write their own verses... perhaps about the villagers' stories the group have just invented. It is called 'The Mad Merry Pranks of Robin Goodfellow' and is easily located online. You might like to choose and perhaps simplify a few verses. Consider the 'shape' or 'form' of the poem, and invite pupils to write new verses.

The stolen child

An anger to alter seasons: Oberon and Titania

The play shows three different worlds:

- the world of the noble people – the dukes and queens
- the world of the supernatural – fairies, sprites, hobgoblins
- the world of the working men – the comic mechanicals.

During the play, the three different worlds interact and come into conflict. Much of the comedy comes from the clashes when different worlds collide – they don't fit together.

> Let's look now at the world of the fairies. We will begin with some questions: Who here believes in fairies? Ghosts? Witches? Angels?
>
> If I asked you in Shakespeare's time, most of you would say 'Yes' to all of these. The King of England (King James) wrote a whole book called *Daemonology* in 1597. 'Fairies' weren't airy-fairy, silly, effeminate things, as we might think of them now... they were real to probably the majority of English people, certainly to the common people. And the woods (or forest) were where they were at their most powerful. In Shakespeare's play, the fairy world is organised like a society, with a king (Oberon) and a queen (Titania).

The fairy world and the human world met at certain points... as we saw with Puck. But there is *one* point of contact which terrified the human world more than anything else – the spirits *stole* human children! Sometimes they replaced them with troll or goblin children.

In the play, Oberon and Titania have fallen out very seriously; their anger is so deep that it has changed the weather across the land. They have fallen out over a stolen child – a beautiful Indian child – the jealous king wants the child as his own, but the queen wishes to keep control of him. Puck says this:

> *The king doth keep his revels here tonight:*

[*the king is on his way here*]

> *Take heed the queen come not within his sight:*

[*keep the queen away*]

> *For Oberon is passing fell and wrath.*

[*Oberon is incredibly angry*]

> *Because that she as an attendant hath*

[*because the queen has*]

> *A lovely boy, stolen from an Indian king.*
> *She never had so sweet a changeling;*
> *And jealous Oberon would have the child*
> *Knight of his train to chase the forest wild*
> *But she, perforce withholds the loved boy.*

Ill met by moonlight...

Now display the text of a simplified version of the argument between Oberon and Titania. It is taken from Act 2, Scene 1 (provided at the end of this chapter).

Enter Oberon and his servants to one side, and Titania and hers to the other.

OBERON: *Ill met by moonlight, proud Titania*

TITANIA: *What, jealous Oberon? Fairies skip hence.*
          I have forsworn his bed and company

OBERON: *Tarry, rash wanton. Am I not thy lord?*

TITANIA: *Then I must be thy lady.*

OBERON: *Why should Titania cross her Oberon?*
          I do but beg a little changeling boy
          To be my henchman.

TITANIA: *Not for thy fairy kingdom. Fairies away!*
          We shall chide downright, if I longer stay.

OBERON: *Well, go thy way.*

After checking understanding, invite pupils to try out the scene. As well as the king and queen who speak, there are servants on both sides who play an important part in the scene by adding dramatic tension and eyeing their enemies on the other side. This is helpful, because not everyone needs to speak the lines. After exploring and performing the scenes, move on to discuss the situation.

> What do you think about that? They've stolen a child and now they're arguing over who has custody of him. Would you like to look at the reality of this? Shakespeare says very little about it, in fact, Titania explains that it wasn't a changeling or stolen child at all. But, given the spirit world's history of child-stealing, can we believe her? Puck says the child was 'Stolen from an Indian king'. Let's look at this subject a little more closely. [*You might continue:*]
>
> Three things come to my mind:
>
> ● What was it like for the child who was stolen and for the parents who lost him? The king and queen arguing reminds me of divorced parents arguing over who 'gets' the children.
> ● The 'father' wants the boy to be brought up as a 'proper' boy: to hunt, to learn to fight. The 'mother' wants the boy for herself and to keep him sweet and pure: she 'crowns him with flowers'. Is he better off with 'mother' or 'father'?
> ● The child was stolen because he was 'beautiful'.

Our changeling child

Now move on to some 'pictures' in the centre of the circle from the story of a fairy child abduction – making them as we go. Use a simplified version of a Story Whoosh! – a 'Picture Whoosh!' (see Chapter 2).

● The parents putting the child to bed the night before he disappeared or was 'changed'.
● The child being taken – who did it? Who was there? What was the human child exchanged for? Something was put in his place!
● The morning the changeling child is discovered. The parents' reactions.
● The human child in Titania's court; and the changeling child in the human world.

Discovery scene

Invite the group to form small groups of three or four. We are going to explore the moment of discovery of the missing child. One person is the human mother, one the father, others are servants, or other children in the family. One person has just found the child gone, and must tell the others. What do they say? It is two seconds *after* the discovery has been made.

TIP   We suggest two possible limitations to the drama, which are often useful for diverting pupils' scenes into new imaginative territory:

● Either: at the start of the scene there is silence. For the first ten seconds, no-one speaks ... then the characters can speak only one sentence each. These sentences must be chosen very carefully. They can have as much *silence* as they like, but language is limited.
● Or: (an idea from Jonothan Neelands) the scene takes place with the characters sitting back-to-back on the floor. Their physical expression is limited; they must rely entirely on speech, and listen to each other very carefully.

The scenes should now be improvised and prepared for sharing. After the class has watched each one, ask them to report what they saw in the family. What did they understand? Who has power in the family? Who showed guilt? Who seemed to take responsibility? Who seemed to be hiding something? What questions do you have for any of the characters? etc.

Letters between worlds

You need: agèd paper and quill pens; reflective period music.
Discuss how old the stolen child is; we (and Shakespeare) don't say 'baby'.

> Can we agree that the child is old enough to talk ... and even to write? Ok. The child has gone from the family home. See this paper and these pens. In this situation, there are two people who write letters that may be never delivered:
>
> ● a 'kindly' spirit/fairy tells the child they will deliver a letter to his mother and father – so he writes
> ● the mother or father believes that, if they leave a letter for the stolen child under a hawthorn bush on the edge of the forest, it will be taken by the fairies and delivered – so he/she writes.
> ● If Shakespeare had written these letters, what would you expect to see in them? 'Old' vocabulary, blank verse, pictures painted with words? We are now going to write these letters. Choose who you would like to write as.

Offer the agèd paper and quill pens. Now give pupils time to write in silence. Introduce some reflective period music.

Once the letters are complete, ask for volunteers to read their letters, perhaps pairing up child with parent. As each is read, ask for the *child* letters to be handed to you as the kindly fairy; and for the *parent* letters to be piled on a single spot, as if being laid under the hawthorn bush. Accomplish this with some ceremony.

A final dramatic twist

Narrate as you enact the following:

> **The kindly fairy holds the child's letters in her hand. She has promised to deliver them safely. She knows it would give the child great comfort to know he is still in contact with his parents. But will she dare to disobey the queen in such a fashion? What if the queen found out? She would destroy her! What will the kindly fairy do?**

Now, invite your assisting adult or a pupil to take up the farmer's monstrous stick and enter the space. He has been watching. He saw the mother put the letter under the bush on the edge of the wood. He understands straight away what the letter is. He walks to the letters, looks around. Would it be kind to steal the letters now? He knows the fairies will not come for them; such kindness is a myth. The king and queen would never allow it. In the morning, the mother will return to see that the letter is gone. Would it be kinder to let her find the letter untouched, or to allow her to believe it has been delivered to her child? (Discuss with the group what might be done. Then . . .) He takes the letter and leaves the scene. Choose one of the pupils to play the mother. The mother comes back and sees the letter is gone. Is the farmer being kind? Is it ever right to deceive someone to make them feel better? Discuss, but do not be afraid of leaving the question completely *open* in the end. It is a genuine human and moral question. Allow space, if it should be necessary, for pupils to discuss their own personal response to this section of work: abduction, separation and loss are issues that can be felt deeply by young people.

In defence of Titania?

We return to the play. There are two conflicting stories of the stolen child: Puck's account that he is a stolen Indian child and a changeling; and the other story, from Queen Titania herself, that he is the child of a human friend of hers who had died. Who should we believe? Does Puck have a reason to lie? Does the queen?

> **Look, the queen has written a letter to her subjects, the spirits of the forest. Look and listen. (See the letter at the end of this chapter.) Who do *you* believe?**

You might go on to hot-seat the queen about the story, or to question her servants. Or you might just leave the question hanging.

The mechanicals

We met the key figures earlier, in their homes. When they are not at work, they are an amateur dramatics group who put on bad plays. They are in the woods, rehearsing a play to be performed at the big royal wedding (of Theseus and Hippolyta). Shakespeare loves to make these amateurs look ridiculous. Remember when we first started, we talked about 'The clowns, who don't know they are clowns'? This is who we will look at now. They are:

● Peter Quince: a carpenter, and the director of the play. Tries to be the boss but is often bullied by the most confident actor, Bottom.

- Nick Bottom: the overconfident weaver chosen to play the main part, Pyramus. He thinks he's really good and wants to be the star all the time. (Later, Puck will give him an ass's (donkey's) head and Titania, under a spell, will fall in love with him.)
- Francis Flute: the bellows-mender chosen to play the leading woman, Thisbe, in the play because he has no beard and a high, squeaky voice. He's insulted to be chosen to play a girl.
- Robin Starveling: the tailor, who ends up playing the part of 'Moonshine' (the moonlight).
- Tom Snout: the tinker, who ends up playing the part of the wall that divides the two lovers.
- Snug: the joiner chosen to play the lion. Snug is really bad at roaring, but still worries that he will frighten the ladies in the audience.

Being funny: Red Nose Day

You need: a set of simple red noses, preferably with elastic; a bright robe for you as 'King of Clowns'; 'clowning' music.

In this section we consider the nature of comic acting: a difficult skill and a difficult prospect, but essential for dealing with Shakespeare's comic parts such as our mechanicals.

> Is it easy to be funny? No, you have to be *fearless*; to not worry about looking silly. In our normal lives, one of the worst things that can happen to us is that people laugh at us (any stories to tell on this?) Well, if you're a comic actor, you have to *invite* people to laugh at you! But it's different, because you *want* them to laugh . . . it's as if *you're* laughing *first*!

> Would you like to have a go at thinking about how to be funny? You will need to join the ranks of the glorious clown. You will need a mask – the smallest mask in the world . . . the red nose! I'm going to play the King of Clowns. You are going to 'audition' for me to join the 'Legion of Clowns'.

> In threes, prepare how to say, in a comic fashion – 'I(we) am(are) clowns, and we come, O King of Clowns, to claim our place in the mighty Legion of Clowns!' If you are successful, the King of Clowns will welcome you to the Legion with a 'honk' on the nose. You must now prepare a short comic routine in a small group. Consider, what sort of clown will you be: a sad one, a victim, a clever one, a sly one, an energetic one?

After an amount of time for preparation, don your clownly cloak, give yourself a throne and prepare to receive your new clowns. Of course, they will all pass their audition and be admitted.

States of tension/points of concentration*

These approaches are used here as an accessible way in, both to comic physicality and to our mechanicals. Both techniques rely on establishing special ways of distinguishing characters: firstly by the amount of tension in their body; and secondly by giving the character a 'leading point' of their body. You will need to throw yourself into this in order to gain maximum benefit and have maximum fun with your children.

States of tension

Invite the group to walk around the space normally as themselves. Then, by demonstrating each one, teach the following 'states of tension', from the *least* to the *most* tension.

- No tension – *jelly* on the floor – you are lying on the floor quivering, giggling.
- Some tension – *very cool* – you are walking around with a deep swagger.

---

*   We believe the origins of both sets of ideas here lie with the Lecoq School of Theatre, Paris. The current telling of the approach has been worked up in classrooms over many years and, though probably original in part, it is certainly a pale imitation of the original, for which we apologise to anyone who might notice!

- More tension – *relaxed* – you are walking around effortlessly smiling.
- Normal tension – you are walking around as a '*normal*' person.
- Nervous –*twitchy* – you are walking around unsure of others, avoiding eyes.
- *Scared* of everything – you are walking around leaping and screaming at the slightest thing.
- *Petrified stiff* – you are turned to stone by fear – squeezing yourself inward, aching.

Once everyone has mastered this range of characters, play the game of calling out the various states and asking pupils to adopt the character immediately. Ask pupils to think about which state of tension their clown was most like.

Points of concentration

Here every character is defined by their point of concentration – the point of their body that 'leads' them around (such as the nose, chin, feet, shoulders, groin!) It can be thought of as the part of their body that might enter a room first. Again, you will need to demonstrate; try several, and ask pupils to copy you. Notice how their point of concentration also affects how the rest of their body moves. Every point gives you a new character. Once established, ask pupils to give their clown character a point of concentration; as we progress, each pupil's clown character is developing. All pupils are now walking around the room with a unique character. Now think – if this is their body, what might their voice be? Give your character a voice, and practise it with just the word 'Blah!' Have conversations with other characters with *just* the word 'Blah!'.

The bus-stop – a scene for six

Invite the pupils to form groups of five or six with a variety of character-types in each. We are going to make a simple scene with the characters; you might think about *both* the states of tension and the points of concentration. Ask the group to think about a *public* place where people have to be together but don't usually speak to each other; this is a physical comedy, so it needs as few words as possible. For example, a bus-stop, a waiting room, a queue in a post office, on a train, etc. Each group needs to choose a place, imagine their characters having to be there, and see what happens. Suggest that groups think about the characters' relative *status* – who is more important – or thinks they are! This is physical comedy... the clown music will cover the silence. Finally, suggest that the scene needs a task; for example, they all want to be at the front of the queue, or someone needs to be served very quickly. Prepare and watch.

Back to Shakespeare

You need: red noses, scripts (ideally handwritten on agèd paper rolls to add a note of authenticity). The preceding work should have loosened up pupils' sense of physical self and promoted a spirit of play. We return now to consider Peter Quince's troupe of amateur players, referred to in the play as 'rude mechanicals', meaning 'simple workmen'. Look at the list of mechanicals again – they are clown characters with distinctive, funny walks, funny mannerisms, funny voices. Ask pupils to think of the groups they have just been working in.

> This is the group we will work in to act out one of Shakespeare's great scenes. Who in your group is going to be which character? Is the clown led by his nose going to be Peter Quince? The clown led by his stomach, Bottom? The group's first job is to cast the scene, making any adjustments to character that you feel you need. Now you're really going to need to find a voice for your character; simply hearing your voice might be funny.

Introduce to the group the edited script (provided at the end of this chapter), and perhaps model the potential voices by reading it through yourself. Then send groups to work on the scene. A few suggestions for further support are as follows.

- Make a label with card, string and crayons for each character to wear and identify themselves.
- Create a line-up to show their relative status and how they feel about each other; perhaps as if they travelled by bus to come here.
- How might they greet each other?

For an extra (but realisable) challenge, ask pupils to try and learn their lines and perform without scripts. Now prepare; perform; then discuss, from the point of view of the pupils-as-actors, doing this comic scene and what the scene tells us.

Some extension ideas

A writing task

An actor's journal: this has hopefully been a fun but challenging task. Ask pupils to write down what it felt like to be doing this. 'Today I became a clown...'. Their journal should include a description of the work and a personal reflection on how they felt throughout the experience and about the character they played.

A watching task

Available online is a film of The Beatles having a go at the mechanicals' later scene, in which they perform their terrible play of *Pyramus and Thisbe* for the Duke's wedding. It takes place before a rowdy live audience, and might capture the spirit of an Elizabethan audience. Search for it online.

The lovers' story

The course of true love

Early on, in looking at the play, we said there were *three worlds*: the fairies, the clowns and the human lovers. The human side of this play is the final world we will look at. The story here is about falling in love with the wrong people – it's like a *farce*, where ridiculous problems ensue from simple mistakes... but it all turns out all right in the end.

TIP   The play is a *comedy* because it ends in *integration* – people/things coming together – a marriage (or several!). The opposite is a *tragedy* which ends in *disintegration* – things falling apart – death (often multiple deaths). Let's make a 'Story Whoosh!' of the lovers' story.

- The lovely Hermia wishes to marry Lysander.
- But her father demands that she marries Demetrius (who also loves her).
- Hermia's best friend, Helena, is a little jealous of Hermia (and fancies Demetrius).
- To escape from her father's demands, Hermia and Lysander run away to the forest.
- Demetrius follows them, and Helena follows Demetrius.
- In the forest, Oberon tries to help by giving Demetrius a love potion so he will love Helena.
- But Puck puts the potion in Lysander's eye – so he falls in love with Helena.
- He then puts it in Demetrius' eye, and he also falls in love with Helena.
- Helena gets very vexed, thinking they are both teasing her.

- The boys fight over her.
- Oberon has had enough, and sorts the problem out.
- He reverses Lysander's spell so that he may love Hermia again.
- And leaves Demetrius to love Helena – to Helena's delight!
- Hermia's father changes his mind and they all get married. Hoorah!

Would you like to finish off our work with a game? Let's play the '*A Midsummer Night's Dream* lover's game'!

The lovers' game

This is another version of 'The Shakespeare stage game' (see Chapter 4). During the game we reiterate the characters, their relationships and the farcical energy of their situation. Explain that the game is similar to a game pupils might know as 'Man overboard/Captain's coming/Torpedoes, etc. It involves the group learning, remembering and reacting to a set of instructions that you will now teach them by demonstration! Indicate where in the space they should imagine the audience to be; then explain the terms 'up-stage', 'down-stage', 'stage-left' and 'stage-right' (see Chapter 4). These are the calls the group need to learn:

- *up-stage* – all turn to face up-stage as indicated, then Freeze!
- *down-stage* – all turn to face down-stage as indicated, then Freeze!
- *stage-left* – all turn to face stage-left as indicated, then Freeze!
- *stage-right* – all turn to face stage-right as indicated, then Freeze!
- *Hermia* – all throw a lover's shape and shout: 'O Lysander!' (or sing the song – 'Herm and Sander up a tree, K-I-double-S-I-N-G!')
- *Helena* – find a partner – one says 'Ahh! Demetrius'; the other screams 'No!'
- *boys* – find a partner – walk angrily at each other and say 'Grrr! She's mine!'
- *Egeus – coming!* (Hermia's miserable father) – shout 'Hide!' and crouch
- *Theseus – coming!* (the Duke) – everyone stand to attention
- *wedding bells* – the end of the play – everyone holds hands, takes a bow and shouts 'Ding Dong Ding Dong'.

Once the full list of calls has been established, the group will walk around to await your instructions, which you will call randomly and energetically.

As you close the game, finish on a final 'wedding bells', at which the whole company will be holding hands and bowing. Stop the action and explain that the wedding and the coming together of everybody is exactly how the play finishes. And at the final moment, Puck steps forward to make a final farewell to the audience, saying,

> *If we shadows have offended,*
> *Think but this and all is mended*
> *That you have but slumbered here*
> *While these visions did appear.*
>
> *Gentle, do not reprehend*
> *If you pardon, we will mend…*
> *Give me your hand if we be friends*
> *And Robin shall restore amends.*

Suggest that we all repeat these last two lines (a couplet) a few times, and end on a general festive shaking of hands.

The story jigsaw

The 'Story jigsaw' activity is a way of summarising and then cementing the whole story of the play. It is a simple group sorting exercise, which can then be realised as a dramatic presentation (see Chapter 2).

● Prepare the envelopes containing the story jigsaw (available at the end of this chapter).

● Invite groups to open the envelopes and sort the story into the correct order.

● Check the sorting.

● Create tableaux and 'transition movement' to tell your part of the story.

● Perform with music as a final, summary performance.

TIP The correct order will be on the original sheet.

A teacher's crib sheet

Background information

- Written around 1594 or 1596 (and probably performed straight away).
- Published in the First Folio in 1623 after Shakespeare's death.
- The story is probably Shakespeare's most original. The story that Bottom's players act, *Pyramus and Thisbe*, is taken from Ovid's *Metamorphoses*, which Shakespeare may have read in Latin at school. It is very similar to the *Romeo and Juliet* story that he wrote at around the same time.

Brief summary of story

- To escape a forced marriage, Hermia runs away into the woods with Lysander, pursued by Demetrius and Helena.
- A group of workmen also enter the woods to practise a play for the duke.
- The King of the Fairies, Oberon, wishes to teach his wife, Titania, a lesson. He sends his servant, Puck, to make a love potion.
- Mischievous Puck gives Bottom the weaver a donkey's head; the enchanted Titania falls in love with him!
- Puck gives the human men the love potion and both fall in love with 'plain' Helena.
- Oberon restores order, forgives the queen, and pairs up the human lovers to everyone's satisfaction.
- A wedding feast is held, and Bottom and his men perform their terrible play.

Main characters

- Hermia: a young woman in love with Lysander, but expected to marry Demetrius.
- Helena: her 'plain' friend in love with Demetrius.
- Demetrius: wanting to marry Hermia.
- Lysander: in love with Hermia.
- Oberon: King of the Fairies.
- Titania: Queen of the Fairies.
- Puck: the king's servant, a mischievous sprite.
- Bottom: a weaver.
- The other mechanicals: Quince, Snug, Flute, Snout, Starveling.

Other things

- It was a very shocking thing to Shakespeare's audience that the queen falls in love with a donkey! This is very daring; Queen Elizabeth herself was referred to as the 'Fairy Queen'. People were executed for having 'relationships' with animals!
- Puck, if anyone, is the main character in the play. He is also called Robin Goodfellow. He is an ancient character from European folklore. Shakespeare's rival Ben Johnson wrote a popular poem called 'The Mad Merry Pranks of Robin Goodfellow'.
- Written at about the same time as the terrible tragedy of love, *Romeo and Juliet*, *A Midsummer Night's Dream* contains a comic shadow of the tragedy in the form of the hilarious *Pyramus and Thisbe* play; perhaps he wrote this play as the antidote to the other.
- At the height of their fame The Beatles performed the *Pyramus and Thisbe* play on television in front of a live, heckling audience (find it on YouTube).
- *A Midsummer Night's Dream* is still one of Shakespeare's most popular and regularly performed plays.

Facts and legends for pupils

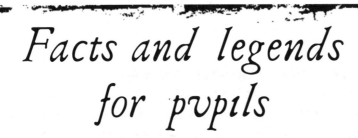

The play takes place in Athens, the capital of Greece, but there doesn't seem to be anything 'Greek' about it!

Puck (the 'main' character – if there is one) is a character probably known by the people of Shakespeare's time as an ancient spirit. His name, in various forms, appears in all sorts of European myths.

We tend to think of 'fairies' as 'Tinkerbell'-style, feminine creatures, but as you can see from the play, in earlier times they were much more dangerous, mischievous, malevolent: they steal children, change the weather with their anger, taunt humans.

The queen falling in love with a 'donkey' is a very dangerous and shocking idea (it was a crime punishable by death!)... even worse, Queen Elizabeth herself was sometimes thought of as 'the Fairy Queen'! – this might be why the final words of the play are Puck's cheeky apology for offending the audience.

The play was written early in Shakespeare's career; it is a story that seems completely original to Shakespeare – most others are 'borrowed' from history or other sources.

Professional theatre (with permanent buildings and actors paid full-time to act) was a new thing in Elizabethan England; with Bottom and the mechanicals making their ridiculous play, Shakespeare seems to be taking the mickey out of amateur theatre companies.

The play is set during the May Day celebrations, which were highly popular and raucous holidays; some have complained that Shakespeare calls the play 'Midsummer Night's Dream', when May Day isn't in the middle of summer!

When Shakespeare mentions the terrible weather that Oberon's argument has caused, he could very well be referring to the disastrous weather of the 1590s, which is sometimes called the 'little Ice Age'. We think of human behaviour changing the climate, and many Elizabethans thought the same... but they meant by their bad moral behaviour!

The story of Pyramus and Thisbe is borrowed from the Latin writer Ovid – who Shakespeare probably studied at school as a boy in Stratford (Ovid is also famous for stories in which people turn into animals, like Bottom).

A page of famous lines

'The course of true love never did run smooth'.
'Love looks not with the eyes, but with the mind'

Lord, what fools these mortals be!'

'…every mother's son.'

'I'll put a girdle round about the earth
In forty minutes.'
'My heart Is true as steel'

'I know a bank where the wild thyme blows'

'The true beginning of our end.'

'If we shadows have offended,
Think but this and all is mended
That you have but slumbered here
While these visions did appear.
Gentle, do not reprehend
If you pardon, we will mend…
Give me your hand if we be friends
And Robin shall restore amends.'

A Midsummer Nights Dream **A Story Whoosh!**

Once upon a time in Athens, a father brings his daughter before the duke to force her to marry the person *he* wants her to. The duke says she must. The girl, Hermia, decides to run away to the woods with her lover. Hermia tells Helena, who tells Demetrius (the man Hermia should marry), who decides to follow them.

. . . Whoosh!

Some local workmen – Quince the carpenter, Bottom the weaver, Starveling the tailor, Flute the bellows-mender, Snout the tinker, Snug the joiner) have decided to perform a play for the duke's forthcoming wedding. They agree to go into the forest to practice in secret.

. . . Whoosh!

Meanwhile, in the woods, the King and Queen of the fairies are having a fierce row about who should get a human child that the queen has stolen. The king sends his servant Puck to make a potion to drug the Queen.

. . . Whoosh!

Demetrius and Helena are in the woods, and Oberon overhears them arguing. Oberon, the King of the fairies, decides to help Helena by making Demetrius love her. He tells Puck to give him the love potion he has made as well.

. . . Whoosh!

Puck gives Bottom a donkey's head and terrifies his friends. The sleeping queen is drugged with a love potion. When she wakes, she falls in love with Bottom and his donkey's head! Puck also makes a mistake and drugs Lysander instead of Demetrius. When he wakes up, he also falls in love with Helena. Oberon gives the other man, Demetrius, the same love potion, and he *also* falls in love with Helena. She is furious.

. . . Whoosh!

Lysander and Demetrius prepare to fight one another for Helena. Puck tricks them into walking round and round the forest in circles until they collapse on the ground in exhaustion. He then leads Hermia and Helena to the same place and puts them to sleep as well.

. . . Whoosh!

King Oberon takes charge. He finds Titania and releases her from the donkey-loving spell. He also releases Lysander from the spell that made him love Helena . . . so he may love Hermia again. He leaves Demetrius to love Helena . . . making her happy again.

. . . Whoosh!

The duke arrives. When the new situation is explained, he allows Hermia to marry Lysander, and Demetrius to marry Helena. Theseus decides to invite the lovers to get married that day, during his own wedding feast. Together they return to Athens, are married, and Bottom's terrible play is finally performed. Puck tells the audience that if anyone disliked the play, or was offended, that they should imagine that it was only a dream.

. . . Whoosh!

A story jigsaw

Hermia is told by the Duke and her father that she must marry Demetrius or be executed, or put in a 'nunnery'. She runs away with the man she loves, Lysander, into the forest.

Hermia and Demetrius follow them.

Some local workmen agree go into the forest to rehearse a play for the forthcoming wedding of the duke.

In the woods. A great argument is raging between the King and Queen of the fairies. The queen has stolen a beautiful Indian boy-child who the king wants to have for his own.

Oberon, the angry king, sends Puck to find magical flowers to make a potion to trick the queen and force her into giving him the stolen child. She will fall in love with the first person she sees upon waking up.

Oberon decides to help Helena by making Demetrius love her by using the same potion.

Queen Titania is asleep on a woody hillock. Oberon drops the magic juice on her eyes.

Puck mistakenly puts the flower-potion in Lysander's eyes instead of Demetrius's. Lysander falls in love with Helena! Then Demetrius falls for her magically too. Helena is furious because she thinks they are teasing her.

The workmen are in the woods to practise their terrible play. Puck gives Bottom the weaver a donkey's head.

Queen Titania wakes, sees Bottom with the donkey's head – and falls in love with him.

King Oberon takes charge. He releases Titania from the spell. He releases Lysander's spell . . . so he may love Hermia again. He leaves Demetrius to love Helena . . . making her happy again.

The duke's wedding takes place. Helena and Demetrius, Hermia and Lysander also marry. Bottom and the actors perform their play. Oberon blesses everyone.

Resources

Name cards for Puck, saying:

Puci, Old Norse

Puce, Old Swedish

Pwci, Welsh

Púci, Irish Gaelic

Putz, Old German

Púcel, Old English

A message from Queen Titania:

My subjects,

Let it here be known. I have been much wronged;

Misrepresented by the gossip-mongers

Of my very Lord, the king. Know you this…

The child is no stolen changeling puking brat

His mother was a votaress of my order

Mine sweet and gentle mortal friend.

Many hours we have sat upon the Indian sand

And laughed and passed away the balmy days

In hot and spicy air. In giving birth

To this very child, she died a mortal death.

It is for her that I have taken now

This beautiful boy as mine own and must remain.

Your queen, Titania

Oberon and Titania's Argument – Act 2, Scene 1

Enter Oberon, the king of the fairies one side and Titania, the queen on the other. Both with their own group of loyal fairies.

OBERON: *I'll met by moonlight, proud Titania!*

Recognising him and stopping.

TITANIA: *What jealous Oberon?*
Fairies away, I have foresworn his bed and company.

OBERON: *Tarry, rash wonton, am I not thy lord?*

TITANIA: *Then I must be thy lady.*
Why are thou here?

OBERON: *Why should Titania cross her Oberon?*
I do but beg a little changeling boy
To be my henchman.

TITANIA: *The fairy lands buy not the child of me*

OBERON: *Give me the boy!*

TITANIA: *Not for thy fairy kingdom. Fairies away!*

Exit Titania and her fairies.

The mechanicals' rehearsal scene (Act 1, Scene 2)

Enter Quince the carpenter, Snug the joiner, Bottom the weaver,
Flute the bellows-mender, Snout the tinker and Starveling the tailor.

QUINCE:	*Is all our company here?* [taking out a scroll] *Here is the scroll of every man's name.*
BOTTOM:	*First, good Peter Quince, say what the play treats on: then read the names of the actors and grow to a point.*
QUINCE:	*Marry, our play is 'The Most Lamentable comedy and most cruel death of Pyramus and Thisbe'*
BOTTOM:	*A very good piece of work, I assure you. Now, good Peter Quince, call forth your actors by the scroll. Masters spread yourselves.*
QUINCE:	*Answer as I call you. Mick Bottom the Weaver?*
BOTTOM:	*Ready. Name what part I am for, and proceed.*
QUINCE:	*You, Nick Bottom, are set down for Pyramus.*
BOTTOM:	*What is Pyramus? A lover or a tyrant?*
QUINCE:	*A lover, that kills himself most gallant for love*
BOTTOM:	*That will ask some tears in the true performing of it. If I do it, let the audience look to their eyes: I will move storms!*
QUINCE:	*Francis Flute the bellows maker?*
FLUTE:	[his voice high-pitched] *Here, Peter Quince*
QUINCE:	*Flute, you must take Thisbe on you*
FLUTE:	*What is Thisbe? A Wandering knight?*
QUINCE:	*It is the Lady that Pyramus must love.*
FLUTE:	*Nay, faith, let me not play a woman; I have a beard coming.*
BOTTOM:	*Let me play Thisbe too. I'll speak in a monstrous little voice* [in a deep voice*] *'Thisbe. Thisbe'* [in a high voice] *'Uh, Pyramus, my lover dear!*
QUINCE:	*No, no, you must play Pyramus; and Flute, you Thisbe.*
BOTTOM	[disappointed*]: *Well, proceed*
QUINCE:	*Snug the joiner?*
SNUG:	*Here Peter Quince*
QUINCE:	*You must play the lion's part*
SNUG:	*Have you the lion's part written?... for I am slow of study.*
QUINCE:	*It is nothing but roaring*
BOTTOM:	*Let me pay the lion too. I will roar that I will make the Duke say, 'Let him roar again, let him roar again!'*
QUINCE:	*You can play no part but Pyramus!*

Puck's closing speech:

If we shadows have offended,

Think but this and all is mended

That you have but slumbered here

While these visions did appear.

Gentle, do not reprehend

If you pardon, we will mend…

Give me your hand if we be friends

And Robin shall restore amends.

[Final words, Puck, Act5, Scene 1]

* These are *our* suggestions, not Shakespeare's.

A Midsummer Night's Dream scheme structure map

Section	Drama approaches	Possible curriculum opportunities
The forest waits		
Exposition and discussion	Discussion; teacher as story-teller	Oracy; developing vocabulary; history
Soundscape	Soundscape; whole group enactment	Literacy: sense of place; geography: environments
Narrative elaboration	Use of symbolic props; story-telling	Literacy: use of symbols, character and narrative introduction
Shape-shifter game	Gaming in context; movement work	Literacy: characterisation; PE
'This is the forest of...' – an all-senses performance poem	Whole group writing and performance	Literacy: all-senses poem; writing for performance
The whole story – a Story Whoosh!	'Story Whoosh!'	Narrative understanding
The animals who saw...	Characterisation; small group play-making; reported story; writing in-role	Literacy: building a character, writing a reported narrative from multiple perspectives; science (animals and environments)
Puck		
Exposition and text	Teacher exposition; consideration of text	Literacy: listening for meaning; textual awareness; historical text;
Puck laughing and moving	Characterisation; physicality	Literacy: building a character, developing empathy
The irate farmer: teacher in-role	Teacher in-role; hot-seating	Oracy; questioning; history
In a village home	Small-group play-making; occupational mime; scene setting; characterisation	Script-making; history; technology
Puck captured!	Teacher in-role; whole group drama; modelling	Oracy; moral education; art (3D clay modelling)
The stolen child		
An anger to alter seasons: Oberon and Titania	Discussion and exposition	Literacy: narrative structures; history; moral education
Ill met by moonlight...	Small-group script work	Literacy: script for performance; historical script
Our changeling child	'Picture Whoosh!'; small-group improvisation	Literacy: dramatic structures, characterisation, play-making; personal and moral education
Letters between worlds	Writing in-role; teacher in-role	Literacy: letter writing in context; moral education; music
In defence of Titania?	Presentation of text	Literacy: textual analysis
The mechanicals		
Being funny: Red Nose Day	Discussion; small-group play-making; physical comedy (clowning)	Personal development; history (of theatre)
States of tension/points of concentration	Performance technique; developing character; small-group play-making	History (of theatre); personal development; PE
Back to Shakespeare	Script work in groups	Literacy: using a historical script
Some extension ideas	Reflective writing	Literacy: personal reflective writing
The lovers' story		
The course of true love	Teacher exposition; Story Whoosh!	Literacy: narrative understanding
The lovers' game	Gaming in context	Literacy: narrative understanding; PE
The story jigsaw	Story jigsaw; summative performance	Literacy: narrative understanding; problem-solving

We offer the chart above as a starting point. There are a whole host of learning opportunities in a rich drama experience that would have been exhausting to list: developing positive groups, expanding language opportunities and vocabulary, developing self-image and confidence, fostering imaginative responses, to name

Resources needed	Teachers Notes
Setting of space for drama	
Associated representative props	
Roll of lining paper, individual pieces of paper, coloured pens	
Story Whoosh! sheet for teacher	
Agèd paper, pens/quills	
The text displayed	
Farmer's monstrous stick	
Plasticine (clay)	
Copies of text	
Agèd paper, quill pens; reflective period music	
Copy of text	
Red noses; king-clown's robe; 'clown' music	
Paper and pens	
Copy of 'Story Whoosh!'	
Prepared story jigsaws; appropriate music	

a few. Also, as you translate the work into your own classroom you will, we hope, create for yourself a whole unanticipated flood of new opportunities for learning. The heart of such learning is the rich experience we all hope to build.

8 Romeo and Juliet – scheme

'What light through yonder window breaks?'

Pre-word: the jig

At a recent visit to Shakespeare's Globe Theatre on London's fair south bank, the tour guide was excited to describe to us how all of Shakespeare's plays... tragedy, history, comedy... probably ended with a company jig. The dead would rise, the killers smile, the tortured groundlings perk up as the actors performed a riotous, frantic dance of closure, and perhaps even sometimes led the audience in a maniacal conga through the Elizabethan streets.

Information about Elizabethan theatre is so scant that it appears the statement is perhaps based upon one visitor's account, but such a good and plausible idea shouldn't be ignored! It was good business sense; whatever horrors the play might show, however broken by grief the crowds might be, the jig leaves the audience quite literally with a dance in its step. As they pour out into the streets, their excitement and vitality is likely to burst into the surrounding community – a great advertisement. Nobody wants a miserable-looking audience leaving their theatre.

In this scheme of work, we have made use of the jig principle. There are moments of intensity and seriousness here, which we give ourselves the ability to step away from instantly with the pressing of the 'jig button' – at which the whole of *our* company will break into a riotous jig. Clearly, this will involve some preparation: you will need to devise and learn the simple steps yourself and teach them to the class. We have discovered one beautiful, cheeky example of such a final moment on the stage of the London Globe with director–actor Mark Rylance, from a BBC broadcast of *Richard II* (search *YouTube* for 'end of play jig'). This piece formed the extent of our research on creating a jig, and we were able to simply borrow and adapt a string of moves in order to create an original jig ourselves. Alternatively, we have also accomplished the moment by simply playing the jig good and loud and, after a loosening-up activity, asking the group to copy first *us* in a succession of moves, then individual pupils who are able to improvise a move. The routine created shouldn't be an exact science of dance – it should be raucous, joyous and liberating. We commend you to brighten your day: go and watch the Mark Rylance video!

The jig we have chosen to use is the Will Kemp Jig. Will Kemp was a fellow shareholder of Shakespeare's theatre company, and legend tells that it was for Will Kemp, celebrated comic actor *cum* clown, that Shakespeare wrote many of his most famous comic parts: Trinculo, Touchstone, the various fools. This jolly tune is said to celebrate an event known as 'The Nine Days' Wonder' in which, in order to win a bet, Will Kemp danced a jig from London to Norwich, a feat that took nine days. It is a distance of around eighty miles!

Verona, city of rapiers

You need: Italianate, renaissance music; a stage or sports rapier, or pictures of rapiers; a large drum that will give a military or marshal tone.

The stand-off game

This game is a version of simple 'walking circle' games such as 'Traffic lights', 'Stop–go', etc. Here the action of the game is used to build a sense of the location of the play.

Instruct the group that they may move only on your drum-beat. Test the accuracy of their stopping and their stillness. Now hold a steady rhythm, allowing the group to make a longer, but still controlled, journey around the room. Once the basic action is established, introduce the following complications, each of which you should first model.

- Members of the group still move only on your pulsing rhythm.
- When you stop on *one* heavy beat, everyone should stop at the next person they meet and hold a steady, threatening, dangerous look (no laughing!).
- But now, when you stop on *two* heavy beats, everyone must crouch, touching the floor and looking around in fear.
- And when you stop on *three* heavy beats, everyone should shout: 'Do you bite your thumb at me sir?'.

Now develop the sense of this place. Continue to play the game and give the signals, but narrate as you do so, and develop identification with the characters who walk these streets.

> You are the people of Verona. This hot and ancient city. Here, all walk with their hands on their rapiers. A 'rapier'. Not many years ago ... before the techniques to smelt and grind the double-edged, razor-style blade of rapiers like these ... we fought with broad-swords – heavy, vicious weapons which we would struggle to lift and swing around our heads. To fight with a broad-sword would be a brutal, monstrous battle. But a rapier – a fine, beautiful and deadly razor ... it cuts both ways and, with a simple, gentle touch, could slice your organs from their bloody pits! And spill them on the city's ground. And light enough that we may hang them from our belts and carry them always at our hand. Ready for the careless look ... that will provoke a bloody, deadly fight.

As you continue through the game one more time now, 'harden' your voice so it supports a more intense and heightened performance of the tension of the street.

> This is the everyday life of the street on which you live. Walk the streets.

> What person are you? In this dangerous place, everyone knows who you are and where you fit in; fit in to the pecking order. *You* know where you fit in the pile. You know your place! You might be powerful, a fine swordsman, belonging to a powerful family, you might be known as a hothead, as dangerous, as someone who has fought many duels and won them all, someone easily provoked ... someone who might fight over a look ... or, you might be someone at the bottom of the pile, someone who lives in fear of giving or receiving a bad look, someone who keeps their head down, someone who avoids eye contact, someone who lives in fear of their life ... every day, here on these streets.

Walking the streets

Now invite the group to clear a space. Out of the general sense of the dangerous street, we are now going to construct a more specific scene and invite pupils to take on a particular character: old, young; involved in violence, not involved; master, servant; beggar, fruit-seller. You are to create a 'Whole group tableau' (see Chapter 2).

> This empty space before us is the street. The empty space is calling for *you* to fill it. To fill it with life; with characters you are going to imagine now. Not everyone is a rapier-wielding, hot-headed young man. Think: who else would you expect to see on this street? Think about the *different* kinds of people there might be, the extremes of age, wealth, fearfulness ... and everything in between.

When you know who you might be, you're going to enter as this person, take up a position, and hold it. We will build up a precise street scene, one at a time.

Allow the scene to build.

Now turn on the sound of the street. No movement yet. 'Thought-track' each character (see Chapter 2) quickly with a tap on the shoulder; hear their contribution to the street scene. Turn the whole sound on again. Explain that, of course, these people are all interacting. When you clap your hands, you are going to bring the scene alive in sound *and* movement. Ask pupils to consider exactly what their character is *doing* on the street; if you ask them, what will they say? 'I need to sell...; I need to find...; I need to meet...; I want to buy...' Ask a few pupils to tell us, but say you assume *everybody* knows their purpose here today.

Clap!

Allow the scene to open and develop. You are looking for pupils to become absorbed in their characters and in their living-through of the moment. Be prepared to stop, spotlight individual sections of activity, and carry on. Characters might be invited to interact with a range of others.

Freeze! Explain that, for the next few moments, the characters are not going to speak to anyone, but they *are* going to continue to move. As they move silently, they are thinking. Ask pupils to respond to these ideas and to prepare to answer the questions for their own character:

- Is this a place you like to live?
- These streets are your home. Are these streets a place where you feel 'at home'? How *do* you feel?
- When you stand at the threshold of your door, about to step into the street... how do you feel?
- What do you take out with you? For protection? For defence? For luck?

This is a place of hot blood and passion and violence. Let's talk to the people whose street this is.

Now ask the questions that you have just anticipated. The scene should move in silence until you beat the drum. All then freeze in character, and you pose each question, tapping individual pupils on the shoulder to invite their responses.

(Shaking their head to indicate they do not wish to answer the question is acceptable.) Pose each question again, and take up to five answers each time. Repeat each answer yourself, for the sake of clarity and to add value.

Listen carefully to the people of the street and extend their ideas with further questioning.

Finally, explain that the scene is going to come alive for the final time on your drum-beat.

Now that we've discovered some very interesting things about these characters, we're going to try something *difficult*. When I beat the drum for the second time, the people of the street are going to begin talking again... but this time, they're going to say the things they think, but do not, or *dare not* say. Do you all understand that? Do you think it's true that we all have thoughts going on in our heads all the time that we know we *can't* say? Well, today, these people are going to tell us those secret thoughts. We're going to learn what they *really* feel about living here on the streets of Verona and the people they meet every day.

On beat *one*, walk. On beat *two*, talk.

Again, allow the pupils to become absorbed in their characters. Expect a loud hubbub of noise. Now, as before, freeze the group and tap each pupil on the shoulder to bring their voices alive and listen to each of their inner thoughts.

The poem of Verona

Finally, say:

> If you could capture all that your character and the others around you feel about this city of yours, what would you say? If you were to complete this sentence root:
>
> 'Verona, our city of . . . ',
>
> what would your character say of it?
>
> Your sentence might include details of the *physical* street . . . What it looks like, feels like, smells like, sounds like; or how people *experience* it . . . how they fear, daren't stop, keep their eyes to the floor, etc.

TIP Using a sentence root (see Chapter 2) encourages a more careful and selective use of language; it encourages the crystallisation of thoughts *at this moment* in the direction of the poet. Pupils will be able to use and extend the dramatic language that you have been encouraging and modelling throughout the sequence. Prompt a variety of responses . . .

> As you walk around the room and invite lines from pupils with a tap on the shoulder, repeat the sentence root before each suggestion. Alternatively, invite the pupils to give the sentence root themselves *before* their completed sentence.

In this way, you allow the moment to emerge from the drama experience within some supported spontaneity. It is a simple step to creating a piece of whole-group, dramatic poetry. We will move from 'creating' mode to a 'performing' mode.

> Your sentence root . . . 'Verona, our city of . . . '

Explain that this is such a rich and imaginative picture of the streets of Verona that we would like to capture it so that we can keep it. There are a number of options here.

- Make a simple digital recording of the pupils as they speak – walk around with a hand-held dictaphone and offer it to each speaker.
- Make use of an available 'other adult' who notes the lines as they are spoken by the pupils. Ideally, this should be anticipated as a task so that the practicalities of pen and paper do not interrupt the flow of the work.
- Invite pupils to form groups of four or five. Together they are going to write a performance poem called 'Verona, our city of . . . '. Each verse is about five lines long and begins with the words 'Verona, our city of . . . '. Ask the groups to write down the poem they create on small rolls of rough lining paper (suggesting manuscript). Collect these together on a wall, having first made a simple centrepiece yourself with the title 'Verona, our city of...'. Explain that each contribution is a verse in a whole-group poem. Stand the group in front of the poem, and ask them to think about how they are going to speak their verse out loud: all together, shared out, two people to each line? After a little time to prepare, perform the poem.
- Individual pupils could now be handed paper and quills to write a letter to someone who lives elsewhere, telling them of recent events in Verona and their feelings about the city they live in. This is 'writing in-role' (see Chapter 2) and might be used as an 'out of drama' task later.
- Another 'out of drama' classroom task might be to consider the ideas we have generated and create individual poems about Verona's streets and its people.

Back to the work on the streets.

Children of Verona

There are *some* people on these streets who do *not* carry rapiers, who do *not* fight for their honour at the drop of a hat... people who, to the violent men of this city, are almost invisible... who? Children, women, the elderly, conscientious objectors?

How would it feel to be one of *these* people; to be a child?

Children of Verona. These are your streets. This city is your home. You want to stay away from these streets. Your mother wants you to stay away from these streets. But you have to cross these dangerous streets twice every day – once to make your way to school, once to return.

Give the signal for everyone to crouch (two bangs on the drum).

In the morning, the streets are often quiet and you pass through the debris and patches of blood of last night's violence.

Invite the children to pass through the streets and look around them.

What do you see? [*Take their ideas.*] You meet your best friend as usual and walk the streets together.

Invite the groups to make pairs, firstly creating a tableau of the pairs walking together, then inviting the action to happen; the children walk and talk, reporting what they see and how they feel as they go. On your signal, the whole group stops and some sample pairs continue to move and talk.

So the children cross the sleeping city and arrive at school.

The city wakes... and the citizens crawl from their houses... and grow angry at last night's attacks and plot the revenge they will take this day... as the feuding gangs sharpen their rapiers... Verona's children must return to their homes...

Let's bring the street to life again as we did before, but this time, let us take out five of the adults created earlier and put back in five children, at the *other* end of the day when they must cross the bustling city again to return home.

Choose these five people and ask them to stand on the edges of the space. Invite the rest of the group to return to their street characters. Revisiting the drum and movement sequence, build up the sense of threat from the street. Freeze! Speak to the 'children' on the edge of the space.

The drum beats its marshal tone and the street comes to life, loud and aggressive, the children enter...

Give a quick indication of a stop–start, action–freeze sequence. The drum is the signal, as before. In each pause, question the children as they cross the streets. Keep the pace up.
Develop the sense of jeopardy for the children...

You may be only a child... and almost invisible to these warring men... but you also belong to a family... and it is the families who are at war here... and everybody knows which family you belong to... who your father is... who your brother has killed, who your uncle has slighted... You can't hide... you won't be *fought*... but you're still the enemy... everyone who looks at you knows it... How will you move? How will you feel?

Stop!

You are spotted. A group of men are standing with their rapiers on their belts. They stop you. They want to speak to you. Decide quickly, do they belong to *your* family or to your *enemy's*?

With a gesture, quickly indicate for these groups of men to form. Each of the five children must have a group to meet. Allow the scene to begin on your signal. Spotlight individual groups.

The mothers

> Look. Your mother waits at the door of your home. She's standing on the threshold... waiting, waiting, fearful...

Quickly allocate a mother to each child. Send them to the edge of the space as before. Give two bangs of the drum so all crouch. Speak to the mothers.

> You're waiting at the door. Who are you waiting for? Where have they been? How do you feel? What do you want to say to the men who make these streets so dangerous? What did you say to your child this morning before they left? What will you say when they return? Can you see them coming? What can you see? Is this a place you want to live? Your son may grow up to be one of the men who carry the rapiers. What would you like to say to him? Do you think this is a place where children can live as children?

> Look out into the street. Something's happened! A fight has started. You can hear shouting, arguing, the clash of rapier steel, cries of pain, the rumble of a hundred feet. Look out and see where your child is. He's running! Running! Is he being chased? Panic!

Invite a moment of panic from everyone. Then, with an almighty final bang of the drum and shout of Freeze! – draw the moment to an end.

> This is Verona, the city where the story we're going to explore happens. It's the city where Romeo and Juliet were born into families who were sworn enemies; where they lived as children. These are the streets they walked through. Do you think they have a chance of surviving? [*Discuss.*] And it's the city where they died having barely reached adulthood.

Discussion

Come out of drama mode. Invite the group to sit and reflect.

> Can you imagine living in a place like this? What would it be like? Do you think there are places like that *today?* Where? What would that be like? Why do places become so bad, so dangerous? What would life be like in that real place; for a child, for a mother, for a person involved in the violence? I wonder if they would like to escape. I wonder if that's why Romeo seems so desperate to *fall in love* in the play.

The prince

You need: the prince's cloak.

This is Verona in the seventeenth century. It's a city with a wall around it. It's a hot Italian city. Shakespeare probably had never been to Italy... the story isn't his... it is an older story that he uses and does wonderful things with. To the people of England in Shakespeare's time, Italy was often seen as an alien, 'hot-blooded', dangerous place.

> Does it feel like a place that doesn't have any law? Where no one is in charge? Do you know the name that is given to a place that has no authority, no law? It's called an anarchy. Well, Verona isn't an anarchy. It *does* have a ruler. Someone *is* in charge. The authority in this place is the Prince... Prince Escalus.

> I wonder if you can tell a lot about rulers, leaders, kings, (teachers?), other kinds of people in charge from the state of the place they rule? What do you think? What sort of ruler must he be, if this is the place he rules over? [*Discuss.*]

> When the prince looks out from his palace tower over the city... [*begin to act this character as you describe the scene and ask the questions; if you have a noble cloak to hand, put it on*]

> ...and hears the sound of fighting, and sees the flash of rapier blades sparking in the night... I wonder what he thinks about the city he rules over... I wonder what he feels...?

Strike a pose as the prince. Look out over your dangerous city. Invite pupils to image what he might be thinking as he looks out. Invite them to stand one at a time and strike the pose that *you* are striking... and then to speak.

> Reflect on what has been said by the prince. How does he feel? Does he like being the Prince of Verona? What would he rather be doing? How does he feel about his subjects? When he comes to speak to them to stop the fighting, he says [*have this displayed or show the words now as you speak them*]:

> *Rebellious subjects, enemies to peace,...*
> *...You men, you beasts... On pain of torture*
> *Throw your mistempered weapons to the ground...*

> And he calls himself 'your movèd prince'. What might 'movèd' mean? [*upset, sad, angered*]. Would you like to speak to him?

Explain that you are going to play the part of the prince for a few minutes, and that pupils will have the chance to question him. What sorts of questions would you ask the Prince of Verona?

Place yourself suitably. We suggest having a chair from which you can answer questions, and a balcony window from which you can view the city and later shout to your rebellious subjects. There should be space between in which you can move; throughout the 'hot-seat' (see Chapter 2), you could be 'acting' the streets that you can hear through your balcony window. Perhaps gather the pupils to sit in front of you on the floor in order to enhance your character's authority.

Begin your hot-seating with the image of a man looking very tense, irritated, angered. When he notices the pupils looking at him, he might be annoyed. Insist that the pupils always address you as 'My liege...', a nicely antiquated form of deferential address. In Dorothy Heathcote's phrase, you are a 'Man in a Mess'. The following might help to fill in some details of the character*.

> I am the Prince of Verona. I didn't ask to be. It was given me by my father. It is a poisoned chalice; an impossible, dangerous responsibility. I threaten, I execute, I imprison, I banish, but the blood of the warring people of Verona runs so hot and so thick and so deep. No man can control the hatred of these streets. No man. When I visit the king and the other princes of Italy; when we meet with the Pope at the Vatican's holy rooms to speak, to plan, it is always, 'Prince Escalus, how is Verona? How are your warring streets? How are Montague and Capulet? How many are dead this month? You need to get a grip, Escalus. You need to take control!' I tell you. No one can control these streets! What do you have to say to me, subjects? You have questions? You have advice?

Now take the questions as they come and seek the pupils' advice.

Here's a spiky question of our own, that might capture the prince's problem: how can a person *lead* something they don't really *control*?

At the end of the questioning, come out of role and reflect on his predicament.

In Shakespeare's play, we begin with a sword fight (we'll look at it soon). The prince looks from his balcony in his tower over the city down into the street, and screams to stop the fight between the two warring families. Ask the pupils: will you help the prince stop the fighting? Now step back into character quickly and say:

---

* We are indebted to drama practitioner Jan Linnik for some of the character's basic attitudes here, which were derived from work with teachers.

I see the sparks of their rapiers light the sky. Another fight has begun. I can hear the roar of the men and the cries of the children in their beds as they listen. I would have it stop. But if I call to them now, they would not hear. Would you help me call? Together we will make such a noise as would stop all Verona. Stand, my friends, call after me.

> *'Rebellious subjects, enemies to peace,....*
> *... You men, you beasts... On pain of torture*
> *Throw your mistempered weapons to the ground...'*
> *It grows quieter below.*
> *and then he says this... [calmly, dangerously]*
> *'If ever you disturb our streets again*
> *Your lives shall pay the forfeit of the peace'.*

Stop. What has the Prince just said?

Fight again and you will be executed by the law, by me!

Imagine taking responsibility for such a wild and furious place!

Would you like to look some more at the world and people of Verona? Let's go inside some of their houses, and then let's jump forward a few years in time.

'Two households, both alike in dignity'

You need: the scripts for these scenes, suitably displayed or prepared.

Teacher exposition

I wonder what it's like inside the four walls of the houses of these two warring families (the Montagues and Capulets) Shakespeare says they are 'alike in dignity'. So, both equal in status, wealth, importance. They are important families in Verona. Perhaps they are like the important dangerous families of the mafia! 'Mafia' is an Italian word and an Italian 'thing'... like Verona; though we don't know that the Montagues and Capulets make their money from illegal activities!

Romeo lives in the Montague house and Juliet in the Capulet house. In the play, Shakespeare takes us inside the houses and families and lets us see how they behave; importantly, he lets us see how the parents and children treat each other, and talk to and about each other. What do you think it's like in the Montague or Capulet house? [*Discuss.*] Would you like to act the scenes inside their houses and to use Shakespeare's words?

We need to make groups. In each group there will be a small number of people actually speaking, but also some servants. A really interesting thing about these very rich houses is that they have servants who *see* and *hear* everything, but have to pretend not to be there; who live at the heart of the house, but have no power at all. I wonder what they might say when they're on their own? I'm going to give you the lines that Shakespeare writes, but also, when the 'important' people have left the scene (or before they come in), we're going to let the servants speak; so some of you will be speaking Shakespeare and some of you deciding on your *own* words to say.

Having explained the arrangements, you may help the pupils make the groups. You might encourage them to make groups in consideration of which pupils feel comfortable speaking Shakespeare at this early stage, and which would rather create their own words.

Inside the families

There are two scenes to deal with. We present the edited text below, but you might find it best to display this simple text in large letters around the room. Having said that, giving your actors a text to handle, and perhaps even learn, could be an interesting proposal here. If this is your plan, you could offer them the script on small rolls of mock manuscript for added interest.

The scenes come from:

● Act 1, Scene 1 – between Romeo's friend Benvolio and Romeo's parents. Romeo isn't in the scene, but they are talking about how worried they are about him.
● Act 1, Scene 3 – between Juliet, her nurse and her mother.

Romeo's scene

Servants standing around, awaiting orders and listening in.

LADY MONTAGUE:	*O, where is Romeo? Saw you him today?*
BENVOLIO:	*So early walking did I see your son.* *Towards him I made, but he was ware of me…* *…gladly fled from me.*
LORD MONTAGUE:	*Many a morning hath he there been seen,* *With tears augmenting the fresh morning's dew,* *Adding to clouds more clouds with his deep signs.*
BENVOLIO:	*My noble uncle, do you know the cause?*
LORD MONTAGUE:	*I neither know it nor can learn of him.*

They exit to continue the scene. The servants are left behind, and may react and speak briefly.

Juliet's scene

In this scene, the nurse (a servant) speaks but other servants wait and listen.

LADY CAPULET:	*Nurse, where's my daughter? Call her forth to me.*
NURSE:	*What, Juliet!*
JULIET:	*How now? Who calls?*
NURSE:	*Your mother*
JULIET:	*Madam, I am here. What is your will?*
LADY CAPULET:	*We must talk in secret…* *How stands your disposition to be married?*
JULIET:	*It is an honour that I dream not of.*
LADY CAPULET:	*Well, think of marriage now.*

They exit to finish the scene. The servants are left behind, and may react and speak briefly.

In setting up the pupils' work on the scenes, explain that Juliet is only thirteen, but in that particular time and place, thirteen was not too young to be married. How do the pupils feel about that?

Also explain how the servants standing around and watching can be very interesting to watch in a scene. The silent servants can be like an audience on stage, and their reactions can be interesting and sometimes funny. Shakespeare's servants are often very funny – like the nearly toothless nurse in this play.

After pupils have prepared and you have watched the scenes, ask the pupils:

- Are there any words in the scenes that are unusual? That you don't understand? That you really like?
- What do the scenes tell you about Romeo, and then about Juliet?
- What's the matter with Romeo? He's in love with Rosalinde, who doesn't like him, but you might like to speculate how a young man in this city might feel despondent in a more general way. Think of all we have imagined about the city. In the midst of all this tension and violence, maybe he is desperate for affection, for love. Rosalinde is a missed shot... he is (perhaps) searching for Juliet!
- What do the scenes tell you about the families?
- What do they tell you about how parents treat children, and how children behave to their parents? Are both families the same? I wonder why not? Why they treat their two children so differently? (Perhaps because one is a boy and the other a girl?)
- What do they tell you about the servants in the wealthy houses?

These scenes happen the same day that Juliet and Romeo meet. They're only hours away from finding each other! Shakespeare calls them 'star-crossed lovers'. What does that mean? That 'fate' – the stars – is against them. That they haven't a chance! We know what happens to them, don't we? Within days of their meeting, they are dead! The clock is ticking. Get ready for a jump! Get ready for some time-travel!

The Golden Juliet

You need: masking tape; subdued, Italianate renaissance music; an old, faded 'plaque' with the words 'Juliet – star-crossed lover'.

Preparation: mark the corners of a square on the floor with the masking tape. Make a small square in the centre of the space and perhaps place a small staging cube in the centre of it (for a plinth). Play the music.

The statue in the square

Clear the central space and the square.

> We're in Verona. It's several years *after* the deaths of young Romeo and Juliet. This is the city's main square: the Palazzo Ducale. It's the very heart of the city. And here, on this plinth, stands a statue of pure gold. And under the statue is a plaque. And on the plaque it reads: 'Juliet – star-crossed lover'. [*Show the plaque and discuss what it means.*] The people called her 'The Rose of Verona'.

> The statue has been there for many years. So long, in fact, that many people have forgotten the story of Juliet; of how she loved Romeo from the other side of town, from the family of her father's sworn enemy. Some have even forgotten the statue's name... the plaque is tarnished and faded and hard to read. They have forgotten how the statue was built and paid for by the family of Juliet's secret lover, Romeo. It was built so the city wouldn't forget the terrible results of its deadly feuds. But... they *have* forgotten...

> What might such a statue look like? [*Discuss.*] Would it be a statue of the dead Juliet? Would she have her arms out in some kind of gesture? Would she be lying, kneeling, standing, reaching? What expression would be on her face?

[*Take a volunteer. Place her on the plinth and cover her with one of the large sheets.*] We don't know what the statue looks like. But we're going to find out...

On the day of Romeo's and Juliet's deaths, the two warring families surrendered into each other's arms. Their feud had gone too far. It had destroyed the families' most precious jewels... their children. Romeo's father, Montague, swore on that day to raise a statue of pure gold of Juliet... and Juliet's father, Capulet, vowed to do the same for Romeo. Now, only the Golden Juliet survives. I wonder why? Was the Romeo statue ever made? Is there a reason why it wasn't?

The stone-masons

The prince instructed the many workshops and sculptors of the city to work on *this* and nothing else. To produce their ideas for what the statue should look like; a statue to commemorate how the rampant, wild violence of the city destroyed the young.

The sculptors and their workshops would each make a statue and the prince would choose the one he wished to be placed in the centre of Palazzo Ducale. [Take the 'statue' away now...]... on the empty, waiting plinth.

You are the stone-masons, the sculptors, the city workshops. You are working for this greatest honour – a statue to last for all time.

Now divide the class into five or six groups. Each group is a city workshop. It might have a sculptor, apprentices, labourers, foremen, slaves. One person needs to be the stone... the statue. This person will need to be happy to be carefully 'sculpted' by the others.

- Ask the group to decide on roles in the workshop.
- Ask them to quickly *make a tableau* of the moment when the square slab of stone arrived from the quarry.

Discuss how a gold statue might be made. Ask for information. Imagine how it might happen. Explain that the statue might be sculpted first out of stone...; then a detailed mould made from the stone sculpture; and finally the gold would be smelted and poured into the mould to make the final statue.

- Ask for a *second tableau* of the first chiselled cut into the stone.
- Ask for a *third quick tableau* of the finished stone statue.
- *Fourth*: the pouring of the smelted liquid gold.
- *Fifth*: the breaking-away of the mould and the first sight of the gold statue (it probably still needs touching-up and polishing!).

Ask the groups to each choose one of these tableaux to bring alive. Groups go to their chosen tableau. When you indicate with a drum-beat, the scene comes alive. In this scene... which will be spontaneously improvised... we want to see what discussions are had about what the statue should look like: its pose, its face.

After a moment's preparation, begin the scenes.

'Spotlight' scenes – that is, freeze them all apart from one that you spotlight, which carries on for all to see. Spotlight each in turn, questioning as necessary in each scene for clarity.

It's time for each workshop to make their final decisions and reveal their own, final 'Golden Juliet'. The prince is coming. The statues are all brought to the square, covered in cloth until the moment they are revealed. The prince will expect every sculptor to be able to explain what has been made, and why. Prepare this.

Presenting to the prince

Invite the groups to bring their statues forward into the square. To pose their statues, cover them with the sheet and to leave them there to await the prince's judgement.

A pupil is invited to play the prince. You are the city's chief architect, and it is your job to show the prince the statues that have been made.

Having chosen a prince, show him/her great reverence and lead him to the square. One at a time, visit each statue. Introduce each statue with an Italianate family name: the Carlucci Workshop, The Matrizzo Workshop, the Aramano, Palluccio, Medici, etc. The members of each workshop bow to the prince as he is introduced. Pull away the cloth and reveal each 'Juliet'. Ask the sculptor of each statue to step forward, and invite the prince to ask questions. The prince is deep in serious thought. This is a momentous decision.

Step everybody out of role for a moment. What is the prince looking for in the statue? Which statue will do this? Which statue would *you* choose? Try and establish a consensus, and make *this* the decision that the prince comes to.

The selected 'Juliet' is led to the plinth and placed on it. Ask everyone to withdraw to the edge of the square again. Continue...

Rose – the song

The great song-maker of fair Verona steps forward. As the people stand and marvel at the Golden Juliet, the singer begins his new song – a song freshly arrived from England – the song he will forever call 'Verona's Rose'. As the singer sings, the people of Verona quickly learn the simple, four-line song... They repeat each line at the singer's request.

Rose, rose, rose, rose
Shall I ever see thee wed?
I marry that I shall
When thou art dead

TIP This song came to us through actors, who explain that this was a traditional song for actors to sing as a warm-up before performances. We can't find a definitive account of its origins, but it probably originates in medieval England, and it is possible, as we like to tell students, that Shakespeare and his men could have stood and sung it before the first performance of all of his great plays, including *Romeo and Juliet*.

Introduce the idea of the 'round' – splitting the group first into two and then into four, and 'conducting' with a wave of your hands each group to begin the song one line after the last. In this way, you can simply and efficiently build up a beautiful, energising piece of community singing in-role.

With the addition of the idea of tragic Juliet as The Rose of Verona (an idea of our own invention), the song becomes wonderfully appropriate.

If you don't know the song, a quick internet search will find a host of versions.

As the group sing for the final time, ask them to step forward and gather around the Golden Juliet. On the final note, Freeze!

The forgotten story

On that day – the day the Golden Juliet is unveiled in Ducale Square – the prince stands proud and thinks he has done a good thing; a great thing. He thinks the statue will make his people remember... and never again turn to blind, murderous feuds. Little does he know! However terrible the story of Romeo and Juliet is, like all things, it will fade. Could the same thing happen again?

Will the statue become just another piece of 'furniture' on the street that people don't see? Look.

As you narrate the next moment, invite pupils to cross the stage in-role as the characters you suggest. Ask pupils to make their own suggestions and to act the part as they speak: children playing chase at Juliet's feet; servants dragging shopping home to their masters; mothers pushing trolleys; teenagers shouting and laughing; people waiting to meet the loves of their lives(!); men passing each other dangerously – their hands on their rapiers. Has nothing changed? Indicate for the street to be empty again.

One day [*gesture for a volunteer*] a young child, a girl, walking through the empty morning streets of Verona to school, feels suddenly that she is being watched. She stops. She turns and looks at the statue she has walked past a thousand times. She talks to it. She looks into the statue's sad, young, golden eyes and says, 'Who are you?' Pause. The girl looks about the square. It has become strangely empty... and silent... not like the heart of a busy city. Is that a tear in the golden eye? surely, a drop of rain? 'Who are you?'

The girl hears music coming from the air. [*Begin to sing again softly and gesture for the song 'Rose' to return quietly.*]

The golden statue stirs. And moves its arms. It looks about Verona's bloody streets. The statue speaks, 'Who am I? You are the first to ask in many years. Do you not know the names of Romeo and Juliet? The story of how they died on fair Verona's streets? No? Then I shall tell you... Sit, my child.' The girl sits. 'This is the story of Juliet, who I was formed to represent so all may remember.'

You are about to begin a full enactment of the story of the play – a 'Story Whoosh!' (see Chapter 2). Here we are attempting what might be called a 'Story Whoosh in-role'. The telling of the story takes place *inside* the story of the statue in the square; it is framed by the situation we are in at this moment.

TIP   You might attempt to tell the story in its entirety from Juliet's perspective as if *she* were the statue. We have chosen to avoid this intriguing complication; but feel free to try. The 'passive' narration of the statue allows for a cleaner line of the story. Maybe you could challenge your pupils to write the story from Juliet the Statue's perspective.

Depending on their level of experience, you may need to explain the 'rules' of a 'Story Whoosh!' But here, try to do this by maintaining the frame. For example:

You are the ghosts of Juliet's story... sitting around the square waiting to be called back to life... to tell your story again. When I mention a place or a name, I will point at you and bring you forward to act out that piece here, in the centre of the square. We might have many people playing Juliet and many Romeos. If I sweep my arm across the stage and say 'Whoosh!', everyone must return to their starting places on the edge of the stage. Would you like to help me tell the Terrible and Tragic History of Romeo and Juliet?

TIP   Ask pupils to think about all the different *locations* that are mentioned in the story. You will be asking them later...

Are you ready to begin? [*Begin formally...*]

'The Tragedy of Romeo and Juliet...'

Please now refer to the Romeo and Juliet 'Story Whoosh!' at the end of this chapter. Practicalities demand that the story here keeps to the central line of the narrative. It is intended as an introduction, not as a comprehensive account of Shakespeare's play.

And as the story ends, the statue of the Golden Juliet is still once more!

Discussion at the end of the story:

Are we all clear about the story? Tell it to me in ten simple steps. What do you think about the story? How do you feel about it? What would you say to any of the characters, if they were here? Whose faults are Romeo and Juliet's deaths? Does it make you think about anything else?

Possible extension

Offer agèd paper, quills and ink. Give pupils the chance to write to Romeo or Juliet, either at the *end* of the story or at some point within it. What would they want to say to them?

Building Verona

You need: a collection of empty, opened and flattened individual cereal boxes; card, newspaper, glue sticks, pens, string, variety of coloured paper, pipe-cleaners, blu-tac, cloth, plasticine, larger boxes, assorted 'junk modelling' materials; a large floor cloth and some scrunched newspaper.

Discuss: what *places* are mentioned in the story, or *needed* by the story? List them. These are the sites of Verona. As each one is suggested, hand out a piece of small card and a pen, and ask the pupil suggesting it quickly to write the name of the place and what happens there. 'The Friar's cell – where Romeo and Juliet are secretly married.' Collect and display these together.

Add a little more historical detail about Verona at the time of Shakespeare. Show the drawing of 1676 by John Speed (a little later). This image is useful because it gives a sense of a city 'contained' within walls and having a variety of topography. Don't let pupils ponder this *too* long... an accurate rendering of the city is not required. It is an imaginative rendering of the landscape of the world of the play using the Shakespearean text as the chief source.

Explain to the group.

We're going to *build* Verona. In fact, we're going to do more than that... we're going to build the whole *world* of Shakespeare's play. [*As you speak, use the large cloth with scrunched newspaper underneath to make a rudimentary relief. Demonstrate how easy it will be to achieve the effect of 'place'.*] Once Verona is built, we're going to add the characters we have discovered there, putting them into the places and situations we have learnt about. Then, we're going to find a way of adding the words that Shakespeare gives them to speak. So:

● one-third of you will build the *place* – Verona – and label each part of it with a beautiful label
● one-third of you will build the *characters* (*this* big – about 8 cm)
● one-third of you will find an inventive way of including the *words* in this model – in some ways, this is the hardest and most important part of the construction. It is Shakespeare's *words* that make the world come to life; why we remember him. You may need to find some of these lines if you don't know them.

Your first task as a group will be to divide up the jobs that make up each group's task – break the 'big' task down into a series of smaller steps and decide how they might be achieved, and who by.

The building of the world begins! (See 'Construction tasks' in Chapter 2.) As explained in Chapter 2, this might be a task that is accomplished in a good, solid hour's labour *or* a more protracted task that might take weeks and be returned to several times. Both approaches have their benefits.

Working with our hands in a focused manner is a great opportunity to talk. Be prepared to encourage further questions about the play.

> Why are these families at war? Do they even remember how it started? I wonder how that happens. Has Juliet brought all this on herself? Is it the prince's fault for not keeping law and order? Where are the police? Do you think it's possible to fall in love at first sight... it's very romantic... do you think it's real? [*I know you're only young...*]. What do you think about the parents? About the friar? Who would *you* blame? Aren't they just stupid, love-sick teenagers who take it too far? Why has this story become so famous? Why has it lasted so long?

When the model is finished, take some time considering how to present it; think about how to light it... perhaps making it a night-time scene... lighting it with a single large torch or lamp, or using small electronic tea-lights placed inside the building that has been made.

Ancient grudge, ancient quarrel: the warring families

The battle lines: Montagues and Capulets

You need: parallel masking tape lines marked on the floor.

> In Verona, there are two families... the Montagues and the Capulets... they are like street gangs, or mafia clans. There is constant conflict between them, and it is they who put the city in a state of tension... often breaking out into vicious sword fights.
>
> Benvolio says, 'For now these hot days is the mad blood rising'.
>
> Mercutio says, 'Thy head is as full of quarrels as an egg is full of meat.'
>
> Listen to those words. Think about what a powerful description they are. What does the line make you think of? They are specially chosen words.

Wonder, in passing, where this conflict might have started, and leave the question hanging. Split the class in two, and send each half to either side of the space. Indicate the parallel masking-tape lines that you have laid on the floor. These are the city's 'battle lines'. On one side are the Capulets (Juliet's family); on the other side, the Montagues (Romeo's family).

> Every day on these city streets, the men of the families face each other in anger, ready to pounce [*model this as you speak*]; ready to 'cross the line'.
>
> The prince has spoken and decreed:
>
> > *If ever you disturb our streets again*
> > *Your lives shall pay the forfeit of the peace.*

Check the understanding of this. If they fight, they will be executed!

> So every day, they go as far as they can up to the line... but don't cross it. If one person were to step *over the line,* then everybody would, and the result would be terrible bloodshed, a fight that can only end in death.

Now, one at a time, pupils walk forward from their current position at the edge of their space and come as far as the battle line – standing with their toes *behind* the line: first a Montague; then a Capulet. As they come forward and strike a pose, hand on rapier, they speak their family name with pride, attitude, threat – 'Montague'/'Capulet'. Maybe some will also speak their enemy's name with derision [*model this*]. At the line, each actor strikes a pose (a tableau) which shows their extreme hatred of the enemy they are facing across the line. Slowly, every member of the group arrives and we build a whole-group tableau.

When all have arrived, step forward and introduce the 'eternal loop' of…

> *Do you bite your thumb at us sir?*
> *I do bite my thumb, sir!*

This is the constant state of conflict between the sides. Always provoking, cajoling, threatening… but fearing to cross the line.

'Loop' the two lines to make a sequence of three repetitions. The groups will repeat the lines in an ever-increasing cycle of aggression – louder, sharper, angrier. Model how the emphasis and intonation might be changed each time to develop the effect of the lines. Between each repetition, there should be a strong silence filled with looks and body language. Perhaps use your drum to indicate the start of each cycle. Switch families each time. So the sequence will go:

[*Drum-beat*]

> *Do you bite your thumb at us sir?*
> *I do bite my thumb, sir!*

[*Silence.*]

> *Do you bite your thumb at us sir?*
> *I do bite my thumb, sir!*

[*Silence.*]

> *Do you bite your thumb at us sir?*
> *I do bite my thumb, sir!*

[*Silence.*]
[Repeat.]

In a final sequence, ask them to repeat many times and to raise the tension of the scene as you raise your hand higher and higher, as if it were a volume control.

> This is the constant 'stand-off'. But sometimes it boils over and someone steps over the line!

Point at someone and say,

> Sampson has had enough and screams, 'Draw, if you be men' [*indicate for the actor to perform the line*]. Benvolio sees what is about to happen and tries to stop them, shouting [*point to a new actor*] 'Peace!' [*again, the actor performs the line*]. But hot-headed Tybalt sees red [*quickly choosing another actor on the Capulet side*] and shouts, '…peace? I hate the word… As I hate hell, all Montagues, and thee!' Tybalt crosses the line and steps into the 'no-man's land' where blood is spilt. All the Montagues scream 'Down with the Capulets!'

> All the Capulets scream 'Down with the Montagues!' And *everyone* steps over the line! Rapiers drawn. Freeze!

Indicate to the whole group that we are going to turn on the *sound* of the fight that now happens… but not the action… there will still be no physical contact.

Allow the sound to continue for a few moments. Then Freeze!

> When blood is spilt and life taken, the passion fades away as quickly as it had come. Mercutio falls at Tybalt's hand. Tybalt falls at Romeo's sword. [*Indicate for the actors playing Tybalt and Mercutio to fall and lie still.*] Too late, the fighting men see sense and walk slowly back to stand

across the line... and turn to see the damage they have done... [*indicate for the group to do this as you narrate the moment*].

When the space is clear, Mercutio and Tybalt are left lying alone in the space.
The prince returns [*play this part*] saying, 'Where are the vile beginners of this fray?'

> Everyone knows what the prince has sworn... Does anyone answer his question?

Either allow this moment to continue as a spontaneous improvisation and see where it goes to... or Freeze! this moment and leave it hanging. Or enquire: 'Does anyone remember from the Whoosh! who the prince thinks is responsible and is banished from the city?

The button: Shakespeare's Great Lost Flashback

You need: a small, antiquated clothing button.

> How does such a thing as this conflict between the two families begin? There is hardly a clue in the play. It's an argument that is lost in 'the mists of time'. Do you know anything about how big arguments start over little things? Any stories you could tell? Does anyone understand why such things happen? Maybe it's about respect or dignity – people wanted to be treated with respect... and if they *aren't* they either give in or they fight back; but why whole families? Can anyone explain? [*Discuss.*]

In the following section, we move on to more pupil-directed invention, in which pupils work in small groups to solve an interesting dramatic problem. This is a mode that contrasts effectively with the earlier sections, which involved a lot of teacher-led whole-group work. (See 'Small group play-making' in Chapter 2.)

Hold the small button high in front of you on a single, extended finger. In your speech, model a heightened, antiquated tone and vocabulary in anticipation of the task you will set.

> Behold! A button! A nothing! A trifle!... A button!

> Imagine. This almighty battle between the Montagues and Capulets... This 'ancient quarrel' that has *always* been... that may have begun *before* the memory of anyone now living... this battle, that we will know will end with the deaths of Romeo and his Juliet... this battle... began with a button. This button. All the terrible events of this story turn on... *this button*.

> Now, Shakespeare didn't do flashbacks... his stories are all told in straight lines... they are what we call 'linear'... like a straight line. This happened, then this, then this... But what if he had done... if he had written a scene to tell us just how the feud between the families had begun? What would that scene look like? It would be 'Shakespeare's Great Lost Flashback Scene'.

> Some questions to consider:

> * What were things like *before* 'the button incident'? Were the Montagues and Capulets friends, neighbours... maybe even related?
> * What could possibly have happened over something as apparently insignificant as a button?
> * It seems like an almost funny thing... that it starts with a button... but it's a very serious and scary moment.
> * Remember, this is a scene written by Shakespeare. If it were, what would you expect to hear? Different words? 'Old' words? Images? 'Poetry'? Different word orders? Maybe even some rhymes? Depending on your group, you might speak about 'blank verse' and invite them to write in 'iambic pentameter' – simply put – ten 'beats' per line.
> * You're going to write this scene in a small group – and then perform it for us.

Alternatively, once written, you could swap the scripts between the groups, so that pupils perform another group's script and see their own performed.

It might be helpful to suggest the following development process.

● Discuss and decide what might have happened. How long ago was it?
● Who was involved? What were their relationships to each other?
● What was the specific *moment* when it occurred?
● Talk through the moment. Build the scene. Write the scene.
● Make the scene feel and sound Shakespearean. (An added interest might be to offer quills, ink and agèd paper.)
● The scenes are rehearsed.
● The scenes are performed.
● The scenes and the events depicted are discussed.

> Some questions: How might things like this ever end? Do you have to wait until it turns into a tragic disaster, like Romeo and Juliet? How can we stop such terrible things? Could anybody have said anything to make it stop? Maybe at an important moment? Would you like to do a 'drama experiment' to see if we could change the story?

Go back to the main story of the play – perhaps use the construction model and the lines we have shown there.

> Can anyone think of anything that a person ... maybe a child ... might have said to stop them in their tracks ... to interrupt them at the moment and make them *think*? Think of a moment where someone might have stopped the 'tragic inevitability'* of the story ...

As we did in the 'Story Whoosh!', call up three moments and build them in the centre of the circle. One pupil suggests a moment; others enact that moment, first as a Freeze! and then bringing it to life. Then the person who has made the suggestion is invited to *interrupt* the story, stepping forward and speaking their challenge. This is a moment of simple 'Forum theatre', in which the audience can intervene and influence the action (see Chapter 2). After each suggestion, discuss its impact. Would this change the story? Discuss as seems appropriate to your class.

   Now – jig!

The trial of Juliet

Juliet: what we know so far

You need: masking tape, torn scraps of paper (or sticky notes)*.

   Before embarking on the trial of Juliet, it is important to ensure that pupils' understanding of the play in general, and Juliet in particular, is secure enough before taking on the roles. In this first activity, we are going to draw together *everything* we now know about Juliet. You will also develop the understanding of her character by adding further information as the section progresses. The opening activity is a version of what has been called, 'Role-on-the-wall', in which the group gather together all pieces of information known about a character, one piece at a time, and display them on a wall for the group to view and ponder.

   An interesting couple of developments that might enhance the activity are:

● Turn a digital projector onto a blank wall. Project a good quality, appropriate image of Juliet at

---

*   if you use this phrase, it will need some unpacking itself!

*   I picked up the creative use of masking tape from Professor Alan Owens, and have come a develop a feel for roughly torn, cheap, coloured paper in preference to the fine-edged industrial precision of copier paper or sticky notes. I can't help thinking there is something 'real', human, pre-digital about it, which fits with our general project. Sometimes we like to call the paper pieces 'clouds' ... which can be developed with a preliminary activity of 'making clouds' – an attractive, gently comic proposition!

body height (so pupils can approach the image and make their contributions straight onto it). There are an extraordinary number to choose from online.

- Or, project the image, mark the outline of the image with the masking tape and then turn off the projector – the outline will remain.
- Or, ask a female pupil to stand against the wall. Either you or the pupils mark around her with masking tape so that, when she moves away, her outline is left behind.
- Then write 'Juliet' in simple letters formed with tape.

Taking time to prepare for the activity raises its value and significance; it makes for a ritualised space and a sense of seriousness.

Now. Ask pupils to think about *everything* they know so far about Juliet. No fact is small enough to be insignificant. The list should include:

- simple facts about her: relationships, age, place of birth, nationality, etc.
- facts about her life
- what happens to her
- how she feels
- what she says
- what people say about her.

Be clear that we are going to collect *everything*. Be prepared to add further information.

Having prepared the wall, produce a huge pile of torn paper (about postcard-sized) and black pens. Explain the task, and invite pupils to offer 'bytes' of information. As each is suggested, hand out a piece of paper and invite the pupil suggesting each idea to write it on a 'card' and add it to 'Juliet-on-the-wall'.

The display will grow. Expect the first ideas to come thick and fast, the second wave to be more hesitant, and the third wave to be punctuated with awkward silences. Explain that this is all part of the process.

When it seems that the group has dried up, take a close look at the display together as a group. Be prepared to add any other pieces of information or understanding that you might have yourself.

Now read 'Juliet-on-the-wall' as a simple 'performance poem', adopting a simple form using 'Juliet...' as a sentence root (see above and Chapter 2). For example:

- Juliet, a girl of thirteen
- Juliet, from the city of swords
- Juliet, who disobeyed her father
- Juliet, who would be wed
- Juliet, a Capulet... etc.

You might invite the group to be part of this improvised performance by whispering the first word, 'Juliet...', each time. End of a flourish of 'Juliet...!'

Ask the pupils to reflect on their feelings towards Juliet:

Do you like her? Is she stupid for doing the things she does at thirteen? Is she acting older than she is? Why is she? Is she spoilt? Do you feel sorry for her? Do you think she really loves Romeo? Should she disobey her parents? Sneak behind their backs?

Prepare to offer opposing understandings in order to produce a balance of thinking about her, in preparation for the following activity.

> Some people think Juliet brings it all upon herself. That she is guilty of lots of things – deceiving, lying, bringing shame. Would you like to put Juliet on trial and try to find out the truth?

I accuse... (J'accuse)

You need: a display version of the courtroom plan (Figure 7).

Take up the posture of a learned barrister. You are the 'Instigator' ('Teacher in-role'; see Chapter 2). Find some old, heavy books to hold, perhaps. Speak to the group and outline your role, your task... and the next phase of our work: 'The Trial of Juliet'. Your role is very much 'devil's advocate'. Enjoy it!

> Ah, the lovely Juliet! What shall we say of the most beauteous Juliet of Verona? You all know her well? Correct? Well, my dear ladies and gentlemen, you have been summoned here today to *this*, our great Court of Justice, to take part in a trial... a most portentous trial... that will decide the fate of men... of *this* man, Honourable Capulet. Juliet's father. He is accused of bringing destruction down on his own daughter's head by insisting that she marry the worthy Paris.
>
> But, good ladies and gentlemen of the Court, this is not the trial of this old and broken man... this is *the trial of Juliet*!
>
> Juliet has nobody to blame for her own death but herself. Had she been a good and obedient child, who honoured her father and obeyed his loving instructions... this tragedy would have been over before it began. Juliet was a haughty, irresponsible, foolish teenager – a moody, tiresome, disobedient child who knew nothing of the ways of real love. *She was a drama queen!* And she died at her own hands... Suicide... because she couldn't get her own way! A despicable, selfish child who has broken so many hearts in our fair Verona!

Stop.

Now come out of role and check understanding of the situation you have placed the group in.

Explain that we are going to make a whole-group drama, in which *everyone* plays a role, and this whole space is the court.

> Now, because this is a 'drama court', the normal rules of life don't apply. Can we all agree these things to make it work?
>
> ● As in some big trials, there won't just be one lawyer... there will be a team of five [*this also means there are more parts for everyone*].
> ● Even though Juliet is dead at this point in the story... we're going to give ourselves the power to call her here anyway. Stranger than that... we're going to call five Juliets – it will be a big part for whoever plays Juliet, so we are going to 'distribute' the role (share it out).
> ● We're going to give ourselves the power to call witnesses: Juliet's father, mother, nurse, cousin, friends, the friar, Romeo? When we call a witness, a new actor will step forward to take on the part... but we're also going to give ourselves the power to 'tag' the character, as in 'tag-wrestling', where someone can touch them on the shoulder and take over from them.
> ● Anyone who is not playing a specific part at any time will be a member of the jury... and this jury has the power to ask its *own* questions.

Explain that you are not sure what such a court would look like. In a 'normal' court you would probably have (mark these out in space as you describe) a judge, the accused on their own, a witness box, defending and prosecuting lawyers, a jury, a gallery of people watching. Take out the rough plan of *this* courtroom that you've prepared. Explain that you thought it might look something like this... (see over)

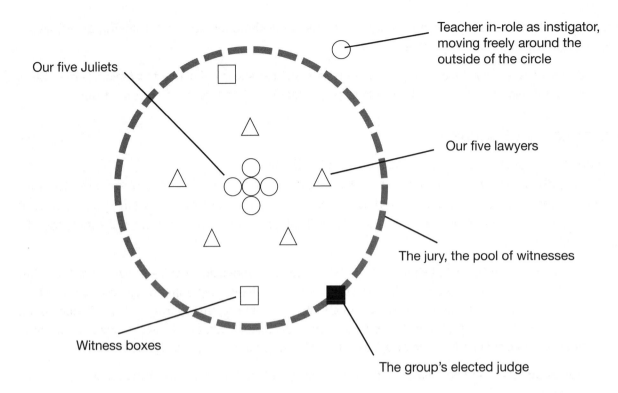

Our five Juliets

Teacher in-role as instigator, moving freely around the outside of the circle

Our five lawyers

The jury, the pool of witnesses

Witness boxes

The group's elected judge

Figure 7 The trial of Juliet – possible layout of the court

Point out that before any court case, there is a whole lot of preparation to be done: lawyers have to prepare their case and collect their facts; witnesses have to prepare their statements, their testimony (that they will swear to be true). We are going to do this preparation now.

Recap on the different parts we will need. Allow pupils to choose the part/s they would like to play in the drama; remember – five lawyers (defending or prosecuting!), five Juliets, a Capulet (father), other characters as witnesses. Who might we like to call? Actors volunteer to take these parts when the time comes. We also need to elect a judge. Who would be a good judge? Discuss and elect. Choose your jury.

TIP   You might like to add another layer of structure by creating character cards in advance. These might be simply name cards, or offer some more detailed and helpful information. You might also think about creating 'accusation' cards for the lawyers. This will all depend on your judgement of the group's understanding of the characters and narrative. To deepen the response, you might set an individual in-role writing task for each pupil... a piece of homework, perhaps, in which they have to write a simple diary piece by their character on the night before the trial. This will allow them to prepare their stance, organise their thoughts, and deepen their identification with the character they have chosen.

If we were to say that the lawyers have five accusations to make against Juliet... what would they be? Discuss. You might expect:

● You disobeyed your father and mother by refusing to marry the noble Paris... a good match.
● You wilfully (on purpose) fell in love with a Montague! Your family's mortal enemy. You dishonoured your family.
● You carried on the relationship with Romeo, even though he killed your cousin Tybalt. You shamed your family.

- You went behind your family's back and *married* Romeo in secret... without your family's blessing.
- You took *drugs* (poison) to try and trick your family into believing you were dead... so you wouldn't have to marry Paris... but Romeo thought you were really dead... and killed himself in grief... so it's *your* fault *he* killed himself too! Nobody killed you, Juliet, you killed yourself!

Everyone needs to prepare their case... their ideas... their questions... Give a little time for the different groups to come together.

The main characters have attitudes towards Juliet that are expressed throughout the text. Offer these to the whole group as part of the preparation, or give them out to the individuals who might play these people as witnesses. Here are some sample lines.

Lord Capulet – Juliet's father says of his beloved only child:

> *The earth have swallowed all my hopes but her;*
> *She's the hopeful lady of my earth.*

But later, in terrible anger at her defiance he says:

> *Hang thee, young baggage, disobedient wretch!*
> *...get thee to church on Thursday [to marry Paris]*
> *Or never after look me in the face.*

Lady Capulet – Juliet's mother – says:

> *Well think on marriage now.*
> *I was your mother much upon the years*
> *That you are now a maid.*

And later:

> *Do as thy wilt, for I have done with thee.*

The nurse – who has brought Juliet up from a baby, says:

> *Susan and she were of an age. Well Susan is with God;*
> *She was too good for me.*

And:

> *Thou was the prettiest babe that e'er I nursed*

Build the court-room space as discussed – build the 'set' for the scene, and then all walk away from it.

> We're almost ready to begin the trial. But first, let's make sure we know *exactly* what everyone in the courtroom thinks. What is their 'stance' towards Juliet? How do they feel about her? How do *you* feel about her? What do you think about this statement: 'Juliet is a silly, foolish teenage girl who, through her actions, brought about the death of herself and her Romeo'?
>
> What is your stance on this? Your attitude? If Juliet was in front of you now, how would you feel about her? Your character might be sympathetic, aggressive, understanding, disappointed [*model these as you show them*]. Of course, we have five Juliets too – how do they feel, hearing these accusations? Try and show it with your body and your face. Make a tableau/statue of your stance.

You might need to point out that the strong statements *your* character has made as prosecutor might be completely wrong. You have said them so strongly partly because they are such wild ideas. This courtroom will be very divided.

When everyone is clear about their stance towards Juliet, we are ready to begin.

Send everyone to the edges of the space and invite them to enter in-role; witnesses first perhaps, then lawyers, then jury, then the accused, then the judge. Insist on the formality of rising when the judge enters. Give the judge a gavel and something to hammer on... If things go to plan, she or he will need it!

Explain that you are the 'Instigator' of this case. Add the following information, which deepens the situation and raises the emotional and symbolic stakes of the decision to be made. Explain:

> The prince and all his subjects in the city are awaiting the outcome of this case. When the deaths first occurred, we immediately leapt to blame the families and their ridiculous feud. Juliet was then seen as a desperate *victim* of this city's violence. But, as the full story has emerged, people have begun to feel differently about Juliet. Once, a statue of pure gold was erected in the city square. Now the prince has decreed that, if Juliet is here found guilty of responsibility for her own death... the Golden Juliet will be removed and melted down... perhaps to make buttons for the Pope's morning gown!... Juliet will be wiped from the city's memory... and maybe the memory of the world.

Let us begin our trial.

At this point, your role becomes the management of the proceedings. The pupils have had time to prepare their stances and to understand their roles. Hopefully, enough brave young souls will have the drive to speak their ideas and make their case. Others should take up the bait they lay. You will need to offer more or less focus, challenge and stimulation, depending on the group and how they respond to the task.

The procedure of the trial might run:

- opening statements from prosecuting lawyer/s
- opening statements from defending lawyer/s
- examining and cross-examining the accused
- calling witnesses
- closing remarks from all
- the judge sums up and 'instructs' the jury
- the jury votes
- the verdict is given.

This should be a free-flowing, spontaneous improvisation (we might call it a 'simulation'), which is bound by the conventions of the setting (the court) but is driven by participants' commitment to their stance. Inviting the group to take the counter-intuitive and counter-emotional position of being *against* the young victim, who they might be likely to identify with in some way, is an exciting and challenging task which will need all your skills of guile; as Dorothy Heathcote might say, you will need your subtlest of 'subtle tongues'.

After the scene has been accomplished, there is much to be discussed.

Why is the *girl* taking all the blame? What is a 'scapegoat'? Is Juliet being the scapegoat for the city? Should children honour and obey their parents? Should people be free to love who they want? Who's responsible for the situation Juliet lived in? Is Romeo just as guilty? Is either of them really guilty? Who would *you* blame? Did she feel *at home* here in this place? Did anyone? Whose fault is that?

Now – jig!

The Friar: the meddlesome monk

You need: monastic music; simple woollen cloth, a monastic habit perhaps; ink, quill pens, agèd paper (placed strategically around the room on trays so they can be retrieved efficiently when needed).

Give the group some outline historical detail. You are going to tell them an important story about England.

> Shakespeare wrote his earlier plays at the time of Queen Elizabeth I. Her father was Henry VIII. Her mother was Anne Boleyn, who her father had beheaded! Before Henry VIII there were hundreds of monasteries in England. Monasteries were places where men and woman lived to dedicate their lives to God. They had taken vows (promises) to live in poverty, to never marry and to serve God. The monasteries were very powerful... and very rich... places. They respected the king... and lived as his subjects... but their real leader was the Pope in Rome (the same Italy as this fair Verona).

> Henry VIII did an important and radical thing... he separated the church in England from the church in Rome... and made *himself* the head of the church... the Church of England. That's something that's still true today. When the Pope came to England in 2010, it was the first time a Pope had ever been here *officially* and met the Queen... since the time of Henry VIII!

> Separating from the Pope... from Rome... was a very important event that made England and the English people feel proud and different – *almost* all of the rest of Europe continued to follow the Pope. England... an island on the edge of the continent... stood alone.

Before moving on, ask for questions.

Continue.

> The law that Elizabeth's father passed to cut the country away from Rome... also took control of the monasteries... and all their wealth. This made Henry very rich. The monasteries were closed down, and the monks who had lived in them were thrown out... and, like Friar Lawrence here in the play, many lived in simple dwellings in the community, doing anything they could – perhaps being paid to pray for people!

> The friar in the play (Friar Lawrence) lives in a 'cell' (maybe a simple hut) on the edge of the community.

Discuss with the group what the life of a monk might be like in a monastery.

Note that:

- some were *silent* orders... meaning they couldn't speak to each other (maybe once a day), but could only pray
- some ran schools
- some did a lot to help the poor
- the monks say they have given up money, love, relationships, a normal life in order to 'serve God'.

> What do you imagine a monk did all day? How would it feel to be one? Would you like to be a monk or nun? What might be good about such a life?

Ask the group to each take up a position that shows what this friar might look like. Play the monastic music. Suggest there might be different 'shapes' for him: when he is alone in his cell; when he is out and about among people; when he visits the cathedral...

Ask: when people see him coming towards them, how do they feel, what do they think? Drop into *this* for a moment to develop perspective. Ask each 'statue' of the friar to melt into a statue of a person seeing the friar coming towards them. 'Thought-track' these people (see Chapter 2)... Explore the community's response to him. Discuss.

If you could ask the friar a question, what would it be? It might be about his life, the monastery, his beliefs, about Romeo and Juliet and his role in their death. Quickly give out paper and collect these together. They will form part of the activity that follows.

The friar in the hot-seat

Now melt pupils back into the shapes of the friar. He is now on the floor of his cell. Explain the process of creating a 'Distributed hot-seat' (see Chapter 2).

> You are *all* the friar, locked in this moment of time. I'm going to ask the friar questions... some questions that I might already have... and some that will come to me as I look at the shapes you've made. When I ask them, *anyone* can answer; three or four people might answer the same question in a different way. What one person says is going to be true of *all* of you... so don't go against (don't contradict) what an earlier friar says... unless you give yourself a reason to do so... 'I sometimes feel/think like that, but I also sometimes feel/think...'

Address Friar Lawrence:

> Friar Lawrence, I understand you are a holy man... etc.

Be prompted by the 'shapes' the pupils propose; allow them to suggest questions, but also use the questions collected a little earlier.

Be interested to find out about:

- his life
- how people treat or react to him
- how long he has lived out of the monastery. What it was like before, *inside*? What does he miss?

Draw your questioning slowly to include the friar's role in Romeo and Juliet's story. This is a moment of 'reversal', when your approach should become a little more accusatory.

- You married Romeo and Juliet secretly?
- You married them without their parents' blessing?
- You married them when Juliet was only thirteen, and Romeo barely much older?
- You married them, even though they had only known each other for two days?
- You gave this thirteen-year-old girl poison to help her deceive her own family into thinking she was dead?
- Do you feel responsible for their deaths?

> Some people think he is trying to be helpful to a loving couple. He thinks he is trying to end a terrible family feud. Some think he is a foolish, meddling monk. Maybe because he has lived in a monastery for so long... and never had a girlfriend, he makes a mess because be knows nothing about the ways of the world and the ways of love!

Discuss out of role: is it true that, without him, Romeo and Juliet would still be alive at the end of the play?

> Let's put him at his worst moment! He has been trying to help this young couple. It has all gone wrong. He walks at great speed through Verona [*a piece of physical activity feels required right now, as we have been in seated discussion and 'tableau' mode for quite a time*].

> He's walking very suspiciously – not wanting to be noticed, his head down. He knows he has done wrong. He has just sent Juliet away with drugs to make her appear dead... if this is discovered... he is terrified of being found out... Are people looking at him...? 'People are looking at me', he thinks, terrified... 'They know... They know what I have done...'

> The friar lives in a 'cell'; a small, lonely hovel – a single room with perhaps just a hard bed... a stool... and a simple wooden crucifix on the wall.

> He arrives back in the cell and closes the door behind him. As he is here in the cell, Romeo arrives at the tomb and finds Juliet lying as if she were dead. Very soon, the friar will go to the tomb to be there when Juliet wakes, as he promised; but he will find Romeo there dead, and soon after they will *both* be dead. But the Friar doesn't know that…

> He's walking like an animal in a cage: trapped, walking round and round, wringing his hands. Show me how big the cell is, and how he walks around. He walks. He prays. He walks. He prays. He decides… What has he decided to do? Tell me…

The pupils are given a little time to think, and then offer suggestions as to what the Friar's decision at this moment might be.

Take ideas… the friar is considering all of these actions… and he decides to confess all that he has done to the prince. He wants to stop all this before things go too far (he doesn't know they already have).

> He takes up his pen. Reaches for a piece of paper. Writes his confession… he starts… 'My Lord, Prince…'.

Give pupils the chance to write the Friar's letter, either in full, or by offering strips of paper and inviting each pupil to create one key line from the confession. You could then spend time sorting them into a coherent order to make plausibly complete documents. Alternatively, first ask pupils to read out the lines they have written… slowly, one at a time, so that the lines might accumulate to make coherent sense. You might then complete the fuller assembly of the confessions as an 'out of drama' literacy and display task.

Finish the section on a final moment of dramatic tableau.

> As he finishes his confession… a messenger arrives… [*speak as the messenger*…] 'Venerable Friar Lawrence, I come with grim news… it is said young Romeo of Montague is fallen, come hence… your name is given as part-engineer of the unfolding tragedy.'

> When he hears this, how does he react? Show his reaction, and Freeze!

Reflect: although the friar's plans have all gone wrong and ended in tragedy, his first thought was to use the love of the young couple to try and resolve the hatred between their warring families. He is trying to do good.

He says:

> *I'll thy assistant be;*
> *For this alliance may so happy prove*
> *To turn your households' rancour to pure love*

Explain that 'alliance' means Romeo and Juliet coming together, and 'rancour' means hatred. Repeat the lines again.

> And look, in the last moments of the play, *after* Romeo and Juliet are dead, the Montagues and Capulets *do* settle their differences and come together. The price they pay for the peace is terrible; but the friar *is* successful! Do you agree? Discuss – or leave the question hanging.

Now – jig!

Love and Shakespeare's beautiful words

You need: a very romantic, perhaps 'cheesy' piece of pop music that will be familiar to your pupils. This should be cued at the start of the session, so that when you get to the appropriate moment it can be cued-in to comic effect. An old box or chest. Agèd paper.

In the Capulets' garden: the balcony scene

In this section of the scheme, we look directly at the main theme of the play – love. Perhaps this will feel like the more difficult section, given the age and experience of your pupils, but our approach will be to underscore the romance with a spirit of playfulness. It will work through groups (avoiding lovey-dovey pair-work) and it will focus on the sheer lyricism of the language.

> There's no escaping the fact that this is a play about *love*; it is perhaps 'the world's greatest love story'; which is a little strange, because we also know that the lovers both die. It's a *tragedy*. So why *is* it the most famous play in the world? [*Discuss.*]
>
> It *might* be because of the words Shakespeare finds to express the love of Romeo and Juliet... especially at their first meeting... at the ball at Juliet's house... where they see each other across a crowded room... love at first sight!
>
> Ladies and gentlemen, we are about to *get romantic*!

Cue your 'cheesy' love song. Perhaps invite everyone to find a partner and dance along in a comic fashion! Expect a comic effect. Allow the laughter that might come to run itself dry. Now, clear the centre space ready for building the 'real' picture of the ball.

Remind the group of the early stages of the Story Whoosh! We are at the ball at the Capulets' house; a ball in which Lord Capulet has suggested Paris might 'woo' Juliet and make her his wife. Ask the group to join you in creating the image of the ball. Also, find another adult to help this moment work by playing Juliet to your Romeo (or *vice versa*) in the scene that follows. The purpose here is to absorb the attention for this classic romantic moment. Very soon afterwards, the language will lead us into a deeper, less comic appreciation of the lyrical content of the play.

> Here are Lord and Lady Capulet, hot-heated Tybalt, Juliet's fiancé Paris, Mercutio and 'the Montague lads' (who have gate-crashed the party), and many well dressed guests dancing. Juliet [*gesture to yourself*] sees Romeo [*gesture to the assisting adult*] across the crowded room. The crowd seems to melt away.

Gesture for the whole group to crouch down to the floor, leaving you and Romeo standing and clearly visible.

> Romeo sees Juliet and says:
>
> 'O, she doth teach the torches to burn bright!'

Gesture for pupils who have taken these roles to act out the actions you now describe.

> Tybalt hears him and recognises the voice. He knows Romeo as a sworn enemy... a Montague! He calls for his rapier. Lord Capulet, Juliet's father, stops him beginning a fight. They argue. Capulet sends Tybalt away. 'Go to! Go to!'
>
> Romeo and Juliet look into each other's eyes. They speak as if this is a holy, religious moment...
>
> Romeo says: [*taking her hand*]

> *If I profane with my unworthiest hand*
> *This holy shrine, the gentle fine is this*
> *My lips, two blushing pilgrims, ready stand*
> *To smooth that rough touch with a tender kiss.*

> And Juliet replies:
>
> *Good pilgrim, you do wrong your hand too much...*

They go to kiss. Freeze!

Whoosh! [*Clear the stage.*]

[*Hold a quick discussion about the group's response to this.*]

After the party, Romeo sneaks around the back of the house, jumping over a high garden wall, to try and see Juliet again. She's in her bedroom, dreaming about Romeo.

He finds her room and the balcony outside. What follows is *the* most famous scene in the whole world; perhaps the most famous words in the English language. What are they?

Now quickly split the class in two halves; quickly so there is no space for protestation! Decide whether this is best done in boy/girl groups or cross-gendered. We suggest the latter might be best. You might point out that, in Shakespeare's time, women were not allowed on the stage and so Juliet would have been played by a boy actor. Don't be afraid of continuing in a spirit of playfulness ... and trust the language to still create impact.

Tell one half of the group that they are Romeo ... who is looking *up* towards the balcony; and the other half are Juliet ... who is looking *up* towards the sky and then *down* to Romeo.

TIP It is helpful that the two groups are not looking directly *at* each other.

They are going to repeat the words that you give them. Feel free to use as much or as little of the following scene as will work (from Act 2, Scene 2).

They haven't seen each other yet...
Looking up.

ROMEO: *But, soft! What light through yonder window breaks?*
It is the east and Juliet is the sun.
It is my lady, O, it is my love!
O that she knew she were!

Looking up to the stars.

JULIET: *Ah me!*

ROMEO: *She speaks, O, speak again, bright angel!*

JULIET: *Romeo, Romeo, wherefore art though Romeo?*
Deny thy father and refuse thy name;
Or, if thou wilt not, be but sworn my love,
And I'll no longer be a Capulet.

ROMEO: *Should I hear more, or shall I speak at this?*

JULIET: *Tis but thy name that is my enemy.*
What's in a name? That which we call a rose
By any other name would smell as sweet.

She hears him below.

JULIET: *What man art thou!*

ROMEO: *My name, dear saint, is hateful to myself,*
Because it is an enemy to thee

JULIET: *Art thou not Romeo?*

ROMEO:	*With love's light wings did I o'er-perch these walls*
JULIET:	*If they do see thee, they will murder thee.*
ROMEO:	*I have night's cloak to hide me from their sight*
JULIET:	*My bounty is as boundless as the sea,* *My love as deep.*
ROMEO:	*O blessed, blessed night!*

After the scene has been executed, sit and discuss the meaning of some key words. Pose some questions to check understanding.

● Which family does Romeo belong to? And Juliet?
● The first thing Romeo says when he takes her hand is to call it 'this holy shrine', and a lot of religious words are used. Why might this be?
● Juliet says, 'Deny thy father and refuse thy name'... what does she mean? She goes on to say, 'if thou wilt not... I'll no longer be a Capulet'.
● They know straight away that they have a great problem because they belong to the different, warring families. Do you think they should have given up then? Wouldn't that have been sensible?

> Perhaps what makes this so famous is how Shakespeare chooses such exciting and wonderful words. Not just *any* words will do... but specially chosen words... the *right* words, maybe the *perfect* words.

> Is it just me... or are these *beautiful* words? What *are* 'beautiful' words? What does it mean to be 'beautiful'?

The Secretaries of Juliet

Confirm that Verona is a real place: a place that you could visit; a place that many people *do* visit. Here you can see the balcony Juliet may have spoken from, the house where Romeo may have lived, and the tomb where it is said Juliet was laid. All this is very strange, because the people of Verona know the houses and the tomb were only built in the 1930s – and Romeo and Juliet were almost* definitely completely fictional characters. But the power of the story is so strong that people are still willing to cross the world to visit this place.

One part of the legend is especially interesting. If you had a broken heart... if you needed someone to share your problems, to share your love with... you could write to Juliet; you could take a letter there and stick it to the walls of her house, or you could *post* it to her – 'Juliet, Verona, Italy' – and it would arrive, you could even email her... Whatever you did to contact her... you would get a reply! A reply from Verona, from 'The Secretaries of Juliet'.

Imagine *this* box is Juliet's secret chest. In it, the Secretaries collect all the letters that have been written to Juliet... from all over the world... every year since her fame spread. At the bottom of the box are the few remaining things from Juliet's short life... what might be in the bottom of the box? Discuss in pairs or small groups... decide and prepare to come and place them in front of the box. (You might explore this idea further and give the pairs the time needed to model the items they decide on out of white paper and masking tape... which is fairly easy to achieve. Expect to be offered: the dagger, her unused wedding dress, mask from the ball, poison bottle, etc.).

> Think of someone from all of history or all of fiction (stories, plays, films), living or dead, real or fictional. It must be someone who you think might have or have had a broken heart; it could be

---
* Some people think they were real people who died in 1303!

someone famous, or someone fictional, or someone ordinary. They could, if you can think of nothing else, be broken-hearted over something that seems quite small... losing a football match, for example, or scratching a new game disk... but I challenge you to *think* big... Whatever it is, to *you* it's the most important thing in the world at that moment, and there's nobody else who you can talk to about it. So you write to Juliet. Juliet is like a sponge that absorbs all the grief of the world.

You will write your letters and place them in this chest.

And the Secretaries of Juliet will write back to you.

Explain that each pupil will write a letter from a broken-hearted person. They will all be placed on the box. The box will be shaken, the letters mixed, and then *we* will become the Secretaries of Juliet, taking someone else's letter and replying to it ourselves.

Ask the group to think about the *form* their letter will take; this will be each pupil's first decision. For example, if you are Cleopatra writing about her love for Julius Caesar, you might write it on paper that looks like papyrus. If you are a poor Victorian factory child, you might write on a tiny scrap of dirty paper. If you are Princess Diana, you might write on very posh-looking paper with a royal crest. If you're Bart Simpson, you might write on bright yellow paper; or if you're a modern teenager, you might send an email. What does the big bad wolf write on? How about David Beckham? How about Anne Frank?

Think about this: who do you know enough about to be able to pretend you are them, and write with their voice? You might also like to think about what his or her handwriting is like (see 'Writing in-role' in Chapter 2).

After writing the letters, ritualistically place them in the chest, then take the chest away and cover it.

Invite the group to sit in a large circle. Adopt something of a gentle, Italianate accent and prepare to address the Secretaries of Juliet. Explain that this is a real group. You are going to pretend that you are the group. You are all volunteers, people living in Verona who come together on a regular basis... perhaps once a month... to empty the 'Juliet Capulet mailbox'. You distribute the letters between you and write your replies. You offer advice and comfort to whoever writes to Juliet. All are signed 'The Secretaries of Juliet'. Ask the group to simply arrange themselves as the Secretaries in this circle. Address the group.

Honourable Secretaries, you are welcome to this the great house of fair Verona. Where once lived the prince who died regretting he could not control his violent subjects – Montague and Capulet. Now all the world knows the name of Verona for the tragedy that was said to have left unwashable blood upon these streets... the tragedy of Romeo and Juliet.

Now the broken-hearted of the world write to our broken Juliet, and we, the Secretaries of Juliet, shall make our replies. Let us receive this month's casket of broken-hearted letters.

Two members of the group leave the circle and return with the chest covered in a cloth, carrying it with great ceremony. They place it in the centre of the circle. Enter the circle and remove the cloth. Open the box and distribute the letters. Continue speaking as you do this:

Our letters have come from all corners of the Earth, from all times

- -

TIP   You might have put a cloth bag inside the box so that you can now lift the completed letters out and offer them around the circle. Alternatively, if there is a break between these two sessions, you might set up the letters in a circle around the box and perhaps cover them with the cloths used earlier in the scheme. Then, instead of a ritual entry of the box, you could have a ritual 'reveal', at which point the covers are simply lifted.

- -

Once the letters have been distributed, speak to the Secretaries in-role for a final time and commend them to their task in formal language:

> **My Honourable Secretaries, your task is a grave one, you must offer hope to the needy of the world. They await your reply.**

Now you may need to allow the tone to loosen a little. As they read other pupils' letters, there may be some levity – particularly as your introduction of the task (in the interest of differentiated abilities and interests) invited both highly serious responses and lighter responses from a more populist range of characters. You may need to speak out of role and make clear that the Secretaries' job is to take *every* letter that arrives seriously and write a serious response.

The replies might be written in classroom conditions as a literacy task; in drama mode, maintaining the fiction of the situation; or perhaps as a private homework task.

When complete, you might choose to:

- read the pieces in performance mode, perhaps dropping back into role as the Secretaries
- display them – letters together with replies
- create a book of all the letters and responses, one facing the other, make a cover and bind them together to make a complete dramatic artefact.

The tomb: the terrible end

You need: an appropriately selected piece of music – sombre, perhaps something contemporary and 'driving' (explore *Music of the Italian Renaissance* by Shirley Rumsey); a sound effect of a tolling bell.

> **Let us return to the story. Where does all this end? We know already. It ends in a tomb. It ends in death. (It's very depressing!)**

For the last time, set up for a Story Whoosh! The final section concentrates on the actions of the final terrible scene. Think about just what the actions are that make up the movement of the scene. During the Story Whoosh! play the musical track in the background to add a sense of gravity.

The terrible end – a Story Whoosh!

- Tybalt, Juliet's cousin, killed by Romeo, is laid in the Capulets' tomb to one side.
- Juliet has taken the sleep drugs and is also now lying in the tomb, *as if* dead.
- Paris, her fiancé, sits by the body, head in hands, distraught.
- Romeo returns from Mantua – a nearby town, where he has been banished for killing Tybalt.
- The friar's letter telling Romeo that Juliet is faking death has been lost.
- Romeo thinks Juliet is dead.
- Paris challenges Romeo. They fight.
- Paris is killed.
- Romeo can't live without Juliet . . . and kills himself by drinking the terrible poison he has brought with him. He falls dead.
- Juliet wakes. She sees Romeo dead.
- The friar arrives and tells her to flee. She won't. The friar flees.
- Juliet can't live without Romeo . . . she kills herself with a dagger she takes from Romeo's belt.
- The watchmen find the bodies and raise the alarm. The friar is captured and brought back. The prince, the Montague and Capulet families and the townspeople arrive and see the bodies.
- Lord Montague and Lord Capulet come together in their grief and shake hands.

Having run through the action of the scene, ask the group if they would like to try and stage a version of the final scene themselves.

Divide the class into quite large groups. A group of thirty might be divided into two groups of fifteen or three groups of ten.

TIP   Having quite large groups such as these might present organisational problems, mainly the problem of communicating fairly. But the advantage in this instance is that it allows for a distribution of focus. There is a wide range of focus on particular characters in this scene; from the high focus of Juliet to the low focus of a spectator arriving at the last minute. The large group allows for the possibility of very differentiated participation. It also means that when it comes to performing, there are only three groups to watch – a boon perhaps, since the scenes will be quite similar.

Give the groups chance to cast and prepare their scenes. It will be helpful to display the bullet points of 'The terrible end' around the room.

Paris says when Romeo enters the tomb: **"This is that banished haughty Montague"**
Romeo says, as he takes the poison: **"Here's to my love.** (He drinks) **O true apothecary!** **Thy drugs are quick. Thus with a kiss I die!**
The Friar says when telling Juliet to flee: **"Lady, come away from that nest of death."**
Juliet says, when she takes draws Romeo's dagger: **"O happy dagger!** **This is thy sheath. There rust, and let me die."**
Lady Capulet says on seeing Juliet dead: **"This sight of death is a bell** **That warns my old age…."**
Lord Capulet says to his old enemy: **"O brother Montague, give me thy hand"**
Lord Montague says in reply: **"I will raise her statue in pure gold"**
The Prince says to all (the last lines of the play): **"A glooming peace this morning with it brings;** **The sun, for sorrow, will not show his head.** **Go hence to have more talk of these sad things** **Some shall be pardoned and some punished;** **For never was a story of more woe** **Than this is Juliet and her Romeo."**

Figure 8 The Terrible End: character texts

When you sense that the action of the scene has been accomplished, offer the following extension into text.

For the purposes of dramatic impact, write the key character lines onto simple, small rolls of lining paper as mock manuscript. Tie them with ribbon. These can now be handed to the relevant actors.

Allow more time to prepare.

As you stop the work to prepare for the performances, ask if one of the groups would like to volunteer to be interrupted in their performance. This group should go second of the three. Watch the *first scene*. At the end, briefly discuss the qualities of the performance.

Interrupting the action

The *second group* is going to help you conduct an experiment. Earlier ('The button') we talked about trying to stop the tragedy happening by intervening and speaking to the characters. If you could have stopped the action of this final scene... and spoken to the people trapped in the moment... what would you wish to say? Maybe you would want to try and get them to do something different? Or to question them... or just simply tell them how you feel about what they are doing. The scene is like a steam train heading for an inevitable crash... can it be stopped?

Run the scene and allow the audience to nod to you to freeze the action. You will Freeze! the action with a bang on the drum, and the audience members may speak to the characters.

Make the point that the characters *are* trapped in the action of Shakespeare's play. If something *different* were to happen, we would probably be outraged. Let us return to the terrible actions as they *really* are.

Now watch the *third and final* version of the scene.

At the end of the final scene, gesture for the whole group to enter as the people of Verona and witness the tragic scene.

Having cued the tolling bell, enter yourself as the prince and deliver his final closing words for the last time.

> *A glooming peace this morning with it brings;*
> *The sun, for sorrow, will not show his head:*
> *Go hence, to have more talk of these sad things;*
> *Some shall be pardon'd, and some punished:*
> *For never was a story of more woe*
> *Than this of Juliet and her Romeo.*

The End

> This is a terrible and beautiful end to our work. Would anyone like to say anything about it? About how you feel, what you think? We might say *nothing* now and talk later, but if you would like to, [*you might say, by way of modelling a response*] I feel a strange terrible emptiness right here. I know it's only a story... but *such* a story. I wonder why it makes me feel like that? Aren't stories amazing? Isn't Shakespeare amazing!
>
> So. What's probably happening next at Shakespeare's Globe Theatre, straight after the end of the play? That's right...
>
> Jig!

This moment was the reason for the jig. Not only is the Globe's jig good marketing and public relations for the theatre; the raucous, energetic dance also, in the face of tragic death, reminds us that we are alive and living free.

A teacher's crib sheet

Background information

- Written around 1595 and probably performed straight away.
- Published in the First Folio in 1623 after Shakespeare's death.
- The story is Italian, and Shakespeare probably read it in an English version of the story by Arthur Brooke, published in 1562. It wasn't unusual for playwrights to 'borrow' stories from other writers; it is what they *did* with the stories that mattered. There were no copyright laws!

Brief summary of story

- In the city of Verona, Italy, two families, Montague and Capulet, are at war.
- Juliet Capulet is only thirteen, but is expected to marry soon (as was the tradition). Paris wants to marry her.
- Juliet meets and falls in love with Romeo (from the enemy Montague family) at a ball at her own house.
- The friar secretly marries them.
- Romeo kills Tybalt in a duel. The prince banishes Romeo from the city.
- Juliet is due to be married to Paris, and takes a drug to make her seem dead to avoid marriage.
- Romeo hears she is dead and returns from exile. After killing Paris, he takes poison to kill himself
- Juliet wakes and sees Romeo dead. She kills herself with his dagger.

Main characters

- Romeo and Juliet: the young lovers from opposing families.
- Lord and Lady Capulet: Juliet's parents, forcing her to marry.
- Lord and Lady Montague: Romeo's parents.
- Mercutio: Romeo's cousin and friend.
- Benvolio: friend of Romeo.
- Tybalt: Juliet's hot-headed cousin, killed by Romeo.
- Paris: becomes engaged to Juliet, killed by Romeo in the tomb.
- The nurse: Juliet's nurse and maid, who has brought her up since birth.
- Friar Lawrence: a local religious man, who marries Romeo and Juliet and provides drugs for Juliet.

Other things

- In Shakespeare's day, Italy was probably thought of as a wild, passionate place by the ordinary people of England.
- England had split from the Catholic Church under Elizabeth I's father (Henry VIII) ... and *Italy* was where the now hated Pope lived, and perhaps seen as a dangerous enemy by many people in England.
- Some say Romeo and Juliet were real people who died in 1303. Others not.
- The story of *Romeo and Juliet* is similar to the ancient story of *Pyramus and Thisbe*, which appears in Shakespeare's *A Midsummer Night's Dream*, a play written at around the same time (see Chapter 7).
- People of Verona, even today, reply to letters addressed to Juliet and sent to their city; they call themselves 'The Secretaries of Juliet'.

Facts and legends for pupils

As in all of *Shakespeare's* plays, the world's most romantic girl's part – *Juliet* – would have been played by a boy! – Now that's a job!

Romeo and Juliet is probably one of *Shakespeare's* earlier plays – it is *3093* lines long! (Quite short really for *Shakespeare* – *Hamlet* is *4042* lines long!)

The play's full title is The Most Excellent and Lamentable Tragedy of Romeo and Juliet.

Even though the story is almost certainly fictional, it doesn't stop the city of Verona, even today, making the most of the story's fame; you can visit Juliet's balcony, Romeo's house, and the tomb – even though they probably never existed!

Even more than this... If you wrote a letter telling of your own 'heartbreak' and sent it to 'Juliet, Verona, Italy' – it would probably get there and you would receive a reply. There are many people in Verona who call themselves 'The Secretaries of Juliet' and reply to all letters received.

This most terrible tragedy was probably written at about the same time as the jolly comedy A Midsummer Night's Dream; *maybe that's the antidote to this!*

Unlike A Midsummer Night's Dream, *which seems almost completely original to* Shakespeare, *the story of* Romeo and Juliet *is 'borrowed' from Italian stories that* Shakespeare *probably read in English. One short novel is by* Luigi Da Porto. *'Stealing' stories didn't seem to be a problem in* Shakespeare's *time!* Shakespeare's *plays were copied and sold by people standing in the audience!*

A page of famous lines

'Two houses, both alike in dignity,
in fair Verona where we lay our scene'

'star-crossed lovers'

'Do you bite your thumb at me, sir'
I do bite my thumb!'

'A plague on both your houses'

'She doth teach the torches to burn brighter'

'Romeo, Romeo, wherefore art thou Romeo?'

'What light through yonder window breaks,
it is the east and Juliet is the sun'

'What's in a name?

'What which we call a rose my any other name
would smell as sweet.'

'O happy dagger!

'Thus on a kiss I die'

A glooming peace this morning with it brings;
The sun, for sorrow, will not show his head
For never was a story of more woe
Than this of Juliet and her Romeo.

Romeo and Juliet: A Story *Whoosh!*

Come to fair Verona, an ancient Italian city. A city on a low hill surrounded
by a mighty wall. A city of churches, a city of grand houses and lowly homes.
A city of tombs. A prince's city, with a prince's palace. And at the heart of the
city a noble, empty, people's square.

. . . Whoosh!

Two families, alike in dignity, Montague and Capulet. Sworn enemies for all time.
Bringing violence to these city streets. Rapiers on their belts, drawn on a moment's
dirty look. Brawling, duelling, spilling blood. The prince would have his city at
peace. But Montagues and Capulets just fight. 'The next to draw their swords
and fight will die! This city will have peace!'

. . . Whoosh!

Here Juliet, Lord Capulet's most precious girl, attended by her loyal nurse.
The time has come for her to wed, and Paris would take her hand.
A ball shall be held at which Paris might 'woo' the lovely Juliet.
Tonight at the Capulets' mansion home.

. . . Whoosh!

The wealthy of the city, in fancy dress, attend the ball. Music pounds and dancing
flows. Paris, Lord and Lady Capulet, hot-head Tybalt, the lovely Juliet. But who is
this sneaking in – uninvited, with masks to hide their faces – it is the gate-crashing
boys of Montague – the enemies of all here. Mercutio, Benvolio and here . . . the
young pride of Montague . . . Romeo.

. . . Whoosh!

Romeo sees Juliet across the crowded room. His heart flies out.
Juliet sees Romeo. She is his forever. They fall in love! Tybalt recognises the
Montague boys and would draw his sword to fight. Lord Capulet demands peace.
The ball is at an end.

. . . Whoosh!

But Romeo will not leave. He jumps the garden wall looking for beloved Juliet.
Through trees and bushes he risks his life. Juliet comes to her balcony, sighing for
her Romeo, calling, 'Romeo, Romeo, wherefore art thou Romeo?' They speak, and
promise to meet tomorrow to be married in secret.

. . . Whoosh!

Next morning, at Friar Lawrence's humble cell. Romeo requests a wedding. The friar thinks that, by uniting the two families, Montague and Capulet, peace might come to Verona's streets. Romeo and Juliet are married! Then go their separate ways. Will peace come now?

...Whoosh!

Verona's streets again. Tybalt wants to fight Romeo for coming to the ball. Romeo does not want to fight. But Mercutio draws his sword, and Tybalt and he fight. Mercutio is killed and Romeo, angered at his best friend's death, kills Tybalt. Now Romeo must die, as the prince has said... he must leave the city and escapes to Mantua.

...Whoosh!

At the Capulets' mansion, Lord Capulet insists that Juliet must marry Paris... and it must be now! Juliet begs the friar for drugs. He gives her sleeping drugs that will make her appear to be dead. She takes them. The friar will write to Romeo to let him know of Juliet's trick... and they can soon be together. But the letter is lost!

...Whoosh!

In Mantua, lonely Romeo hears that Juliet is dead. He rushes, full-pelt, back to Verona. Then to the tomb. Where Juliet lies. And broken-hearted Paris waits. Romeo and Paris fight. Paris lies dead. Romeo sees the stone-cold Juliet. In his hand, he has a deadly poison. He drinks to join his lovely Juliet and falls dead beside her. Juliet wakes. She sees her secret lover dead. Kisses his lips to take the poison. Then draws his dagger. 'O happy dagger!' And kills herself. Too late, the Montagues and Capulets arrive. The friar is brought. And then the prince. To see the tragic scene.

A glooming peace this morning with it brings;

The sun, for sorrow, will not show his head:

Go hence, to have more talk of these sad things;

Some shall be pardon'd, and some punished:

For never was a story of more woe

Than this of Juliet and her Romeo.

The End. Whoosh!

A story jigsaw

In Verona, two families, Montagues and Capulets, are sworn enemies. The prince tries to control them, but fighting and death can happen at any time.

Juliet Capulet is told she must marry Paris.

At a masked ball, Juliet falls in love with Romeo – a Montague. Romeo comes to her room that night, and they promise to be married the next day.

Next morning, at Friar Lawrence's cell, Romeo and Juliet are married. The friar thinks that, by uniting the two families, Montague and Capulet, peace might come to Verona's streets!

Tybalt picks a fight with Romeo for coming to the Capulets' ball. Mercutio defends Romeo, fights with Tybalt and is killed. Romeo then kills Tybalt.

The angry prince banishes Romeo from the city. He flees to Mantua.

To avoid marriage to Paris, Juliet takes sleeping drugs supplied by the friar so everyone will think she is dead. The friar writes to Romeo to let him know this. But the letter is lost!

In Mantua, Romeo hears that Juliet is dead. He rushes back to Verona.

At the tomb where Juliet lies. Romeo and Paris fight. Paris lies dead.

Romeo sees the stone-cold Juliet and believes she is dead. He takes poison to kill himself.

Juliet wakes. She sees her secret lover dead. Kisses his lips to take the poison. Then draws his dagger and kills herself. Both lie dead.

The Montagues and Capulets arrive to see the tragic scene. The prince declares: 'The sun for sorrow will not show his head'.

Resources

> Two households, both alike in dignity,
>
> In fair Verona, where we lay our scene,
>
> From ancient grudge break to new mutiny,
>
> Where civil blood makes civil hands unclean.
>
> From forth the fatal loins of these two foes
>
> A pair of star-crossed lovers take their life;
>
> Whose misadventured piteous overthrows
>
> Do with their death bury their parents' strife.
>
> The fearful passage of their death-mark'd love
>
> And the continuance of their parent's rage,
>
> Which, but their children's end, nought could remove,
>
> Is now the two hours traffic of our stage;
>
> The which if you with patient ears attend,
>
> What here shall miss, our toil shall strive to mend.

The balcony scene (edited) – Act 2, Scene 2

Juliet hasn't seen Romeo yet… *

*Looking up**

ROMEO: *But, soft! What light through yonder window breaks?*
It is the east and Juliet is the sun.
It is my lady, O, it is my love!
O that she knew she were!

*Looking up to the stars**

JULIET: *Ah me!*

ROMEO: *She speaks, O, speak again, bright angel!*

JULIET: *Romeo, Romeo, wherefore art though Romeo?*
Deny thy father and refuse thy name;
Or, if thou wilt not, be but sworn my love,
And I'll no longer be a Capulet.

ROMEO: *Should I hear more, or shall I speak at this?*

JULIET: *Tis but thy name that is my enemy.*
What's in a name? That which we call a rose
By any other name would smell as sweet.

She hears him below.

JULIET: *What man art thou!*

ROMEO: *My name, dear saint, is hateful to myself,*
Because it is an enemy to thee

JULIET: *Art thou not Romeo?*

ROMEO: *With love's light wings did I o'er-perch these walls*

JULIET: *If they do see thee, they will murder thee.*

ROMEO: *I have night's cloak to hide me from their sight*

JULIET: *My bounty is as boundless as the sea,*
My love as deep.

ROMEO: *O blessed, blessed night!*

*   These are *our* suggestions, not Shakespeare's.

A glooming peace this morning with it brings;

The sun, for sorrow, will not show his head:

Go hence, to have more talk of these sad things;

Some shall be pardon'd, and some punished:

For never was a story of more woe

Than this of Juliet and her Romeo.

What's in a name? That which we call a rose

By any other name would smell as sweet.'

'Do you bite your thumb at us, sir!'

Romeo and Juliet scheme structure map

Section	Drama approaches	Possible curriculum opportunities
Verona, city of rapiers		
The stand-off game	Gaming in context	
Walking the streets	Whole group scene-setting; whole group tableau	Literacy: setting the scene; character development; history; PHSE
The poem of Verona	Thought-tracking; whole group writing	Literacy: poetry/performance poetry, sense of place; history;
Children of Verona	Group improvisation; character development	Literacy: developing empathy and character; moral and personal education
The mothers	Group and solo work	Literacy: developing empathy, alternative perspectives and character; moral and personal education
Discussion	Reflective discussion	Oracy; PHSE (current affairs/geography)
The prince	Teacher in-role; use of text	Literacy: character development
The Golden Juliet:		
The statue in the square	Teacher exposition; discussion	Literacy: developing context, modelling language
The stone-masons	Small-group play-making	History; design and technology (manufacture); oracy
Presenting to the prince	Teacher in-role; whole group drama	Prince's robe
Rose – song	Song	Music; history
The forgotten story	In-story Whoosh!	Literacy: narrative understanding; PE in context
Building Verona	Whole group construction task	Design and technology; art (3D modelling)
Ancient grudge, ancient quarrel: the warring families		
The battle lines: Montagues and Capulets	Whole group performance of text	Literacy: speaking text; PHSE
The button	Group script-writing and performance; discussion	Literacy: writing from an established model; script-writing for performance
The trial of Juliet		
Juliet: what we know so far	Role on the wall	Literacy: depth in character
I accuse... (*J'accuse*)	Teacher in-role; pupils with 'mantle of the expert' (formal roles); small-group preparation; drama simulation; whole group drama; use of text and character	Literacy: use of formal language, contextualising narrative and characters; developing narrative understanding; oracy; development of character; citizenship (legal process); history
The Friar: the meddlesome monk		
History	Teacher exposition	History; RE
The friar in the hot-seat	Individual character work; distributed hot-seat;	Literacy: character development and understanding; oracy
In his cell – writing	Writing in-role	Literacy: empathy; writing from a perspective; formal written language (a confession)
Love and Shakespeare's beautiful words		
In the Capulets' garden: the balcony scene	Use of edited script; Story Whoosh!	Literacy: using script, appreciating language of significant cultural heritage
The Secretaries of Juliet	Teacher in-role; writing in multiple roles	Literacy: letter-writing in context
The tomb: the terrible end		
The terrible end – a Story Whoosh!	Story Whoosh! of single scene; whole group enactment	Literacy: narrative understanding
Group work	Large-group play-making; use of text	Literacy: spoken text of significance
Performance – the prince	Performance; use of text; final words	Literacy: understanding form (tragedy)

We offer the chart above as a starting point. There are a whole host of learning opportunities in a rich drama experience that would have been exhausting to list: developing positive groups, expanding language opportunities and vocabulary, developing self-image and confidence, fostering imaginative responses, to name

Resources needed	Teachers Notes
Drum	
Paper, pens; appropriate music	
Text; prince's robe	
Block; sheets	
Story Whoosh! sheet	
Junk modelling materials	
Masking tape for floor	
Paper, pens	
Paper, pens; projector?	
Paper, pens; chairs for formal setting; masking tape for floor	
Agèd paper, quill pens	
Texts made and displayed	
Prepared script; props: safe stage dagger, vial of poison, sheets of white cloth; safe candles	
Appropriate music	

a few. Also, as you translate the work into your own classroom you will, we hope, create for yourself a whole unanticipated flood of new opportunities for learning. The heart of such learning is the rich experience we all hope to build.

Afterword: Notes for a Festival

We hope you will agree that the preceding schemes offer rich opportunities for classroom exploration. Each has been constructed to be usable and achievable by teachers. Once the challenge of realising them yourself, in your own situation, with your own children, has been embraced, the possibilities are, we hope, wide and deep.

As well as enriching classroom teaching, the schemes might be used within your school in a more expansive way. To explain, we will begin by describing the origin of the schemes.

Background to the schemes

A good few years ago at Egerton Park Arts College, a high school near Manchester, performing arts staff began to teach on a weekly basis in a range of local primary schools. We took as a unifying, high-value theme Shakespeare's *The Tempest*. In this instance, the specialist performing arts staff developed a programme of work on *The Tempest* which used the play as a way into studies of drama, music and dance. In the primary school, staff themselves were able to take the work we had delivered and expand it to serve a wide range of curriculum areas. To give the year's work shape and momentum, we devised a celebratory end-point to be performed in the school's own professional theatre space. We called it *The Children's Shakespeare Festival.*

Following this work, I transferred roles to become a local education authority subject adviser for drama (at Cheshire County Council). The role provided an opportunity to translate the same idea on a much larger canvas with a project we called *The Cheshire Children's Shakespeare Festival*. Our innovation in the new project was to not deliver all of the work ourselves, as drama specialists, but to find ways of inspiring and supporting teachers in their own delivery of quality drama experiences. It is this project which continues to be offered today in my capacity as a freelance drama practitioner, with two performances each year at Manchester's beautiful Royal Exchange Theatre, and with new projects opening up in nearby towns.

At the heart of each of these projects are the schemes of work that explore the chosen texts; they have been tried and tested on teachers and pupils, and expanded for the purposes of this book.

Inasmuch as the schemes derive from a 'festival' situation, they retain the possibility of large-scale, whole-school, public celebrations of your children's dialogue with our great and eternal bard. It is to the possibility of such a festival that we now turn our attention for a short time.

The reason for a festival

Shakespeare's plays were written to be performed; under the pressure of a commercial public theatre, they leapt immediately from pen to stage. His characters, his narratives, his language are there to be seen and heard and understood. It seems a tantalisingly tiny step from the explorations engaged in through the schemes, to the public celebration of your own and your children's responses and re-imaginings.

Of course, performance is not our purpose. To think first of performance is likely to distort our work and make us product-led in an unhelpful way. The approach we take during the festivals is to drive a separation between the 'exploration phase' (during which the schemes are delivered) and the 'performance phase' (in which the results of the exploration are assembled into a coherent, performable form). For festival teachers, the point of shift from one phase to the other is the arrival of our 'commissioning specification' or 'area of focus'. This simple document, unique to each of the schools involved, asks the group to offer an original piece of performance which represents an exploration of just one aspect of the play, as touched upon in the schemes; perhaps the friar, Juliet's family, the city of Verona, etc. The 'spec' will include a key line of text and require such things as Shakespeare's words to be spoken, elements of movement, song, new text written by the children in reflection of Shakespeare's text. Simply because teachers do *not* know their areas of focus during the exploration phase, they are free to give each area of the scheme equal, thorough attention.

Of course, we are not proposing that you establish a city-wide *Children's Shakespeare Festival* on your own (though if you would like to, come and find us and we'll help out!). But within the context of your own school, perhaps you might imagine such a thing happening. A whole-school 'Children's Shakespeare Festival' is something that has begun to happen in our own festival schools, with dynamic teachers taking the work we have done with them and delivering it themselves to their own school staff, who then go on to deliver the schemes to their own classes. On completion of the schemes, areas of focus are duly distributed, and each class works towards a performance in which they will offer a short (ten-minute) performance on their given aspect. At the festival performance, every child is able to take part in a vibrant celebration of the play. No attempt is made to perform the whole text; we are exploring the 'world' of the play, looking at key aspects and characters and speaking the key words. It should open a door on the play for the audience, as it has for the children in their explorations.

The stages in our festivals – and, conceivably, in yours – are as follows.

- Preparation of the scheme – in our case, this involves absorption in the text and source materials and the construction of the scheme; in your case, the 'translation' of the scheme into your own teaching and your own classrooms.

- Delivery of the schemes to the associated staff – having taken the scheme on board, you become the practitioner who delivers the work to staff.

- Staff do their own translations of the scheme into their own classrooms, and perhaps map the curriculum possibilities to serve their learning needs.

- Exploration phase – teachers deliver the schemes to their own classes; a whole-school jamboree of Shakespearean excitement!

- Each class is issued their 'commissioning spec – area of focus' and prepares a ten-minute theatrical piece to meet the needs of the 'spec'.

- The class pieces are rehearsed and performed together as a single presentation – your very own 'Children's Shakespeare Festival'.

We wish you luck in all of your adventuring.
John Doona
john@northwestdramaservices.co.uk

Bibliography and further reading

Shakespeare

Soul of the Age: The Life, Mind and World of William Shakespeare, Jonathan Bate, Penguin, 2008

Shakespeare: The World as a Stage, Bill Bryson, Harper Perennial, 2007

The Cambridge Companion to Shakespeare Studies, edited by Stanley Wells, Cambridge University Press, 1986

Shakespearean Tragedy, A.C. Bradley, Macmillan, first published 1904, studied text 1986

Shakespeare's Language, Frank Kermode, Penguin, 2000

At the Sign of the Swan, Judith Cook, Harrap, 1986

William Shakespeare: The Extraordinary Life of the Most Successful Writer of all Time, Andrew Gurr, Harper Collins, 1995

The texts (all of which include fascinating source materials)

The Tempest, edited by Peter Hulme and William H. Sherman, A Norton Critical Edition, W.W. Norton and Company, 2004

A Midsummer Night's Dream: Texts and Contexts, edited by Gail Kern Paster and Skiles Howard, Bedford/St Martins, 1999

Romeo and Juliet: Texts and Contexts, edited by Dympna Callaghan, Bedford/St Martins, 2003

Macbeth: Texts and Contexts, edited by William C. Carroll, Bedford/St Martins, 1999

Drama – a few places to start

Dorothy Heathcote, Collected Writings on Education and Drama, edited by Liz Johnson and Cecily O'Neill, Hutchinson, 1984

Improve Your Primary School through Drama, Jonothan Neelands, Rachel Dickinson and Shenton Primary School, David Fulton Publishers, 2006

Mapping Drama, Allan Owens and Keith Barber, Carel Press, 2001

Other

Brain-based Learning: The New Paradigm of Teaching, Eric P. Jensen, Corwin Press, 2008

Edward Bond and the Dramatic Child, edited by David Davis, Trentham Books, 2005 [a starting point for understanding Bond's work]

The Hidden Plot, Edward Bond, Methuen, 2000 [important theoretical writings]

Useful websites – background information, facts, electronic versions of the texts

There is an enormous amount of information about Shakespeare, his life and his work online; the information is everywhere. The issue will be, of course, where to start and what to trust. We offer the following sites from the vast array available.

The Folger Shakespeare Library, www.folger.edu – authoritative American Shakespearean institution

Shakespeare Online, www.shakespeare-online.com – author and copyright Amanda Mabillard [good for pupils]

Mr. William Shakespeare and the Internet, http://shakespeare.palomar.edu – author and copyright Terry A. Gray

BBC History: William Shakespeare (1564–1616), www.bbc.co.uk/history/historic_figures/shakespeare_william.shtml – copyright BBC

Shakespeare Resource Centre, www.bardweb.net – copyright J.M. Pressley and the Shakespeare Resource Centre

And, of course

Wikipedia, http://en.wikipedia.org – which will not be your only source, but does collect together a vast array of information and is mediated by a community of people with a real interest in the topic.